The Comfortable Arts
Traditional Spinning and Weaving in Canada

Dorothy K. Burnham

National Gallery of Canada
National Museums of Canada
Ottawa, 1981

© National Gallery of Canada for the corporation of the National Museums of Canada, Ottawa, 1981

ISBN 0-88884-474-3

Design: Virginia Morin

Printing: Friesen Printers

Obtainable from your local bookseller or from:
National Museums of Canada, Order Fulfilment, Ottawa, Ontario K1A 0M8

Aussi publié sous le titre:
L'art des étoffes: Le filage et le tissage traditionnels au Canada

PRINTED IN CANADA

Rights to photographic materials used for reproduction: The photographs have been supplied by the owners or custodians of the works, except for the following–the courtesy of all is gratefully acknowledged: Figs 21, 34, 37, 39, cat. nos 2, 24, 28, 32-33, 36-37, 39-40, 42-43, 47, 55-56, 60, 62, 64, 69, 73, 77, 82, 94, 96, 100, 105-110, 113-114, 117, 129, 131, 144, 146, 149, 151-161, National Gallery of Canada, Ottawa; cat. nos 13, 132, Canadian Conservation Institute, Ottawa; cat. nos 30-31, 34-35, 45, 49, 52, 63, 76, 78, 90-91, 99, 112, 118, 122, 128, 134 (detail), 137, 147, Royal Ontario Museum, Toronto; cat. no. 44, Prince Edward Island Heritage Foundation, Charlottetown.

© Dorothy K. Burnham for all diagrams.

Photograph Credits
Fig. 6, Molly Brentnall, Edmonton; Fig. 37, cat. nos 2, 159, Ernest Mayer, Winnipeg.

Every reasonable attempt has been made to identify and contact the holders of copyright and rights of ownership in regard to reproductions. Errors or omissions will be corrected in subsequent reprints.

Contents

Foreword

The Comfortable Arts exhibition fulfills a promise first articulated in 1937. On 14 October of that year H.P. Rossiter, Curator of Prints at the Boston Museum of Fine Arts, wrote to his friend H.O. McCurry, then Director of the National Gallery of Canada, about a collection in Quebec City. A Boston physician, who was a member of Rossiter's Print Committee, had recommended the textiles collection gathered by a Mr D. Morgan, keeper of a shop opposite the Chateau Frontenac. Rossiter, in turn, brought it to the attention of McCurry:

> What a nice piece of original research it would offer to some scholarly Canadian... and what a chance to rescue something for Canada that was artistic and made there. A nice catalogue with some reproductions in colour!!!

In 1939, the National Gallery did, indeed, acquire some textiles from the estate of Mr Morgan, through the good offices of Dr Marius Barbeau, then Director of the National Museum of Man. These have now been brought together, with examples from many other private and public collections, to offer a history of developments in hand-spinning and weaving in Canada. Mrs Dorothy Burnham is the "scholarly Canadian" who has seized the opportunity to do research on "something... artistic and made [in Canada]."

With this exhibition the National Gallery also recalls a recommendation made by its Board of Governors in the Annual Report of 1943–1944:

> ...exhibitions of Canadian crafts should be organized without delay to demonstrate to our own people the wealth of material ... produced in Canada and to stress the importance of such activities in both rural and urban communities.

As a museum of art, the National Gallery recognizes aesthetic quality, historical significance, and intellectual content in applied, decorative, or the minor arts as in the "fine" arts. Its collections are stronger in painting than in any other medium, but the gift of the Henry Birks Collection of Canadian Silver has supplied another strength. Exhibitions such as this one of Canadian textiles, and the help of scholars from outside the Gallery, are methods by which the Gallery seeks to redress possible imbalances posed by the limitations of its collections. In addition, the generosity of other collectors in making loans to such travelling exhibitions as *The Comfortable Arts* helps to enlarge the experience of all Canadians.

Hsio-Yen Shih
Director
March 1981

(Detail, cat. no. 162)

Acknowledgements and List of Lenders

The organization of this exhibition and catalogue has been a great cooperative adventure, involving Canadians from one coast to the other. To the thirty-seven institutions and the two private owners who are so generously lending their treasures to the exhibition, *The Comfortable Arts*, I give my sincere thanks. Listed by province, they are as follows:

Alberta: Department of Cultural History, Glenbow-Alberta Institute, Calgary; Department of Ethno-Cultural History and Department of Ethnology, Provincial Museum of Alberta, Edmonton; Mrs Tillie Wieczorek, Edmonton.

British Columbia: Doukhobor Village Museum, Doukhobor Historical Society, Castlegar; Museum of Anthropology, University of British Columbia, Vancouver; Department of Ethnology, Vancouver Centennial Museum, Vancouver; Department of Ethnology, British Columbia Provincial Museum, Victoria.

Manitoba: Musée de Saint Boniface, Saint Boniface; Department of Ethnology and Department of Multicultural Studies, Manitoba Museum of Man and Nature, Winnipeg.

New Brunswick: Musée acadien, Caraquet; Village historique acadien, Caraquet; York-Sunbury Historical Society Museum, Fredericton; Musée acadien, Université de Moncton, Moncton; Kings Landing Historical Settlement, Prince William; The New Brunswick Museum, Saint John.

Newfoundland: Newfoundland Museum, St. John's.

Nova Scotia: Nova Scotia Museum, Halifax; Museum of Cape Breton Heritage, Northeast Margaree; Mrs. Hector Campbell, Sydney.

Ontario: Ontario Science Centre, Don Mills; Black Creek Pioneer Village, Downsview; Stone Shop Museum, Grimsby; Doon Pioneer Village, Kitchener; London Centennial Museum, London; Upper Canada Village, Morrisburg; National Gallery of Canada, Ottawa; Canadian Ethnology Service, History Division, and Centre for Folk Culture Studies, National Museum of Man, Ottawa; Ethnology Department and Textile Department, Royal Ontario Museum, Toronto.

Prince Edward Island: Prince Edward Island Heritage Foundation, Charlottetown; Confederation Centre Art Gallery and Museum, Charlottetown; Musée acadien de l'Île-du-Prince-Édouard, Miscouche.

Quebec: McCord Museum, Montreal; Musée du Québec, Quebec; Monastère des Ursulines de Québec, Quebec.

Saskatchewan: Western Development Museum, North Battleford; Museum of Natural History, Regina; Ukrainian Museum of Canada, Saskatoon.

On a more personal level, behind each loan there have been special people – administrators, loan officers, curators, technicians, preparators, conservators, photographers – or sometimes the single employee of a small museum, who have gone out of their way to help me in my quest. To all of them, my warmest appreciation for without their enthusiastic support this venture would have been a dreary labour rather than a joyous experience.

Special thanks to those experts who have kindly read and commented on sections of the catalogue related to their areas of expertise Ted Brasser and Denis Alsford of the Canadian Ethnology Service, National Museum of Man; Dr. Mark Mealing of the School of Doukhobor Studies, Castlegar; my colleagues, Dr. Edward Rogers of the Ethnology Department and John Vollmer of the Textile Department at the Royal Ontario Museum. Any mistakes or omissions are mine, but the generous help of these men has led to the production of a better catalogue.

No major exhibition can be a one-man show. Many people at the National Gallery have been deeply involved in the planning and realization of this exhibition and its accompanying catalogue. I am grateful to the Director, Dr Hsio-Yen Shih, and her Exhibitions Committee, who had the courage to say yes to my proposal; to the Department of Exhibitions, particularly Richard Graburn and Darcy Edgar, who have given their continuous support; to Sylvain Allaire and Ross Fox, the curators who have worked with me and looked after both me and exhibits; to the photographers, Ellis Kerr and Claude Lupien, who have made beautiful photographs when it was impossible for the lenders to supply them; to John Anthony, Chief Installations Officer at the National Gallery, and the staff of Design and Technical Services of the National Museums Corporation, who have worked their usual magic; and to Barbara Keyser of the Gallery's Conservation Department, who stepped into the breach and did necessary conservation with the help of Eva Burnham, Chief of the Textile Division of the Canadian Conservation Institute and her staff. Their timely help and the C.C.I.'s hospitality in allowing the use of their facilities is much appreciated. Added to the careful conservation done by the larger lending institutions, all this has assured the level of "good housekeeping" required for an attractive textile exhibition.

Peter Smith and his staff in the Publications Division at the N.G.C. have not only been efficient in their work, but a pleasure to work with! My thanks to all, and most especially to Pamela Fry, English editor, who has clarified my meanings and smoothed my English; to Hélène Papineau who has given me a voice in French and who was assisted by Bibiane April-Proux, Professor of Weaving; to Colleen Evans who has done the monumental task of gathering illustrations from across the country; and to the designer, Virginia Morin, who has brought all the jigsaw pieces together.

In all dimensions, height or length, which usually indicates the direction of the warp in the weave, precedes width. Fringe measurements are not included in dimensions because so many of the fringes are irregular.

List of Figures

List of Diagrams

(Detail, fig. 11)

(Diagram 2)

Introduction

Things that are always with us and always dependable have a quality of invisibility. From cradle to grave we are surrounded by textiles, yet how many of us ever stop to consider that a complete miracle has been performed by the making of a piece of cloth. The usefulness of textiles is undisputed; life would be unthinkable without them and they can also be very beautiful, with a subtle beauty that is satisfying to the senses of both sight and touch.

From my years of work in the Textile Department of the Royal Ontario Museum has grown a love affair with Canadian textiles. Their quality and sturdy beauty is exciting. The indomitable spirit of the makers is in them, providing a close, personal link with our Canadian past. Several years ago, tired of my favourite subject being treated, at best, as a minor decorative art and, at worst, as something that was only useful for keeping warm and decent, I approached the National Gallery of Canada. I suggested that it was time for Canadian textiles to be treated with the respect they deserved – as an art form – and the Gallery agreed! What *they* then suggested sounded very much like a jail sentence: they gave me ninety days to travel across the country to select a worthy gathering of Canadian textiles. Indeed a "life sentence" would not have been too long for the purpose, but with my ninety days and the cooperation of many people, an exciting selection of material, celebrating the skills of Canadian spinners and weavers, was brought together.

As can be seen by the contents of this book I attempted to achieve a balance between east, west, and centre, but this objective was constantly being complicated by either too much or too little to choose from. My travels were preceded and followed by endless correspondence but, at this point, it was not possible to do any grass-roots research. I had to rely mainly on the museums that are spread across the country, and if these organizations had not yet found textiles, their areas are inadequately represented here.

The eastern half of Canada has been so well explored, textile-wise, during the last number of years that the selection of material was agonizing – so many riches had to be excluded because of lack of space! On the other hand, the western provinces presented quite a different problem, since the time-span of their existence is so much shorter. By the time of western settlement, store-bought goods were fairly readily available, and it was only among a few groups that textile making was really practised as a basic craft. So far there has been little research done on the subject, but hopefully within the next very few years, before pioneer memory dies of old age, researchers will fill out the western picture in much greater detail than has been as yet achieved. I am fortunate in being able to at least illustrate a small group of outstanding western pieces that may set in motion the search for more.

When work was initiated on this project the first title suggested was *Unlike the Lilies – They Toiled, They Spun, They Wove*. Intriguing as it may sound, it was not used. The biblical allusion to the famous lilies that did not spin, but were still able to outdo Solomon in the way of raiment was a little farfetched, and the "toil" sounded dreary. Old-fashioned toil *is* indeed dreary, but mighty few people ever established themselves in this country without undertaking a considerable amount of plain, hard work. The exciting thing is that so many rose above it and, when it came to spinning and weaving, also a heavy form of toil, they did not just make the plainest and roughest fabric to serve their purpose. Instead, they lifted their spirits by spinning a good yarn, dyeing it, and working it into a fabric that would be a pleasure to use.

The title that was finally chosen for this book – *The Comfortable Arts: Traditional Spinning and Weaving in Canada* – tells the story but gives rather a soft impression. That unattractive word "toil" may have disappeared, but it does not change the reality – Canada has not been an easily settled land. Behind all the creations shown in the following pages there lies not only the work that went into the making of the actual fabric, but the preliminary work of draining the marshes, clearing the trees, removing the stones, and breaking the sod, before the fibres for the textiles could be raised and the material finally made. The comfortable arts of spinning and weaving shown here are a true manifestation of the human spirit rising above the difficulties of a pioneering way of life.

The material comes from a wide range of ethnic origins: many of the native peoples; Acadian, Western, and Quebec French; the Loyalists who came from the United States following the American Revolution; those immigrants from the British Isles and Germany who settled in Ontario during the early and middle part of the nineteenth century; as well as that great flood of people of many origins who moved in to fill up the land, as the West opened up in the latter part of the nineteenth and the beginning of the twentieth century. As a result, the dates of the pieces which appear in this book vary enormously. They stretch from quite early in the history of Canada until a comparatively short time ago, but all are from the period of settlement, or very shortly after it, when roots were still being put down in the new country.

The range of material is wide but not all-embracing. Regrettably, the fascinating textile subject of the baskets made by the native and other peoples is just too large for inclusion. Some embroideries are described, but only if the ground fabric as well as the decoration was locally hand-produced. Industrial development is mentioned only where it is an adjunct to the work of local craftsmen. Craft revival is an important fact in the textile production of individuals, and of government-sponsored movements. It is an interesting tale that could provide material for another whole volume, but it is not part of this story. A fairly recent type of textile production, the weaving of materials for ethnic costumes used in multi-cultural festivities is also important. However, it has no connection with the way the early comers, whether from long ago or not so long ago, rose to the challenge of providing themselves with household goods and clothing in a pioneer society.

In the process of selecting material it has been possible for me to handle the different pieces, to turn them over, and to examine them in detail, even using magnification. Neither an exhibition nor a book can provide others with such privileges, so diagrams of some constructions have been included in the hope that the reader can, in some measure, share the pleasure of close observation. This is particularly important with the very fine pieces of native origin, where the work is so detailed and so meticulous

that it is difficult to appreciate with the naked eye the skill and dexterity that went into the making. Nevertheless, even with its diagrams and details of construction this is not a how-to-do-it book. It is a book for the non-specialist, for those who simply enjoy things Canadian and Canada in all its diversity. It is a book for spectators, but as with other forms of spectating – hockey, tennis, whatever – it will provide more fun, and the skills involved will be better appreciated, if some of the limitations and difficulties of the medium are grasped. The following few pages therefore provide a general background, some explanation of terminology, and a little basic textile technology, in the hope of augmenting the visual pleasure provided by this gathering of Canadian spinning and weaving.

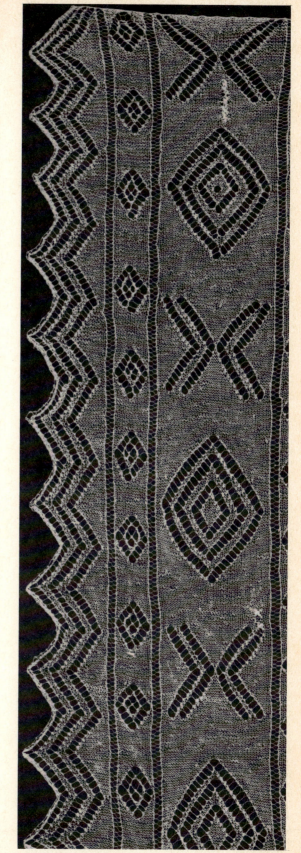

(Detail, cat. no. 158)

Spinners and Weavers.

The roles of the sexes, with regard to textiles, were quite mixed. Among the native peoples the women were the textile-makers, and this was also true for almost all among other groups. However, if there were no daughters in the family, a son might have to help with the spinning. In the case of professionals it was different. Some women wove professionally, using simple household looms. But complex equipment, such as multi-shaft looms and those with jacquard attachment were used by men, and only by those men who had served their apprenticeship as weavers. Complex weaving was specialists' work.

Fibres.

There were a number of fibres used in the production of textiles in Canada. The native peoples had indigenous fibres, such as the inner bark of various trees and bast fibres, quite similar to flax, from the stems of plants like milkweed and nettle. They also used wool from buffalo, mountain goat, mountain sheep, and a special little dog that was domesticated on the West Coast. The pioneers planted flax and hemp, which were used for the oil in their seeds and the fibres in the stems of the plants. Sheep were imported and raised in many areas but, until the country was fairly well cleared, it was an uphill fight to establish a flock and guard it from predators. A shortage of wool is a recurring theme in the history of textile-making in Canada. Machine-spun cotton yarn was imported at an early date and was widely used. At first, it was only available in the form of singles yarn and when a heavier yarn was required it was plyed with a spinning wheel.

Spinning.

The linen and woollen yarns used for both weaving and knitting in pioneer times were largely spun by hand in all parts of the country, and this has continued in some areas until quite recently. Spinning is simply the twisting of fine fibres around each other

so that, with their natural roughness, they cling together and form a yarn. It can be done by twisting between the hands or rolling the fibres on the thigh. A small stick, held in the hand on which the spun fibre can be wound, facilitates the twisting, and various simple methods such as this were employed, particularly in the West. If the stick is weighted, it can be twirled and dropped, stretching attached fibres out and putting the twist in them at the same time. This method was of widespread use among the peasants in Europe and was sometimes used in Canada by the Ukrainians and the Doukhobors.

The most common type of spinning wheel in eastern Canada was the "Great" or "Wool" wheel, such as the one shown in fig. 22. With it, the spindle is held on a mount and is turned rapidly as the wheel is revolved. More advanced types of spinning wheels, with treadles and with the addition of a flyer on the spindle, are found in different forms all across the country (see figs 23, 34, and 37). The flyer makes it possible to pull out the fibres, twist them, and roll up the spun yarn in a continuous action.

Spinning can be done with the twist running either to the right or to the left. There is a very useful notation for the direction of the twist that has come into general use. If the angle of the twist follows the slope of the central bar of a Z, it is said to be "Z-twist," if it follows the slope of an S, it is "S-twist." The plying of a thread is almost always done in the opposite direction to the original twist. If a yarn is described as Z,2S it means that the yarn has been spun in the Z direction and two Z-singles yarns have been plyed together in the S direction (Diagram 1).

Knitting.

There are many ways of making a fabric with only minimal equipment, and knitting is probably the method most familiar to all of us. It certainly played an enormous part in the clothing of early Canadians. Knitting was done from locally handspun woollen yarns in all parts of Canada, wherever there were sheep. It was of far wider use than weaving, but as it was plain and mainly utilitarian, very little early knitting has survived (see cat. nos 106, 107, and 144).

Braiding.

This technique was used by both the native peoples of the Great Lakes region and the Quebec French, particularly for the making of ornamental sashes (see Chapter II).

Weaving.

Weaving consists of two separate elements of thread that interlace. One element is made up of a number of threads, called the warp. The warp threads are held in some way, possibly only hanging from a bar, but more usually wound on a frame or stretched on a loom. The other element, a single thread called the weft, is worked through the warp, over and under the threads from one side to the other, and is then returned under and over other warp threads. This side-to-side movement of the weft is continued, forming a woven textile. Weaving can be done completely by hand, but it was long ago discovered that, with the help of a series of sticks and string loops, the openings through the warp could be made quite quickly and easily. The opening through the warp threads is called a shed, and the addition of a shedding device to a weaving frame turns it into a true loom.

The true loom was not used by the native peoples of Canada. Their remarkable weaving was done with the passage of the weft through the warp, formed entirely by hand. It did not make their weaving any less beautiful or expert – just more time-consuming. The weaving device used by all other groups in Canada was very similar to the hand loom which is shown and described in fig. 28. Other loom frames might be more solid or less solid, and the parts might vary a bit, but in general the illustrated loom is the type common to all parts of the country. It has four ways of making shed openings, and the shed making is controlled by wooden shafts on which there are string loops, called heddles, through which the individual warp threads are carried. Simpler looms have just two shafts but more complex looms, which were used particularly in Nova Scotia, New Brunswick, and Ontario, sometimes had as many as twenty shafts. Another, even more complex handloom, the jacquard loom, with a shedding system controlled by a series of punched cards, was used by professional weavers in Ontario during the middle and latter part of the nineteenth century.

Handlooms were usually quite narrow. The shuttle carrying the weft thread was thrown through the shed opening from one of the weaver's hands and was caught by the other hand at the other side of the warp, so the width of the warp was limited by the weaver's reach. This meant that anything wide, like a blanket or a coverlet, was woven in two separate widths and was seamed down the centre of the piece. The centre seam is the tell-tale sign of a handwoven piece and is also, if the pattern comes together neatly, the sign of a good weaver. It took considerable skill and experience to weave a web so evenly that the two parts matched exactly. Occasionally we find wide handwoven pieces without a centre seam, because there were a few wide looms that were operated by two weavers, one at either side. There were also looms equipped with a flying shuttle, a sort of sling device that was one of the early inventions of the Industrial Revolution, which allowed the weaver to control a shuttle on a width wider than his reach. As a centre seam is normal with wide handwoven pieces, it is not as a rule remarked upon in the following catalogue descriptions.

Basic Weave Constructions.

There are three constructions that are basic:
1. Tabby is the simplest form of interlacing warp and weft (Diagram 2). Each weft passes alternately over and under single warp threads across the width of the warp and returns through the reverse shed. Tabby can be woven on a loom with only two shafts.
2. Twill requires more than two shafts on the loom. Two common forms are illustrated, each requiring a loom with four shafts. The first is a 2/2 twill (Diagram 3) and the warp and weft interlace, using floats of two threads with a step over one warp thread on each successive passage of the weft. Diagram 4 shows a 3/1 twill with the warp and weft interlacing by floating over three threads and then being tied down by one thread. There are many varieties of twill constructions, some of which are much more complex than the above. A number of twill constructions

1 Spinning; S, Z, and ply

2 Tabby

3 Twill, 2/2

are discussed and illustrated in the following pages.

3. Satin, the third basic weave, is important in other parts of the world but was only used by one Canadian jacquard coverlet weaver (see cat. no. 139). For its effect, satin depends on a construction with long floats unobstrusively bound down. The construction used in Canada (Diagram 5) is the simplest possible version of the satin weave. It has a float of four threads, with the single thread ties distributed so that they are less obtrusive than the stepping that characterizes twills.

Weft-Twined Weave.

This is a different type of weave construction from the basic three, and was very important in the weaving done by the native peoples. It is really a basketry technique, adapted to the weaving of flexible fibres. There are many versions, but the simplest (Diagram 6), has two wefts handled together, enclosing a warp thread, then twisting around each other before enclosing the next warp thread. Other versions of the weave are shown in Diagrams 13 to 20, 22, and 23. The direction of the twining may be described by using S and Z, as in the notation for spinning.

Tapestry is a weave that creates a pattern by the use of weft threads of different colours that do not pass across the full width of the warp. Instead, they work backwards and forwards, interweaving only with the part of the warp that is required for a particular colour area of the pattern. The weft threads often turn around on adjacent warps (see cat. no. 160), leaving slits between the different colour areas (Diagram 7), or they may link and turn on a common warp thread (see cat. nos 149, 150, 151, and Diagram 93). Usually, tabby is the basic weave used for tapestry patterning, but twined weave is also used (see cat. nos 11, 12, 14, and 15).

Brocading is a way of patterning a weave by working extra wefts backwards and forwards in limited areas above a ground weave. It is a technique of many variations. The false embroidery of cat. nos 8 and 9 is technically a brocading technique. More normal versions are found in the Quebec coverlets, cat. nos 48

to 52, and in the Ukrainian piece, cat. no. 151, and Diagram 94.

In the diagrams of the weaves, for the sake of clarity, the threads are shown spread apart. The actual fabrics are more compact. In some of the diagrams, to increase the understanding of a given weave, the individual threads are shaded where they would be visible on the surface of the weave, but are shown in line only where they would be hidden in the weave (see Diagrams 20, and 83 to 90). Most of the diagrams also show the weaves as being balanced in weight and spacing between warp and weft. Although this is often the case, there are times when it is not. In woven fabrics there are all possible variations of heavy and light and closely and widely spaced threads, from totally warp-faced materials to those in which only the weft is visible. No matter what the spacing of weight of the warp and weft, the constructions are constant, utilizing one of the basic weaves, which may be decorated in one or more of a number of ways, many of which are illustrated in the following pages.

4 *Twill, 3/1*

6 *Weft-twined weave, simple type*

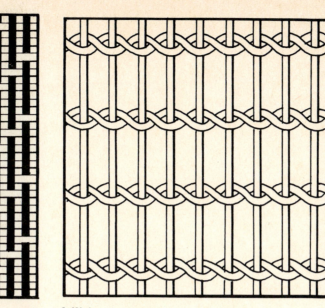

5 *Satin*

7 *Tapestry, split type*

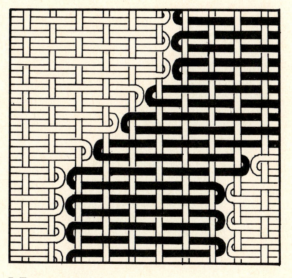

(Detail, cat. no. 12)

Canada was a multi-cultural land long before the coming of the Europeans and, in textile making, as with all other aspects of the culture, there was great variety. It is not possible to present a full range or even a balanced selection of examples, but the following items have been chosen to show as many techniques as possible and particularly to emphasize the marvellous textile skills and artistic ability that was to be found among the native peoples in every part of the country.[1]

There were many kinds of weaving frames but there were no true looms in use among the native peoples. In their weaving, the working of the threads was entirely manual, consequently slow, and there was no incentive for the development of the kind of utilitarian weaving that would depend for its practicality on rapid production. If a blanket or a garment was needed, the skin of an animal was a much easier source of material than the laborious converting of native fibres into woven cloth. This does not mean that textiles were not made. Basketry and mat-making were done on a large scale, but when the same techniques that were used for making these practical, and often very beautiful articles, were adapted to fine, flexible fibres it was not to produce utility objects, but ritual or prestige items that were more like fine jewellery than textiles.

The art of spinning was well developed among the Indians. Spindles and spindle whorls were used on the West Coast, but in much of the rest of the country thread was spun by simply twisting the fibres between the hands or by rolling them on the thigh. These are not fast processes, but produce perfectly good thread. Sewing in pre-contact times, and for long after, was done with a thread made from animal sinew, split, and then rolled as in simple spinning. Sewing with sinew could be done without an eyed needle. An awl was used to punch a hole for the stitch and the sinew was shoved through the hole without benefit of needle. Skill and patience were not lacking among Indian women who were the makers of textiles.

Early textiles are usually of better quality than later ones and it is tempting to say that the introduction of trade goods led to the decline, but the facts do not bear that out. From the evidence of existing material, it is plain that the introduction of trade goods provided a stimulus and the highest point in the artistic production of Indian textiles came after trade goods were available. The Indian women took the woven cloth, beads, ribbons, metal ornaments, fine steel needles, and good sewing threads and used them in their own inventive way to supplement and decorate their native materials. Quality improved, and did not decline until considerably later, when other pressures came into play.

Among several native communities there were slaves, but it was not like the great ancient slave-owning societies of other lands, where there was such a large mass of cheap labour that it could be applied to all sorts of useless luxuries, like the making of impossibly fine textiles or the building of pyramids. One cannot help but question the time-factor in connection with the more special textile creations. We know that women were the textile artists, but how did a busy Indian wife look after children, cook, chop wood, prepare skins, make clothing, and so on, and yet manage to find time to perfect her textile skills and to produce beautiful and non-essential luxury items? The answer may be relatively simple. In pre-contact and early contact times, the idea of monogamy was not part of Indian life, and an expert hunter often had more than one wife. It is an intriguing thought in these days of "women's liberation" to wonder if the liberty for a woman to be a creative artist came from the cooperation of another wife within a family unit. Monogamy is certainly not the only reason for a decline in the quality of textile production, but it may be a hidden contributing factor.

1 Man's "rabbit-skin" parka   about 1955

Looped netting, height 1.3 m
Northern Ojibwa, Weagamow Lake, northern
Ontario

Rabbits, correctly speaking, "varying hares", are often plentiful in areas where there is a great need for warm coverings and where larger, fur-bearing animals may be scarce. As their skins are fragile and tear easily if joined by sewing, other simple techniques have been used to convert this resource into warm blankets and coats. If each animal skin is cut spirally it produces a long, narrow strip of approximately three metres in length. These can be twisted to form firm, fur-covered cords that can be worked together in various ways to make a fabric that is light, flexible, very warm, and fairly durable. The working of rabbit strips is very ancient, and has been practised over wide areas of North America since prehistoric times. This coat has been looped, stitch on stitch (Diagram 8). The looping was done on a simple frame, with the different parts of the coat made separately, then joined by lacing with fur strips. As with other textile techniques, this method of making coats and blankets was considered women's work. It required about six days and up to two hundred skins to make a large blanket.[2]

Royal Ontario Museum, Toronto (959.50.67).

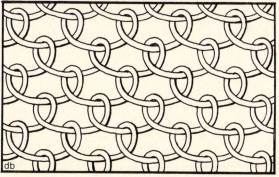

8 Looped netting

2 Hunting bag   early twentieth century

Looped netting, 27.0 x 44.0 cm
Athapaskan, Northwest Territories

Strong, light, flexible, open bags of various sizes, but roughly of this same form, are characteristic of western subarctic regions. The mesh is made of fine strips of rawhide, called *babiche*, worked in the same simple looping technique used for the parka (cat. no. 1). These hunting bags were often lavishly decorated, and the mesh of this one has several rows of the looping in which an extra twist has been inserted (Diagram 9), as well as many carefully-made tassels of knitting wools, tied off with beaded skin strips. The top is finished with fine beads, silk ribbon, red flannel, and a handsome band of quill weaving. In this case, skilled native techniques and materials have been enriched by a limited use of trade goods.

Manitoba Museum of Man and Nature, Winnipeg (H4.3.38).

9 Looped netting with extra twist

3 Pair of snowshoes   about 1911

Swallowtail type, 86.0 x 55.0 cm
Montagnais, Les Escoumins, Quebec

The frame of these snowshoes is a single piece of birch, a wood that is light, tough, and resilient and much used for snowshoes. The shape is the wide, rounded form used in northeastern Canada. The lace, cut from a caribou skin, interweaves by working backwards, forwards, and diagonally across the frame in a well worked out sequence that makes a hexagonal mesh. Each line passes over another line and under the following one in every direction in which it runs.[3] The subtle pattern on the toe has been made by putting a twist in as the web is formed (Diagram 10). This type of lace, used for snowshoes and many other articles, is called *babiche*, and is simply a fine rawhide strip. Long lengths can be made by cutting round and round a circular piece of skin. *Babiche* is used wet then, on drying, it shrinks, thus tightening up the work and producing a strong and very firm fabric.

Royal Ontario Museum, Toronto (956.160.5).

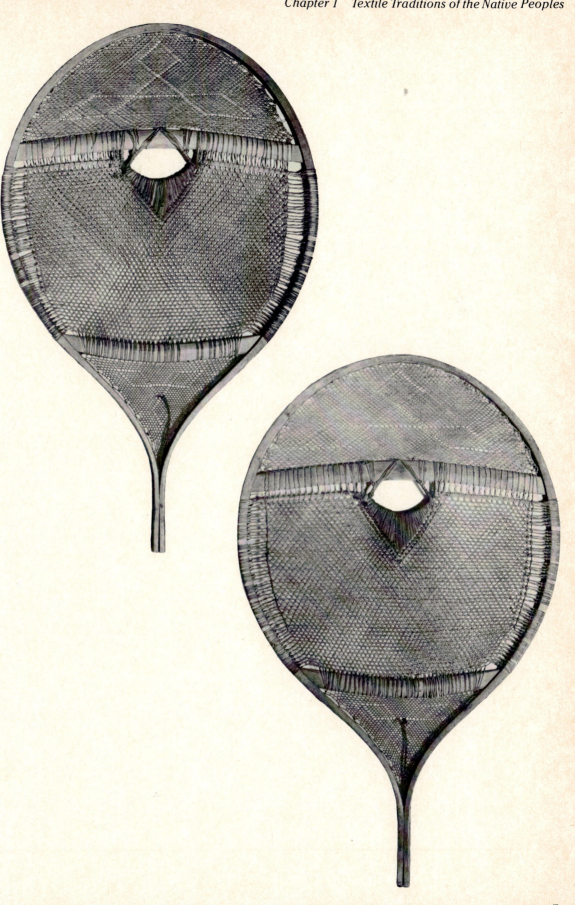

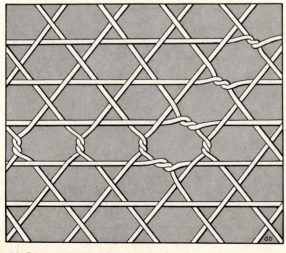

10 Snowshoe lacing, hexagonal

4 Pair of snowshoes   early twentieth century

Athapaskan type, 1.43 x 0.29 m
Kutchin, South Mackenzie River, Northwest
Territories

Snowshoe frames in the Northwest are made
from two lengths of wood and are often
pointed at each end, where the two pieces
meet. This beautifully-shaped pair has
pointed heels but the wood is carefully bent
and spliced over the toes, making them
smooth, raised, and rounded – ideally suited
to the snow conditions and the terrain for
which they are intended. The lacing of toe
and heel sections are of very fine *babiche* in
the usual hexagonal mesh. The central
portion, which needs extra strength, is made
in a way that is obviously based on a basketry
technique. A vertical lacing is held at
intervals by a stiff element, passing across
and bound firmly into place by a flexible
element. This form of square lacing is a
weft-twined weaving technique (Diagram
11).

Royal Ontario Museum, Toronto (22198).

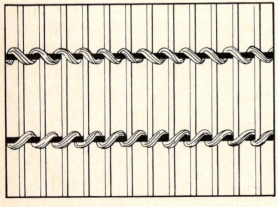

11 Snowshoe lacing, square

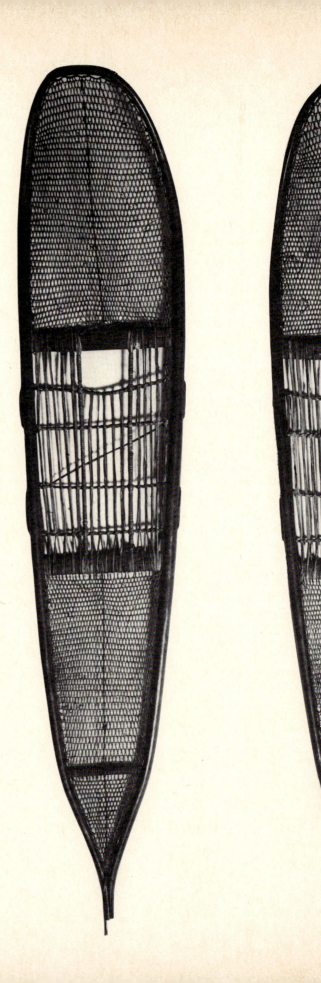

5 Mat of cedar bark   early twentieth century

Tabby with twill patterning, 2.10 x 1.21 m
Haida, British Columbia

Mat-making is a very ancient form of textile production. It was practised in many areas of Canada, using any available vegetal materials such as reeds, bulrushes, grasses, osiers, and, on the West Coast, the inner bark of cedar trees, either shredded, or split into fine strips as in this piece. Mats were used for all sorts of household purposes; for creating some degree of privacy in communal living quarters; and, occasionally, even for sails.

Mats were usually made on simple frames with two uprights and a cross-bar, from which the warp could be suspended. Warp and weft were interlaced by hand, often worked diagonally down from an upper corner. The basic weave of this piece is tabby, with alternately natural and black warps and wefts. The pattern is created by making twill or two-thread skips in a regular sequence on diagonal lines (Diagram 12). These floats change the usual thread crossing of dark over light and light over dark, to dark over dark and light over light. By this simple means, the vertical lines of the pattern are turned into horizontal ones and the pattern of concentric squares is formed. When a pattern such as this is created by the order in which two or more colours are used, in combination with the weave construction, it is called a "colour and weave effect."[4]

Royal Ontario Museum, Toronto (HN 223).

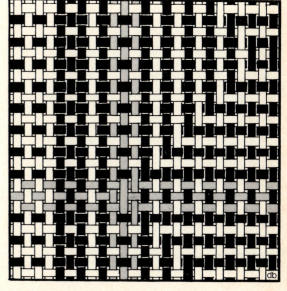

12 Bark mat, colour and weave effect

Weft-Twined Weave

Weft-twined weave, an important prehistoric textile technique of world-wide distribution, is a simple form of weaving. It is performed manually, with weft threads twined around each other in either an "S" or a "Z" direction as they enclose each warp end, or group of warp ends, in turn. Probably the oldest use of weft-twining was with comparatively stiff fibres for the making of baskets. It is still a popular basketry technique, but it is also a form of weaving that is adaptable to flexible fibres.

Among the native peoples of Canada, the weave had a wide distribution and many variations. The simplest is like that used for the bark fibre cape (see Diagram 6, and also cat. no. 10), with widely spaced pairs of wefts twined around each warp in turn. A firm fabric, as shown on the undecorated parts of the bags in cat. no. 9, can be made by spacing the wefts closely (Diagram 13). If the wefts are twined around two warp threads instead of one, the weave is often varied by alternating the pairs of warps to be enclosed on succeeding rows. When the wefts are closely spaced it results in a weave with a diagonal effect (Diagram 14).[5]

If weft-twined weaving on split pairs is done with the wefts spaced widely, the result is like a lattice (Diagram 15). In all types so far described, the weft threads twine around each other with a half twist, changing places with each twist. There are also versions of the weave with the wefts making a full twist around each other, each maintaining its position on either the face or the reverse of the fabric (Diagram 16).

Twined weaving with a full twist may have one fairly stiff weft element that always stays on one side of the fabric, and which is wrapped into place by another flexible weft element (Diagram 17). There are great possibilities for patterning if half twist and full twist are combined with wefts of two different colours (Diagram 18).

15 Weft-twined weave, widely spaced on split pairs

16 Weft-twined weave, fully twisted wefts

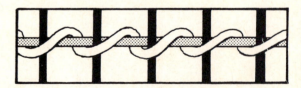

17 Weft-twined weave, fully twisted with stiff element

13 Weft-twined weave, firm

14 Weft-twined weave, closely spaced on split pairs

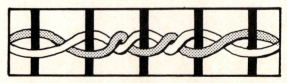

18 Weft-twined weave, half twist and full twist

6 Bag mid-nineteenth century

Weft-twined and twill weave, 36.0 x 46.0 cm
Ojibwa, Algoma District, Ontario

This bag was used to store objects of special
significance, and is of great rarity and
interest. Two springy sticks planted upright
in the ground with a cord between them
would have provided support for the warp
threads. The weft would have been worked
round and round them, forming the weave
entirely by hand, just as in the weaving of a
basket.[6] The wool, in shades of brown, red,
yellow, and orange, is very irregularly spun
and may be reworked ravellings from trade
cloth. The weave is plain 2/2 twill between
bands of a weft-twined weave on split pairs of
warps (S-twine). The wefts used for the
twining are in two colours and, by a change
of the order in which the colours are used, a
chevron pattern is formed in this otherwise
unvaried weave (Diagram 19). The rows of
dots are simply made by the enclosing of
three rather than two warps with each twist
of the weft-twining.

Royal Ontario Museum, Toronto (HD. 12572).

19 *Weft-twined and twill weave*

9

7 Wampum pouch   probably late
eighteenth century

Double-faced weft-twined weave,
11.5 x 16.5 cm
Great Lakes area

This small pouch is associated with the Penn
Treaty wampum belt, which is also in the
Royal Ontario Museum. Belt and pouch came
to the museum together, from an early
collection and, when folded, the width of the
belt fits neatly into the width of the pouch.
Traditionally, the wampum dates from 1682,
but the pouch was probably made for the belt
after it was brought to Canada by the
Delaware, who settled in Ontario at the end
of the eighteenth century. A native bast fibre
in natural, black, and grey-green is used
a small amount of red wool. The technique is
a complex weft-twined weave (S-twine),
done on pairs of warp threads. The warp is
separated into two layers that exchange

places to produce patterns (Diagram 20). On
one side of the pouch there is a turtle and, on
the other, chevrons. A number of bags woven
in this way have survived, particularly from
the Lake Michigan area. This piece, with its
Canadian connection, is unusual and is a
particularly fine and early example.

Royal Ontario Museum, Toronto, Oronhyatekha Collection. Gift of the Independent Order of Foresters
(911.3.130).

20 Weft-twined weave, double-faced

8 Burden strap   before 1780

Weft-twined weave with false embroidery,
centre 61.0 x 5.5 cm
Probably Ojibwa, Eastern Great Lakes area

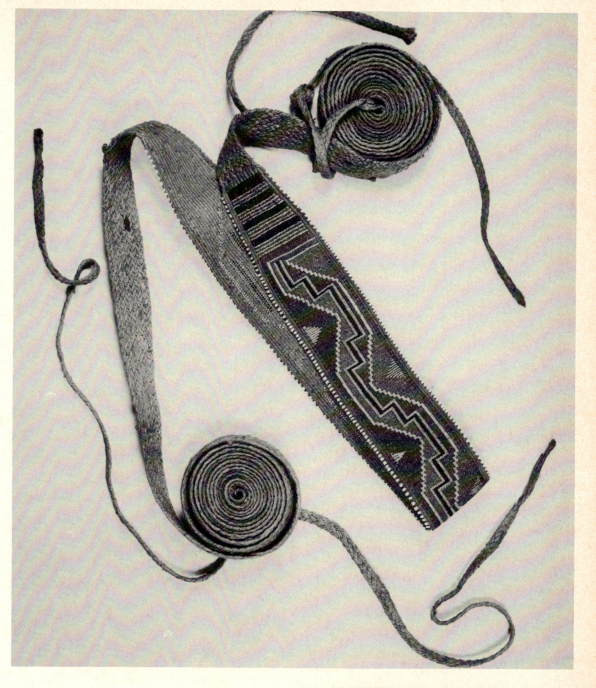

This beautiful burden strap was one of the
Indian "curiosities" that Sir John Caldwell
took with him when he went back to Ireland
after serving with the British Army at Niagara
and Fort Detroit between 1774 and 1780. it
has been published as Ojibwa,[7] presumably
because Sir John was made a chief of the
Ojibwa tribe, but others in the small surviving group of such pieces have been attrib-
uted to Iroquois and Huron. Whatever may
be the exact tribal origin it is an outstanding
example of the skill and artistry of early
textile work from the eastern Great Lakes
area. The form is functional, with a central
band to be placed across the forehead and, at
either end, long braided cords to secure a
heavy load across the back. The basic
material is a native bast fibre, worked in
weft-twined weave (Z-twine). As the ground
was being woven, white, yellow, orange, or
blue moose hair was wrapped around each
weft thread as it came to the face, forming a
very precise and detailed pattern by a
method that is usually called "false embroidery." The technique is the same as that
shown in Diagram 22 with cat. no. 9 but, as
the moose hairs are fine, several are used
together and are wrapped more than once
around each lift of the weft.[8] The edge warps
carry opaque white beads and are bound by
every second passage of the wefts, distrib-
uting the beads evenly along the sides of the
band (Diagram 21).

National Museum of Man, Canadian Ethnology Service,
Ottawa, Ontario. Speyer Collection (III x 237; neg no.
74-7986).

21 Beaded edge of burden strap

9 Pair of bags   about 1900

Weft-twined weave with false embroidery,
56.0 x 38.0 cm, and 56.0 x 42.0 cm
Plateau area, British Columbia

These bags are of a well-known type that was
made by various Indian tribes of the Plateau
area in the mountains of the northwestern
United States and southeastern British
Columbia. They were made as everyday
utility items for storage and carrying bags,
but were also used for trade with the Indians
of the Plains. In that area, they were treated
as something more special and have survived there in use as medicine bags. This pair
belonged to the artist, Edmund Morris, who
is well-known for his portraits of the Plains
Indians.[9] They have been roughly joined by a
band of buffalo hide, probably so the artist
could use them as saddle bags. The technique has a basic fabric of simple weft-twining
(Z-twine; see Diagram 13) and, as the weave
was done, each weft thread as it came to the
surface was wrapped by a variety of natural
fibres (Diagram 22), mostly shredded corn-
husk. Knitting wools in black, green, red, and
brown were used for patterning. The central
parts of the bags are completely covered by
this false embroidery, a technique that is also
much used for basketry patterning.

Royal Ontario Museum, Toronto, Morris Collection.
Bequest of Edmund Morris (913.14.136).

22 *Weft-twined weave with false embroidery*

10 Shoulder cape early twentieth century

Weft-twined weave with painted design, 0.6 x 1.03 m
Probably Nootka, British Columbia

Salmon and wood are the two great resources on which the economy of the native peoples of the West Coast has traditionally been based. Salmon provided an easily obtained staple food and wood provided almost everything else. The use of wood for houses, totem poles, and boxes is obvious, but wood was also converted into various forms of basketry and provided a very useful raw material for the weaving of clothing.[10] The inner bark of both red and yellow cedar trees was processed in different ways for different textile purposes. For garments, it was softened by pounding and shredding the fibres, some of which were used unspun, as in the warp of this cape, while for firmer cords like those in the weft a twist was put in by spinning. Clothes were not much used in early times but, when needed, blankets, wrap-around dresses, and capes such as this were used for protection from rain and cold. The weave of this cape is in the simplest of weft-twining techniques with widely spaced wefts (Z-twine; see Diagram 6).

Royal Ontario Museum, Toronto (HN 1296).

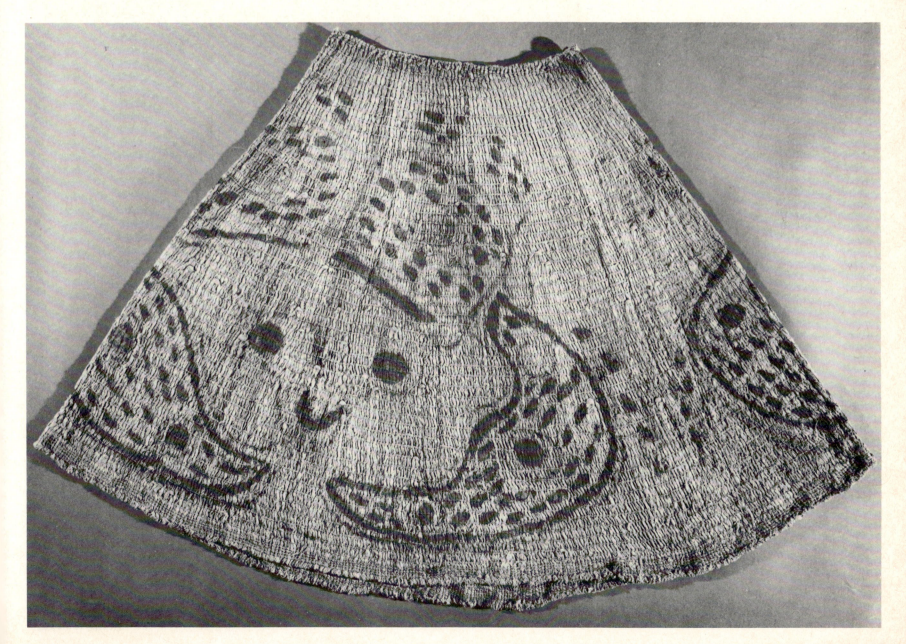

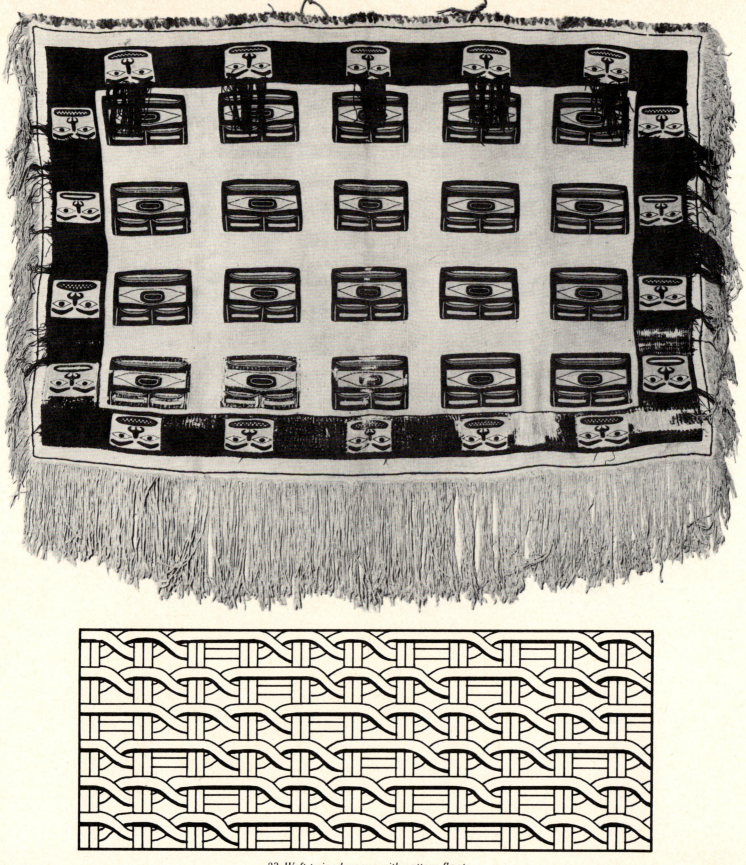

23 Weft-twined weave with pattern floats

11 Shoulder blanket about 1840

Weft-twined tapestry weave, 1.05 x 1.62 m
Tshimshian, Nass River, British Columbia

The masterpieces of West Coast Indian weaving are the elaborate tapestry-woven blankets which were made by using a combination of weft-twining techniques. Cedar bark fabrics were for everyday use, but these productions, made mostly from the limited supply of mountain goat wool, were for festivals. This is an early blanket of rather strange design. It is thought to have been made to celebrate the massacre of an enemy at Kincolith village on the Nass River, and trophy heads form the border.[11]

The frame on which such blankets were woven consisted only of two uprights and a single cross-bar. The free-hanging warp was divided into sections, and weaving was done in a limited area at a time, with the areas merging and changing as work progressed. Any vertical slits left between different sections of the weave were joined by sewing. Both the warp and the weft of this blanket are of mountain goat wool. The weave is very close and firm. The ground is twined (S-twine) on repeating pairs of warp threads, producing a strong vertical rib that is patterned by diagonal lines, formed by the wefts enclosing four warp threads instead of two in a regular stepped sequence (Diagram 23). In the motifs, other weft-twining techniques have been used.

Royal Ontario Museum, Toronto (927.37.142).

Figure 1: Chief Minisqu' of Gitlakdamsk, a Nishga village on the Nass River, wearing the blanket illustrated in cat. no. 11. The photograph was taken by Dr Marius Barbeau. National Museum of Man, Ottawa, Ontario (neg. no. 69696).

12 Tunic   early twentieth century

Weft-twined tapestry weave, 100.0 x 63.0 cm
"Chilkat" type, British Columbia

A West Coast Indian chief in full regalia was
just as impressive as the most gorgeously
attired medieval king or the Emperor of
China. Under a shoulder blanket with complex totemic designs, an apron with similar
patterning might be worn, or, for particular
opulence, a tunic of this type. Tunics were
woven in a tubular manner, starting at the
neck, and shaping the garment during the
weaving by adding or subtracting warp
threads as required. With a head-dress to top
off the magnificent figure, there could be no
doubt that the wearer was important. The
time and skill required for the making of such
a garment meant that their use was confined
to those of real wealth, either male or female.
The Chilkat, a division of the Tlingit tribe of
southern Alaska, were famous as the weavers
of these luxury items, but their use spread
widely among other tribes and the origin of
the craft is thought to be among the
Tshimshian across the Nass and Skeena
Rivers, in northern British Columbia. In this
type of weaving the warp is of cedar bark,
often covered with wool and the weft is of
finely-spun mountain goat wool. The colour
range is limited: usually natural white, dark
brown shading to black, yellow, and green-
blue. The symmetrical designs are like those
used on painted and carved wooden objects
and are based on the wildlife, both mythical
and real, that inhabits the area.[12]

British Columbia Provincial Museum, Victoria (14506).

Figure 2: Paul Kane (1810-1871), Clallum Woman Weaving. *Kane left Toronto in 1846 to journey across Canada, sketching Indian life as he went west. This oil (46.0 x 73.5 cm) was completed about 1850. The sketches upon which it was based were made between 1846 and 1847, near Fort Victoria on Vancouver Island.[13] The scene is in a lodge of the Clallum Indians, a branch of the Salish tribe. One woman is weaving a blanket on the two-beam weaving frame typical of that area. Although not a fully developed loom, for it has no shedding device, it is a considerable advance on the frame with single cross-beam and loosely hanging warp that was used farther north. As can be seen in the painting, the warp is stretched round the two beams and weaving proceeds from the top down. The work was kept at a convenient height by removing wedges, loosening the tension, and pulling the warp up. The little white dog in the foreground probably represents one of the dogs known to have been kept for their wool. Royal Ontario Museum, Toronto. Gift of Sir Edmund Osler (912.1.93).*

Figure 3: This sketch, A Sangeys Girl Spinning, *is the one upon which Paul Kane based the spinning figure in his painting (fig. 2). It is in pencil and watercolour (17.75 x 12.5 cm), and was one of the sketches made in 1846–1847, near Victoria on Vancouver Island. The woman is spinning mountain goat or dog wool, using a very large spindle in a manner unique to that area. Royal Ontario Museum, Toronto. Gift of Raymond A. Willis, in memory of his mother, Mrs E a C. Wolff, a grand-daughter of the Hon. George Allan, Kane's friend and patron (946.15.226).*

13 Shoulder blanket   about 1880

Twill with tapestry weave borders, 1 x 1.50 m
Coast Salish, British Columbia

The Salish Indians, with their special weaving frame (see fig. 2), have weaving traditions that are quite different from their neighbours, a fact that has intrigued ethnographers for many years. Unlike the fine, twined-weave blankets of the more northerly people, their weaving is coarse, usually in a loose 2/2 twill of heavy yarns, spun with the big spindle from mountain goat or dog wool. Patterning as a rule is a simple check, formed by strips of rag, or sometimes by bands of colour in a finer twill weave. This very special blanket is like the one in the Paul Kane scene and was probably woven only about thirty to forty years after the painting was done. It is a rare type known as a Salish "Nobility" blanket and has tapestry-woven borders, worked in trade wools in bright yellow, red, green, and black. The tapestry areas are woven in a combination of tabby and weft-twined weave. The blanket has four finished edges, due to the ingenious way the warp threads were stretched over the two beams of the weaving frame, and turned on a cord between them (Diagram 24). When the weaving was completed, the cord was withdrawn, leaving a length of cloth with both side and transverse selvages.

Photographs taken early in this century show Indians in gala attire wearing such blankets. Survival of blankets patterned in this way is rare, but many fairly plain old ones exist and in recent years there has been a considerable revival of Salish Indian weaving, both plain and patterned.[14]

University of British Columbia, Museum of Anthropology, Vancouver. Acquired through the National Treasure Emergency Policy (A 17200).

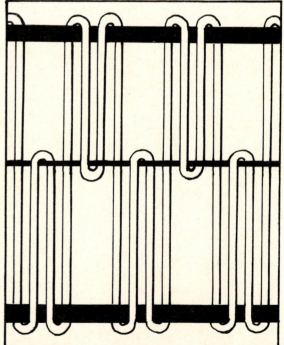

24 Warping on 2-beam weaving frame

14 Burden strap   early nineteenth century

Tabby and weft-twined tapestry weave, 152.0 x 5.5 cm
Coast Salish, British Columbia

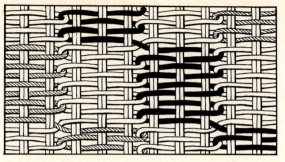

25 *Tabby, check*

This fine burden strap is in the same style and technique as a small group of rare and early Salish blankets.[15] The warp of cedar bark is used in pairs and is entirely covered by a closely-packed weft of wool in natural white, red, and a little green. The wefts do not travel from selvage to selvage, but are carried back and forth in limited areas, producing a tapestry-woven design. In the checkerboard part, the weave is tabby, with the wefts interlocking between the warps (Diagram 25). The diamonds are in weft-twined weave (Z-twine), built up on the diagonal to form the motifs (Diagram 26).

Royal Ontario Museum, Toronto (948.44.1).

26 *Weft-twined diamonds*

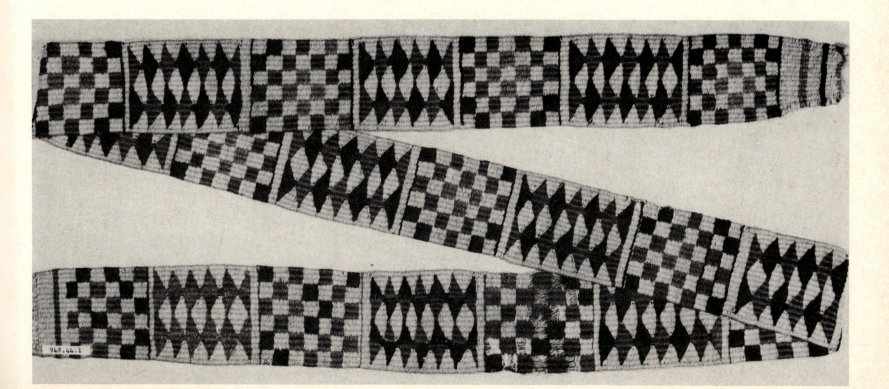

Rigid Heddle Weaving

A rigid heddle is a simple device that provides an easy means of making sheds, or openings, through the warp threads to facilitate the passage of the weft. Rigid heddles can take a number of different forms, but all have a series of slats with holes in the centre and between the slats there are narrow slits. Warp threads are carried alternately through a hole and through a slit. If the heddle is lifted, the warps in the holes are lifted with it, while those that lie freely through the slits remain below. If the heddle is depressed the opposite occurs, and a counter shed is opened up (Diagram 27). With the possibility of opening these two sheds easily, bands for practical uses, such as burden straps, could be woven quickly and efficiently. The use of rigid heddles is widespread among North American Indians, and some consideration has been given to its possible independent invention on this continent. It is now thought that the rigid heddle was brought by early settlers from Europe and to have spread from them to the native peoples.[16]

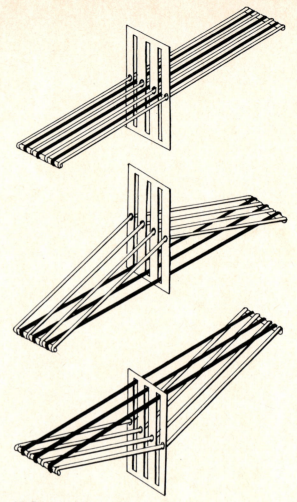

27 Rigid heddle weaving

Figure 4: This rigid heddle is similar in form to European examples that have slats held in a frame but with the wood-working skill of the West Coast Indian, it has been made from a single, solid piece of maple. The unfinished band on it is of fine knitting wools. It was made by the Interior Salish of British Columbia in the mid-twentieth century, and measures 18.0 x 12.5 cm. Vancouver Centennial Museum, Vancouver, British Columbia (AA 1247).

15 Dance apron   late nineteenth century

Warp-faced tabby weave, 0.52 x 1.04 m
Salish, British Columbia

This fascinating piece, a dance apron that would have been worn on ceremonial occasions, is made of joined bands that were woven with the use of a rigid heddle. It is of natural white mountain-goat wool, patterned in red and blue, and the bands are from two different set-ups of the warp: plain stripes, alternating with a simple colour and weave effect (Diagram 28). The edges are bound with a trade cotton, and brass thimbles have been pierced and used as noise-making dangles on the ends of the fringe. Thimbles, being imports, were more exotic and special than the locally obtained puffin beaks and deer hooves that were also popular for this purpose.

Royal Ontario Museum, Toronto (929.37.125).

28 Simple colour and weave effect

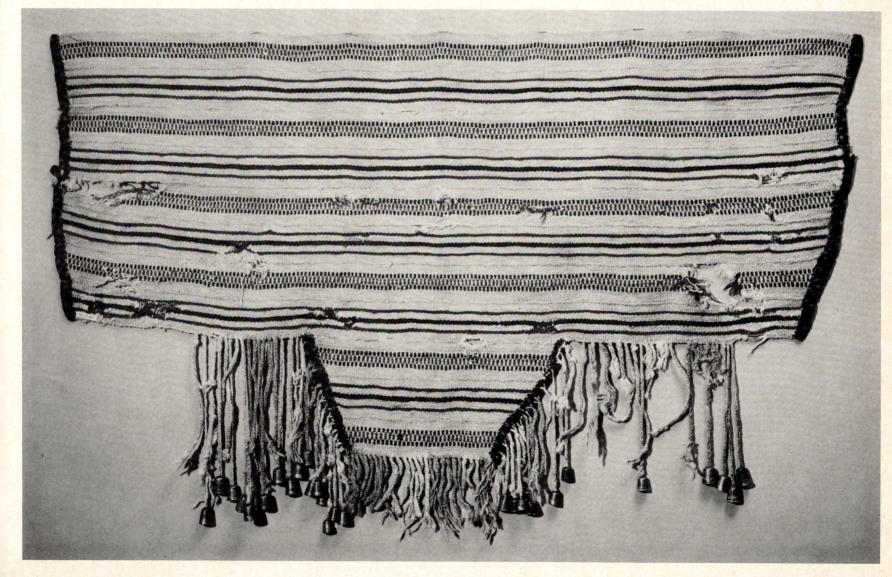

16 Beaded garter   early nineteenth century

Warp-faced tabby weave, 35.0 x 9.5 cm
Ojibwa, Algoma District, Ontario

This decorative garter traditionally belonged to Chief Shingwauk, head chief of the Northern Ojibwa at the time of the war of 1812. It may be an early example of rigid heddle weaving but there are a great many warp threads to be controlled with that kind of a device. The wool is fine, hard English worsted yarn in red, olive green, dark grey, old gold, and black. The small white beads were threaded on the weft and then were placed so as to make longitudinal rows as the weaving progressed, with a bead placed at either selvage as the weft was turned (Diagram 29). The length of the central part of the garter is enough to wrap around a man's leg, just below the knee, and the fringes at either end are long enough to make a firm tie. Probably there was originally a matching pair, but sometimes only one was worn.

Royal Ontario Museum, Toronto, Oronhyatekha Collection. Gift of the Independent Order of Foresters (911.3.77).

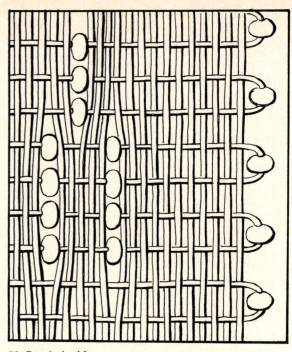

29 Beaded tabby

Quill Weaving

The making of exquisite woven bands with dyed porcupine quills has been practised by Indian women from one side of Canada to the other. The art was fully developed by the time of European contact[17] and, although quill weaving has been largely replaced by the simpler bead weaving, a revival has taken place in the far northwest and the work is of very high quality.

A flexible piece of wood in bow form is the traditional frame for holding the warp, as seen in fig. 5. In early times, both warp and weft were usually of animal sinew. In more recent pieces, commercial thread is often substituted. Only every second thread of the warp is held on the bow. The intervening warps are supplied by porcupine quills that are inserted by the weaver as she carries the weft backwards and forwards. Two weaving motions are repeated to make a tabby weave (Diagram 30). First, the weft is carried across above the taut warp threads and between each of those warps a quill is inserted and is lifted over the weft. Then the quills are pushed down and the weft is carried back over them and under the taut threads.

In the diagram, the band is started, as they often were, with a line of bead weaving. In an actual band only the quills show, giving the appearance of a fine beaded surface. As the short length of a quill runs out, or if it is desired to change to another colour for patterning purposes, the end of the quill is pushed down to the back of the weave and a new quill is worked in. This ease of colour change gives great freedom for the making of complex geometric designs, but the work requires incredible skill and patience.

Porcupines were found in almost every part of Canada and each one provides an enormous number of quills, so there was no lack of the raw material for quill work. One wonders how Indian women ever managed to squeeze the time out of their busy lives to produce these masterpieces. Quills had to be prepared and sorted, for they must be of matching thickness for good quality work. Dye stuffs had to be found, and sinew for the weaving and sewing had to be prepared. Then, after all the preparations had been made, the skills acquired through years of practise could be applied in the hours and hours of patient work necessary to turn the lowly and quite unappealing quill into the glowing decoration that would change a utilitarian object into a very special work of art.

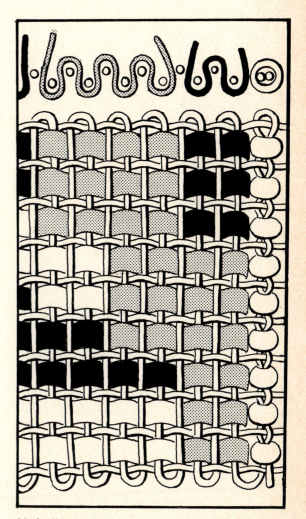

30 Quill weaving

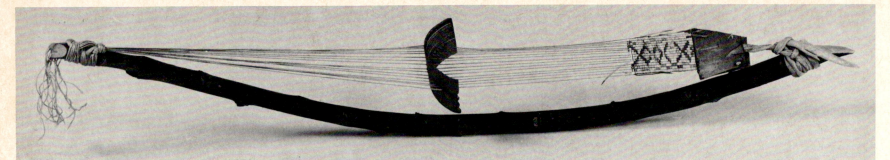

Figure 5: This frame, for the weaving of quill bands, was made by the Tahltan of British Columbia. A flexible piece of wood in bow form holds the warp of linen thread taut. The starting end of the warp is threaded through a folded piece of birch bark. In front of the weaving there is a warp spacer of bark that spreads the warp threads slightly, to facilitate their manipulation. The unfinished piece of quill weaving has a red and purple pattern on a natural white background and the weft thread is a black sewing thread. The frame was made in about 1915, is 52.0 cm in length, and was collected at Cassiar, British Columbia. National Museum of Man, Canadian Ethnology Service, Ottawa, Ontario (VI H 21; neg. no 76-886).

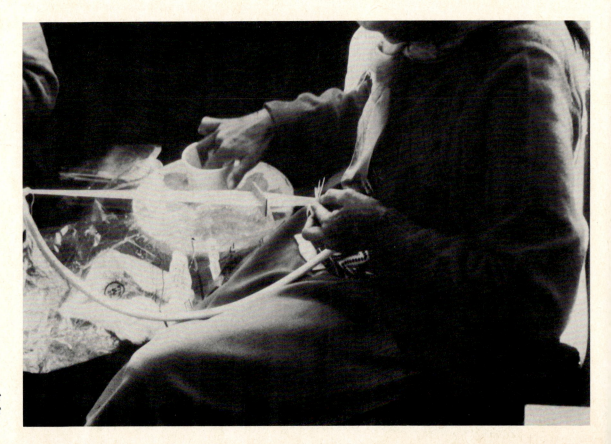

Figure 6: Rosa Minoza, of Fort Providence, Northwest Territories, demonstrating porcupine quill weaving at the Provincial Museum of Alberta, Edmonton in 1975.

17 Pouch early nineteenth century

Sealskin and stroud with quill weaving, 24.0 x 18.5 cm
Swampy Cree, northern Ontario or northern Manitoba

Quill weaving was used to decorate all sorts of things, but by far the most usual articles for such adornment were the ever useful pouches, often found in this form, with two bands of quill work and decorative fringes. This pouch is of sealskin, with woollen trade cloth of the type known as "stroud," in dark blue and red edged with beads (Diagram 31). The quill bands are of identical geometric design in white, red, yellow, and green and are finished at either end with a double row of green glass beads. Below these bands and surrounding the pouch are fringes that are very skilfully made by cutting one side of a strip of skin into fine slivers. As is usual, the cutting is done on the diagonal. The uncut edge of the strip is inserted into the seam and the cut edge provides the fringe. Below the quill bands the fringe is bound with quills and terminates in tassels of red wool. The fringe that surrounds the pouch is threaded with beads, and ends with a short wrapping of quill and a few strands of red wool. The meticulous finishing of each detail is characteristic of Indian workmanship of this fine quality.

National Museum of Man, Canadian Ethnology Service, Ottawa, Ontario, Speyer Collection (III D 565; neg. no. 74-8266).

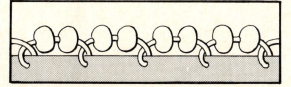

31 Bead edging

18 Pair of moccasins   about 1780

Skin with quill weaving, 26.0 cm
Huron, Great Lakes area

The cut of moccasins varied from tribe to tribe. This pair is a Huron type. The vamp is covered with a quill-woven band, outlined with two different edgings of flattened folded quills, a single quill (Diagram 32), and two quills that interlace with each other (Diagram 33). Quill-woven bands, matching on the two moccasins, but with different patterns on the outer and inner sides of the feet, decorate the ankle flaps, and are finished with short fringes of red hair, held in small metal cones. Cones, usually of tin, were a very popular trimming, once the metal was available through trade. Pieces of early date, such as these moccasins, are as a rule sewn with sinew and the warps and wefts of the quill-woven bands are also usually of sinew. But in this case, both sewing and weaving are of a bast fibre, probably one of the native fibres, such as nettle or milkweed, that produced fibres similar in appearance to flax and hemp.

National Museum of Man, Canadian Ethnology Service, Ottawa, Ontario, Speyer Collection (III H 432; neg. no. 74-8046).

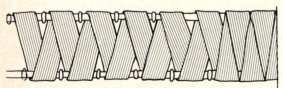

32 Folded quill, single

33 Folded quill, two interlacing

19 Knife sheath with carrying band
eighteenth century

Skin with quill wrapping and quill weaving,
sheath 22.5 x 6.7 cm; band 66.0 x 2.8 cm
Eastern Great Lakes area

34 Edging, quill-wrapped over thong

This knife sheath is faced with a masterly
piece of quill weaving, made to fit the tapered
blade shape of the sheath. Its narrowing form
has been achieved by dropping some warps
as the weaving progressed, as well as
through a careful selection of quills. At the
top of the sheath the quills measure almost 3
mm across, while towards the tip they are
very fine, only about 2 mm in width.

This book is mainly concerned with
weaving, and the great majority of the
illustrations have been selected to show that
technique. But when the whole artistic effect
of a piece is due to the combination of a
variety of skills, one cannot isolate a single
component and ignore the rest.

In this small piece, several other quilling
techniques have been used in conjunction
with the quill-woven band. The edging of the
sheath is quill-wrapped over a thong (Diagram 34). At the top of the sheath there are
three rows of quills that are folded, as in
Diagram 33. The carrying band is of fine
thongs, quill-wrapped in alternating pairs, to
form a decorative lattice (Diagram 35), as
well as in pairs, which are wrapped in a figure
of eight (Diagram 36). The colour of the
quills is predominantly green with red,
yellow, blue, and white – and the effect of the
whole is exquisite.

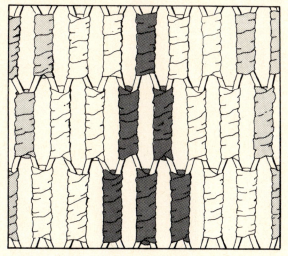

35 Quill-wrapped lattice

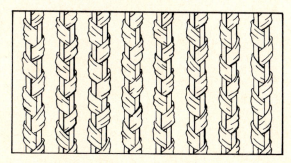

36 Quill-wrapped in a figure-of-eight

National Museum of Man, Canadian Ethnology Service,
Ottawa, Ontario, Speyer Collection (III x 239; neg. no.
74-7911).

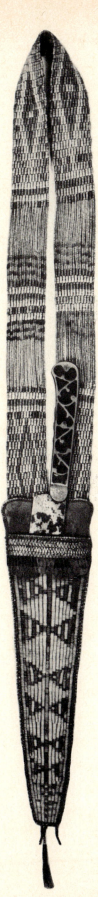

20 Knife sheath with carrying band
eighteenth century

Skin and wood with quill and rigid heddle weaving, quill band 21.0 x 8.0 cm; strap, 57.0 x 4.0 cm
Ojibwa or Cree, northern Ontario

This is an excellent example of the precise ornamentation of every detail of a utilitarian object, turning it into a creative artistic expression. The reason for this creation is a double-edged European steel blade which would have been, to its owner, a treasure of great worth. A setting befitting such a treasure has been created. The knife handle itself has been bound by a pair of thongs, quill-wrapped as in Diagram 36, and is topped off with a beaded fringe. The sheath of wooden slats and decorated skin is covered by fringes of slashed skin that are quill-wrapped and threaded with beads. It is flanked by strips of trade woollens that have been trimmed with beaded edgings and finished with beaded fringe and tassels. All this hangs from a breast piece of fine quill weaving that is suspended from a beaded neck band made of skin strip warps and sinew weft (Diagram 37), which was probably woven on a rigid heddle. The effect of this piece around the neck of a warrior would be as impressive as the finest jewellery and, with the hint of the blade ready to hand, rather more intimidating.

National Museum of Man, Canadian Ethnology Service, Ottawa, Ontario, Speyer Collection (III D 568; neg. no. 74-7051).

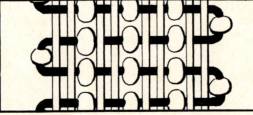

37 Beaded band weaving

21 Man's jacket about 1910

Moose-hide with mink fur and quill weaving,
0.80 x 0.54 m
Slave, Mackenzie River area, Northwest
Territories

This jacket is an excellent example of quill weaving from an area much farther north and west than the previous examples. It is smoke-tanned moosehide, of a fairly straight cut, and has been sewn with sinew. The decoration is lavish, with bands of mink fur edging the fine, quill-woven bands that are on either side of the front opening, around the wrists, and across the pocket flaps. Several joined bands of quill weaving form a yoke across the back of the shoulders, which is also trimmed with mink and is finished at front and back by quill-wrapped fringes. This is a truly magnificent piece, and the thought of the woman-hours of work that went into its making is staggering. Such coats were sometimes made for an especially favoured relative or friend to wear. Presumably, if all had gone well with the owner, this coat would have been worn out some sixty or so years ago. But the coat survives, and the skill of its maker can still be admired, because it was lost in a poker game at Grouard on Lesser Slave Lake in 1910, and the man who won it gave it to the Alberta Museum.

Provincial Museum of Alberta, Edmonton. Gift of Mr W. H. Turton, (H70.166.1).

Bead Weaving

The piercing of natural objects, such as seeds and stones, and teeth and claws, so that they could be used for personal adornment, is of great antiquity in almost all parts of the world, and North America was no exception. From remote times on the East Coast there was considerable production of beads made from bits of shell, polished and laboriously pierced. Probably their earliest use was simply for decoration and, as time went on, they became a useful article of trade with those tribes that did not have access to such attractive raw material.

By the early years of European contact, shell beads had taken on special significance. The beads themselves were known as "wampum" and, by extension, the term came into use to describe woven bands made of wampum beads. These bands were used for many important purposes, such as tribal records, binding treaties, or as important gifts. The bands had considerable intrinsic value in themselves, for the making of the carefully shaped and pierced cylindrical beads was a slow process. The shell that was most used for both white and purple wampum was the "quahaug," or hard-shell clam *(Venus Mercenaria)*. Soon after their arrival, European settlers disrupted the wampum making by introducing easier ways of manufacture. But in spite of that, and of the wholesale introduction of glass trade beads, wampum maintained its position and was of particular importance among the Iroquois peoples.

The actual making of the wampum bands was done in a variety of ways, but many of the early belts seem to be woven in the same technique that was used for the weaving of bands of trade beads. A group of warp threads was held taut, possibly on a bow, as with quill weaving. The beads were threaded on the weft and were positioned between the warps. Then the weft thread was returned across the warp, passing again through the same beads. One passage of the weft was in front of the warp and the other was behind the warp. The process was repeated with row after row of beads, varied in colour, as required for the design (Diagram 38). Two separate weft threads crossing in opposite directions were sometimes used instead of a single one.

When trade beads became common, quill decoration was largely superceded. At first, glass beads were an exotic addition to the indigenous materials, and a touch of the import would be added to a quilled object. Then, as the possibilities of trade beads were explored, it was found that they provided not just a medium for easy copying of earlier techniques, but were an artistic medium in their own right. Indian women, with the inborn dexterity that came from generations of fine craftswomen, exploited the new medium to the full. Beads were used for embroidery in many ways, and bands that were woven with them could be wider and longer and more colourful than the quill woven bands and so became very popular.[18]

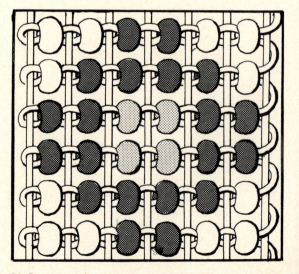

38 Bead weaving

22 Wampum band
early nineteenth century

Bead-woven of shell beads, 66.5 x 4.5 cm
Iroquois, Caughnawaga, Quebec

Traditionally, this wampum band, woven as in Diagram 38, is associated with the Iroquois Indian group that settled at Caughnawaga near Montreal at the end of the seventeenth century. The warp is of fine strips of skin, but the weft is of sewing thread rather than sinew, which suggests a date not earlier than the beginning of the nineteenth century. Other Iroquois wampum bands, associated with the Six Nations Indians in Canada, are probably old enough to have been among the treasured possessions brought with the people when they came to this country from New York State. This band, with its later date, was possibly woven in Canada, using wampum beads brought from the eastern seaboard.[19]

Royal Ontario Museum, Toronto. Gift of Miss E. H. C. Johnson (922.1.43).

23 Shot pouch with carrying band
mid-twentieth century

Band, bead-woven of glass beads, 90.0 x 5.0
cm; pouch, 22.0 x 17.5 cm
Barren Ground Band Naskapi, northeastern
Quebec

The Naskapi Indians of Labrador lived a
hard, mostly nomadic life in a harsh environ-
ment. Yet many of the women had great
artistic ability and managed to find time and
energy to make beautiful things. They are
famous for the skin hunting coats they made
for their husbands. These were decorated
with elaborately painted designs that the
women, quite literally, "dreamed up." It was
very important for a hunter to be properly
attired when hunting the staple of life–the
caribou.

This beaded shot pouch is quite unusual in
its elaboration but, like the coats, it was
probably the result of the belief that good
craftsmanship helped to ensure good hunting. The technique of the woven beadwork
on the band is slightly different from the
standard bead weaving. Instead of a single
bead between the warp threads, two small
beads are fitted into each space. Although
the main interest of this piece in the context
of this book is the expert bead weaving of the

carrying band, it is not possible to ignore
other details of its construction. The band
has a sewn edging of beads on either side,
making a very nice finish, similar to the one
shown in Diagram 31. The pouch itself is very
handsome, with a beaded floral design in
grey, red, and blue beads. The beads were
strung in the desired colours on a thread,
which was then firmly couched down with
small stitches to the black broadcloth
ground (Diagram 39). The edge is neatly
finished with ribbon and a simple, beaded
edging (Diagram 40).

Royal Ontario Museum, Toronto (958.131.131).

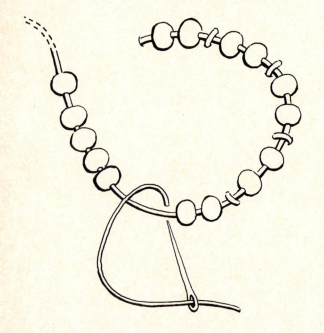

39 Couched bead work

40 Bead edging

24 Neck band   about 1925

Bead-woven with glass beads, 1.94 x 0.15 m
Cree, Lake Athapapuskow, Saskatchewan-
Manitoba border

Bead weaving does not produce a very
durable fabric. It is only as strong as the
threads used for warp and weft and these are
often just light cotton sewing threads which
have to carry the heavy weight of glass beads.
Bead weaving can be very effective when
used, as in this example, for the making of
wide, decorative neck bands or sashes. The
beads are in green, black, brown, yellow, and
blue on a white ground and the pattern is
beautifully drawn and very striking. The
standard bead-weaving technique has been
used and, at either end, the width of the band
has been split into five narrow bands, each of
them woven separately and terminating in a
point finished off with a wool tassel. In early
bead weaving, such as the wampum bands
which were woven with a sinew weft and
were comparatively narrow, no needle was
needed to carry the weft. Wide bead weaving,
such as this, could not develop until after the
introduction of fine, strong steel needles,
made especially for beadwork.

Museum of Natural History, Regina, Saskatchewan. Gift
of Mrs Lucy Baker (1085-6548).

(Detail, cat. no. 30)

Braiding is an important form of Indian fabric construction. From the evidence of existing pieces of early date, it was fully developed very shortly after the time of European contact and is probably an indigenous technique. Unlike weaving, braiding consists of only one element, a group of threads that start from the same point and are then interwoven with each other, with threads changing freely from an active function to an inactive one. The simple three-end construction used for braiding hair is the most elementary form of the technique, but it can be elaborated into the making of wide bands consisting of many threads and producing complex patterns. Cat. nos 25 to 32 provide an outstanding series, illustrating the craft as practised among the Indians of the Great Lakes region. These are followed by examples showing the types produced by French-Canadian women in Quebec.

There has been considerable discussion as to the origin of the complex braiding technique practised in Quebec. The wide, braided sash, *ceinture fléchée*, worn by *habitant* and *voyageur* alike, and which later became an accepted accessory to the winter costume of the fashionable sportsman, has quite the status of a national historic costume for the Québecois. It is almost sacrilege to suggest that any aspect of the garment's construction might have other than a French origin. As is shown in Diagram 50 with cat. no. 34, the technique that makes the complex pattern of the *ceinture fléchée* possible is that the threads, as they interlace, link with each other and make a turn to produce a colour change. There is no evidence that this linking and turning, this interlocking of the threads, occurs in the braiding of any part of the world, France included, other than North America. It does occur in various forms in early Indian braiding. There was considerable interchange of ideas on textile techniques, as on other matters, between native peoples and the early comers from Europe. It therefore seems likely that an indigenous patterning technique was picked up by Quebec women, elaborated and improved upon, and applied to the making of the sashes that were a part of the folk costume. In the folk traditions of Europe, wide belts and sashes were worn as a

support while doing heavy work and were often highly ornamented. The men who went out from Quebec as *voyageurs* on the fur trade canoe routes across the country needed such support when carrying canoes and heavy packs over rough portages and the wide braided sash was a recognized part of their outfit. Later, the sashes became a popular trade item, produced in quantity for the Hudson's Bay Company through a well-organized cottage industry that was centred on the village of Assomption in the Montreal area. With this wide dispersal of the Quebec sashes they, in turn, influenced the Indian productions.[20]

The yarns used for early Indian braiding are of considerable interest. Woollen yarn was not introduced as a direct article of trade to North America until some time after woollen yard goods were available. There were many native textile fibres spun and used in pre-contact times but, once seen, the yarns used for European trade woollens had great appeal, with their soft handle and bright colours. All trade items were used by the native peoples in their own, not in a European, manner and it was not long before plain European woollens were given rebirth in Indian textiles, by the tedious process of fraying out the fibres from a piece of cloth and re-spinning them.

Scattered research has been done on this subject but, to the present time, no definitive study has been published so a few technical remarks concerning the yarns used in the following articles are in order. Spinning among the eastern Indians was done without benefit of spindle. A good thread could be made by rolling the fibres on the thigh. The usual way to accomplish this movement is from hip to knee, which makes the fibres twist in an S direction. Plying is done in the opposite direction to spinning, so the S-twist singles were twisted in a Z direction when plying. European yarns were spun with a dropped spindle, or on a spinning wheel, both of which methods normally result in Z-spun yarn, which is then plyed S. As neither direction of spinning is totally definite for Indian or European methods of spinning, this technical detail is not a point of proof that a yarn has one or the other origin, but it is an indication of likelihood and a useful guide

post. The spinning direction of the yarns used in the items that follow is noted in the catalogue entries.

25 Sash   about 1780

Braided, with beads, 1.32 x 0.11 m
Eastern Great Lakes area

As a part of an Indian man's costume, decorative sashes were for adornment rather than use. Worn around the waist or over the shoulder they may have carried something like a knife, but usually such braiding was a simple luxury, made for enjoyment and show. This braided belt is in a balanced tabby weave and is made of terracotta-coloured woollen yarn (S2Z) that is probably respun ravellings of trade cloth. Every tenth thread is blue linen that would have been obtained by trade, and these linen threads carry small white beads that are positioned as the work is done, so that they form a diamond lattice. At either side of the braid there is a narrow strip in a natural black wool, and this edge braiding links into the body of the braid with every meeting of the two colours (Diagram 41).

Equidistant from each end of the braid there are two bands that are yellow in colour. This is not a mistake, but does present a problem that has not, as yet, been satisfactorly explained. It is a patterning procedure that is known on other early Indian braids. It must have been done either by top-dyeing a yellow belt with terracotta dye, while protecting the bands with some kind of resist, such as clay. Or a discharge must have been applied to those two limited areas of a terracotta-coloured sash for the deliberate purpose of bleaching the colour. Whichever method was used, the black woollen edgings and the blue linen bead-carrying threads have not been affected. The answer to this problem will undoubtedly be found, but whether this strange marking was done for decorative or for magical purposes may never be known.

National Museum of Man, Canadian Ethnology Service, Ottawa, Ontario, Speyer Collection (III x 230; neg. no. 74-7293).

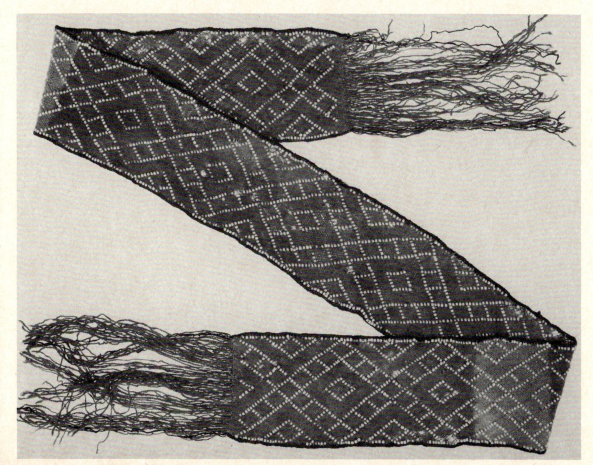

41 *Braiding, interlocked border*

26 Sash   late eighteenth century

Braided, with beads, twined weaving, and
quill wrapping, 1.22 x 0.10 m
Eastern Great Lakes area

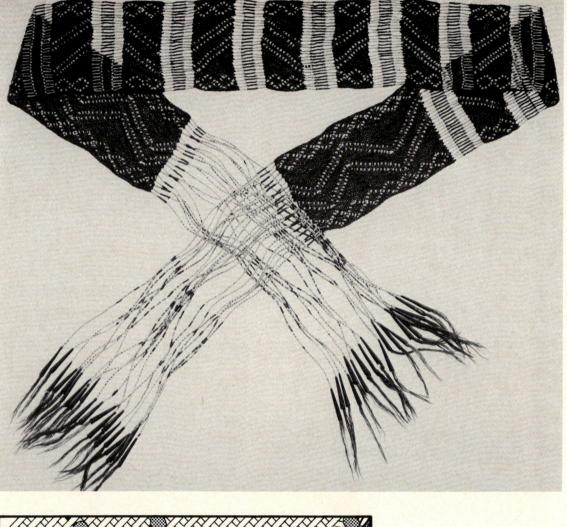

A finer piece of craftsmanship than this
would be hard to imagine. Each element is
worked with precision and the overall design
is a satisfying combination of many elements. The worker was obviously an artist of
great skill. The braiding is of green trade
wool of excellent quality (Z2S) and is on a
fine scale in balanced tabby. At either side
are two blue, bead-carrying threads that
work backwards and forwards, linking with
the green ground and turning to form the
diamond borders. Down the centre of the
band run two zigzag beaded lines, each of
which is double and encloses three lines of
weft-twining in blue wool (Z2S; Diagram 42).
At intervals, the braiding is interrupted and
the yarns are quill-wrapped in narrow
cross-bands. They have a carefully worked
out colour scheme that repeats white,
orange, white, and yellow, orange, yellow. On
either side of the orange quill wrapping there
is a row of white beads, worked as in
standard bead weaving (see Diagram 38).
The long self-fringes at either end of the belt
are beautifully quill-wrapped. The wrapping
is done with each quill finished off, and a
hair-line space left before the next quill is
used, so as to give a regularly repeating
bumpy outline. The fringes terminate in tin
cones. It is truly a masterful piece.

National Museum of Man, Canadian Ethnology Service,
Ottawa, Ontario, Speyer Collection (III x 254; neg. no.
74-7284).

42 *Braiding with weft-twining*

27 Garter pendant   late eighteenth century

Braided, with beads, 40.0 x 9.5 cm
Eastern Great Lakes area

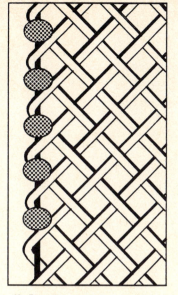

43 Braiding with bead edging

Indian men are shown in early illustrations with decoration hanging from below the knee, either in the form of a garter with decorated fringe or a pendant, such as this, that was secured by a garter. An interesting detail is that at the top, where the eagle feather is attached, there is a short section with no beads, probably where the garter tied over it and had there been beads they would have been uncomfortable. The eagle feather is trimmed with a red feather and a quill-bound slat. The top of the band has yellow ribbon with a beaded edging that would have made an elegant finish, hanging out over the garter. The technique is similar to the previous example, with red wool borders linked in the braiding to the black centre (both wools S2Z), and both areas are decorated with interwoven beaded patterns. The bead-carrying threads are of a bast fibre, and a similar thread carries a row of beads at each of the outer edges of the braiding (Diagram 43). The yarns extend into a braided quill-wrapped fringe, terminating in metal cones and orange hair tassels.

National Museum of Man, Canadian Ethnology Service, Ottawa, Ontario, Speyer Collection (III x 253; neg. no. 74-8268).

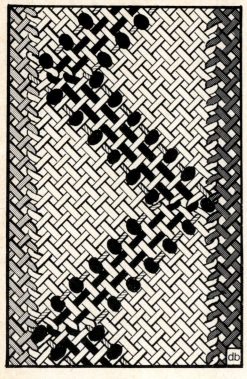

44 Braiding with interlocking bands

28 Sash   mid-nineteenth century

Braided, with beads, 0.75 x 0.12 m
Ojibwa or Iroquois, Ontario

The way that any of the Indian braided sashes were worn is uncertain. This is said to be a woman's sash, but it could equally well have been worn by a man, as in fig. no. 7. Braided sashes are also shown in portraits of Indians from the western end of the Great Lakes, wrapped around the head as turbans.[21] This sash has been made of three bands of differently coloured wools, red, blue, and brown, linked together in the braiding. The wools are definitely of European origin, and are like fine knitting yarns (Z3S). Subtle, fine details are two lines of brown wool between the double zigzag of beads on the central blue strip (Diagram 44) and beads strung on a linen thread that wrap some of the fringes. The sash probably dates towards the middle of the nineteenth century, but is completely traditional in style and very skilled in execution.

McCord Museum, Montreal, Quebec (M1558).

Figure 7: From a Daguerreotype of Chief John Henry Martin, of the Six Nations Indians. He is shown in elegant, fashionable attire, and appears to have embroidered arm-bands covering the lower part of his sleeves and a large game bag on his knee. His costume is completed by a handsome, braided sash, worn over the shoulder like a badge of office, or the ribbon of an order. The likeness was taken in Brantford, Ontario, about 1850. Royal Ontario Museum, Toronto, Chiefswood Collection. Gift of Miss. E.H.C. Johnson (922.1.102).

29 Bag with carrying band
late eighteenth century

Braided, with beads and quill decoration
Bag 17.0 x 27.0 cm; band 100.0 x 7.5 cm
Great Lakes area

Technically, this bag is similar to the early braided belts, but the threads have been handled in pairs, giving a slightly coarser effect. It is braided from green wool (S2Z) with beaded diamonds on one side and zigzags on the other. The bag is bound with green silk ribbon, has three rows of folded quills, and is finished with tin cones enclosing red hair-tassels. The quills are folded, as in Diagram 33, but with two quills of different colours laid one on top of the other, so that first one colour shows and then the other (Diagram 45). The rows of folded quills are bordered by a running stitch with quill wrapping (Diagram 46). It is an early and carefully made piece.

The carrying band, although contemporary with the bag and appearing to match it, was not originally made for it. It consists of two separate matching pieces, almost certainly garter pendants. They are braided from brown and green wool (Z3S) that matches the bag in colour but not in weight and spin. The braiding of the strap is different from anything so far described. With its narrow, black-beaded borders, linked on as the braiding was done, it must certainly be of Indian manufacture. The main body of the braid is, in texture, more like Quebec examples, with the threads closely set when they are inactive, completely covering those threads that are active. The threads change their function from inactive to active at three points where the zigzags of the pattern take place, but there is no linking of threads at these points. They are like the heart of a typical Quebec sash (see cat. no. 34). For a diagram of the weave, see the following piece and Diagram 47. In it, the threads move in pairs when active. In this piece, all threads move separately. This extremely rare piece provides a link between two types of braiding with its beaded, balanced weave borders and the unbalanced weave of the central part.

National Museum of Man, Canadian Ethnology Service, Ottawa, Ontario, Speyer Collection (III x 263).

45 Folded quills, double layer

46 Quilled line

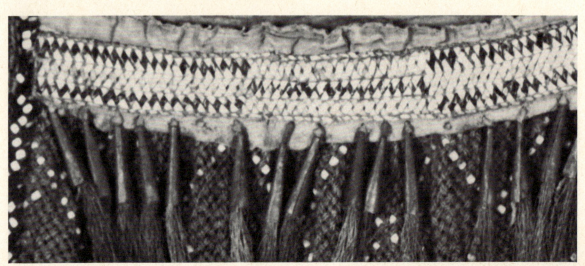

30 Sash   early nineteenth century

Braided, 2.28 x 0.17 m
Possibly Métis, Red River area, Manitoba

This handsome belt is another of the rare pieces that link Indian and French braiding techniques. Unlike the previous example, it does not have the Indian type of beaded border at the sides. It is made of a fine, rather soft trade wool of excellent quality (Z3S) in scarlet, yellow, olive green, and white. This type of braiding (Diagram 47) is an extension of a simple, multiple-end braid that produces a "V" pattern and that was made, particularly for garters, in many parts of the world. In this, as in the previous piece, the basic V-braiding has been repeated across the width, producing chevrons. A sash with this type of patterning shows plainly on the sleigh driver in fig. 8. This English lithograph was based on two watercolour sketches made by Peter Rindisbacher (1806–1834) in the Red River area, between 1821 and 1826. The scene showing the sleigh drawn by dogs with brightly-coloured blankets appears to have been copied from *Winter Voyaging in a Light Sledge*, but the figure of the hooded driver has been replaced by a top-hatted figure with chevron braided sash that is very close in appearance to the man in *A Halfcast and His Two Wives*.[22]

It should be remembered that the men in the Métis community may have been French, but the women were either Métis or Indian, and the women were the braiders. Possibly, in this type of braiding, Métis technique links Indian and French methods, just as the people themselves provide a link between the two cultures.

National Gallery of Canada, Ottawa, Ontario (9631).

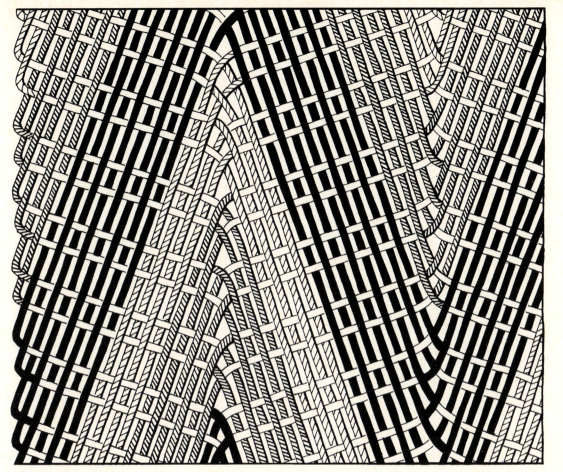

47 *Chevron braiding*

Figure 8: This English hand-coloured lithograph, Gentleman Travelling in a Dog Cariole at the Hudson's Bay (17.0 x 29.3 cm) is based on two watercolour sketches made by Peter Rindisbacher. The clothing of the sleigh driver, top hat, knee-length coat, and chevron-braided sash, similar to cat. no 30, are very like those worn by a Métis man in one of the sketches. Royal Ontario Museum, Toronto (958.141.6).

31 Sash   early nineteenth century

Braided, with beads, 1.66 x 0.18 m
Probably Huron, Lorette, Quebec

The reason for the popular name *ceinture fléchée*, or arrow sash, is made obvious in this braided sash, with its rows of arrow points outlined by white beads. The type is now usually simply called *ceinture perlée*. Beaded sashes are an Indian fashion and probably most of them are of Indian manufacture. It is not practical to tie a beaded sash tightly around the waist, so they were an article for simple adornment, rather than serving the dual purpose of decoration coupled with support that the French expected of them.

Sashes of this pattern and type seem to centre on the Huron Indian area of Lorette, close to Quebec City,[23] but examples are also known from the Maritime Provinces. This piece has been braided in four narrow widths that have been joined by sewing. Occasionally a similar piece is found that was braided in one width. The braiding (Diagram 48), is done so that the bead-carrying threads outline the arrow heads at the top, and a line of thread interlocking makes the colour change at the bottom of the motifs. Colours are fairly standard in all examples of the type and have a red background with a pattern in two shades of green. The yarn (Z3S) is a good quality woollen worsted.

National Gallery of Canada, Ottawa, Ontario (9629).

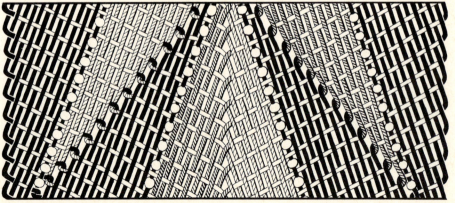

48 Ceinture perlée

32 Sash   early nineteenth century

Braided, with beads, 1.98 x 0.11 m
Probably Huron, Quebec

This is a very handsome and rather unusual version of a *ceinture perlée*. Most of the existing examples are almost identical to the previous piece. This one also has the rows of arrow points made in separate bands and joined by sewing. The technique of braiding is the same, the arrow points are the same, but the balance between the pattern and the red background is freer and, instead of the arrows being parti-coloured, one row is dark green and the other is light green. This sash may be a bit earlier in date, made before the type became set. The yarn is undoubtedly imported trade wool, combed worsted of fine, hard quality (Z2S). It is an excellent piece, even to the beaded finish of the fringes (Diagram 49).

From the evidence of the pattern, the yarns, and the craftsmanship we can guess that it is of Indian manufacture, probably from Quebec, probably quite early in date. It is a frustrating fact that few examples of braiding, either Indian or French, have sound documentation. They have usually passed through a number of hands since the original owner, or even the original collector, before finding safe haven in a museum collection. If they ever did have a pedigree, it has long since been lost, and we are left to play guessing games.

McCord Museum, Montreal, Quebec (8486).

49 Beaded fringe

33 Sash   about 1835

Braided, 1.70 x 0.18 m
French, Quebec

This is a sash with a history. It is said to have belonged to Dr Nelson, who was one of the leaders of the Rebellion of 1837–1838, and it is thought to have been made shortly before that time. The sash itself fits well with this background. It is a Quebec French type, made of the typical imported English wool (Z2S), in the colours of Quebec sashes, red, blue, green etc. The braiding has the usual linking and turning to form the pattern, but it is made in three lengths that are joined by sewing. The texture is rather loose, and the pattern is somewhat erratic, of a type now called "saw tooth," *dents de scie*. All this indicates a date before the quality and the pattern of the Quebec sashes became completely set. Also, Jane Ellice's watercolour sketch of the rebels who held her prisoner in 1838 (see fig. 9) bears witness to the fact that, to a man, the rank and file of the rebels were wearing sashes, and in all probability the leaders were too.

McCord Museum, Montreal, Quebec (M5437).

Figure 9: Watercolour sketch (23.5 x 16.5 cm) of the rebels at Beauharnois by Jane Ellice, wife of James Ellice, who was private secretary to Lord Durham. She and her sister were held prisoner during the Rebellion of 1837–1838 for a week in November, 1838. She recorded the happenings in her diary, and through the window she sketched some of her captors, wearing the characteristic sashes.[24] Public Archives of Canada, Ottawa, Ontario (C-1339Z).

34 Sash mid-nineteenth century

Braided, 2.07 x 0.15 m
French, Assomption, Quebec

Whether the origins of Quebec braiding techniques stem from Indian skills or not, the characteristic Quebec sash, known as a *ceinture fléchée*, or Assomption sash, is justly famous, and among the most admired types of braiding in the whole world. Braided sashes were worn by Quebec men and were particularly popular with those who traversed the country on the fur trade routes. The sashes became an eagerly sought article of trade, and were carried by both the North West Company and the Hudson's Bay Company.

At first, the sashes seem to have come from scattered areas, and were made in a quite individual way. But as the trade for them increased and the quantities of orders multiplied, a flourishing cottage industry grew up which was centred on the parish of L'Assomption, just east of Montreal. Fine worsted wool of top quality (Z3S) was brought in from England, especially for the braiding. It was dyed in a limited range of very fast colours: scarlet, light and dark blue, yellow and olive green, and these were used with white. The wool was issued by middlemen to the braiders, sometimes even warped ready for the braiding. Women worked at home, often helped by children and elderly men. It was a typical nineteenth-century cottage industry, with rigid standards of quality. It was also a typical nineteenth-century cottage industry in that the braiders worked very long hours for very little money!

The industry flourished until towards the end of the nineteenth century. Then, faced with unrest among the workers, the Hudson's Bay Company increased their orders for cheap loom-woven copies from England, and the market was knocked out from under the cottage industry almost overnight.[25]

This sash is an excellent example of the quality that made the Assomption sashes famous. Many like this still survive, evidence to the fact that they were treasured possessions. Most have seen considerable wear, but the wool is of such excellent quality and the weave is so firm and hard that, one hundred to one-hundred-and-fifty years after their making, they are still sound and beautiful. It is interesting to note the technical points that produce the complex pattern. Diagram 50 shows a row of arrow points, similar to those used on the *ceinture perlée*, (see cat. no. 31), and they are formed in the same way, but without the outlining of beads. This is the heart *(coeur)* of the sash and, as here, it is usually of scarlet. On either side of the heart there are lines repeating the side form of the arrow heads. The diagonal rows of thread interlockings are discontinuous, producing the zigzags or lightning flashes *(éclairs)* at the sides of the sash. This is the characteristic pattern of the classic form of *ceinture fléchée*, or Assomption sash.

National Gallery of Canada, Ottawa, Ontario (9639).

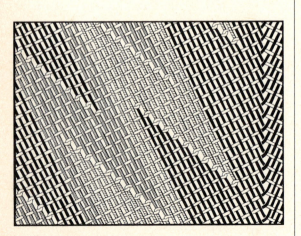

50 *Braiding, Assomption type*

35 Sash   mid-nineteenth century

Braided, 1.70 x 0.20 m
French, Quebec

This large and very handsome sash has a slightly different pattern from the standard Assomption type. Instead of lightning flashes to either side of the central row of arrows there is a diamond pattern (Diagram 51). The rows of thread interlockings are continuous from the side of the heart *(coeur)*, right to the outer edges. This breaks the colour areas up into lozenges. If, as in this example, every second colour-group of threads is in similar tones, either dark or light, diagonal stripes form and show much more strongly than the underlying diamond pattern. Yarns (Z3S) and workmanship are of similar quality to the previous example, but it is probable that the maker was not locked into the regimented cottage industry, and was from a Quebec centre other than L'Assomption. This type is described in French as *ceinture fléchée nette*.

National Gallery of Canada, Ottawa, Ontario (9640).

36 Sash   mid-nineteenth century

Braided, with beads, 1.98 x 0.12 m
Probably Métis or Indian, Manitoba

This strange piece is most likely of either Métis or Indian manufacture. The braiding is very loose, but the wool (Z2S) is spun very hard, which it needs to be, if it is to have sufficient strength to carry the unusually heavy beading. The colours are red, blue, green, and yellow and the pattern is similar to the previous example, with an all-over lozenge pattern. The beads are transparent and quite large, making the sash very heavy in weight and very magnificent in appearance.

McCord Museum, Montreal, Quebec (M4921).

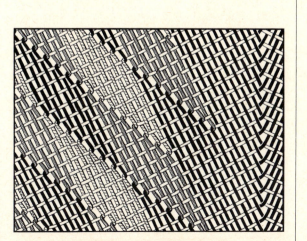

51 Braiding, ceinture fléchée nette

The view we can get of early French weaving traditions in Canada is unsatisfactory. There is no known surviving Quebec hand-weaving from either the seventeenth or the eighteenth century, except the remarkable altar frontal from the Ursuline Convent (cat. no. 37), and although listings of fabrics in inventories are numerous, such records tell little. Quebec was founded in 1608 and we know from written reports that there was hardly any interest in the raising of textile fibres, or the drudgery involved in textile productions. Money could be made in the fish or the fur trade, so imported fabrics were purchased. Times were not always good however, ready cash for imports was not always available, and there were waves of official encouragement for the planting of flax and hemp, the raising of sheep, and the teaching of girls to spin.

Then, in the eighteenth century, the bottom dropped out of the beaver market. As a result, self-sufficiency for the colony became a much more pressing necessity and gradually home production of textiles increased. Throughout the nineteenth century, useful fabrics of many sorts were produced on the farms of Quebec. [26] They were used for both home consumption and as a product that could be marketed in the towns (see fig. 11). These materials were made for simple clothing and household necessities, and, as such, were used and worn out so, even from later times, survival is scanty. We have the great pioneer ethnographer, Marius Barbeau, with his collecting in the rural areas of Quebec fifty years ago, to thank for the fact that even as much as we have has survived.

From the Acadian French areas, actual material is equally scarce and records are not plentiful, but the attitude of the settlers to the production of textiles was different from that of the Quebec people. Settlement in the Bay of Fundy area started in 1604. From the beginning, the settlers were farmers, and the making of textiles was an accepted part of farm work. Flax and hemp were grown and there were also a few sheep providing a small supply of wool. No actual material survives from the early period before the famous 1755 Expulsion when, during the long bitter struggle between France and England for control of North America, the Acadians were forced from their farmlands in Nova Scotia. [27] In a strange way, it is from that tragic upheaval that we know that early Acadian textiles must have been similar to later existing pieces. One group of the dispossessed Acadians ended up in the marshlands at the mouth of the Mississippi River. Here they continued their isolated farming way of life, maintaining their religion, their language, and their customs. The Acadians of Louisiana were separated from the Acadians of the Atlantic Provinces by two thousand miles for two centuries, yet a bed covering woven in "Cajun" country is a recognizable cousin of a bed covering woven in an Acadian community in Canada. Both are tabby weave, since the loom common in both areas had only two shafts, and both are patterned with weft banding. In Louisiana, this is of brown and white cotton, in Canada, of woollen strips. It might be considered that the resemblance of two such simple weavings is only coincidence, but there are many other points of similarity. The bandings used in both areas are carefully worked out in a reversed mirror image, and the balance and weight of the bands in relation to the background is similar. The weights of warp used, and particularly the heavy weight of the wefts, are the same. In both traditions we find one patterning detail used over and over again–a dark and a light weft spun together to make a barberpole line across the weave. The family connection is unmistakable. We can therefore only conclude that the Canadian Acadian and Louisiana Acadian weaving traditions date back to a common origin.[28]

The following pieces provide a range of materials woven in areas of French tradition from Quebec, from Manitoba, and from Acadian settlements in Nova Scotia, Cape Breton, New Brunswick, and Prince Edward Island. Although four-shaft looms were introduced into these areas through contact with other weaving traditions the old basic French loom had just two shafts, and the typical weaves from French areas are all based on the possibilities of that simple loom. The basic weave is tabby, frequently with pattern banding in the weft, and two simple techniques *à la planche* (cat. nos 45 to 50) and *boutonné* or *boutonnue* (cat. nos 48, and 50 to 54) are used frequently in Quebec and occasionally in the other areas to provide colour, texture, and simple patterning.

37 Altar Frontal of the Assumption of the Virgin Mary   early eighteenth century

Twill with wool embroidery, 0.91 x 1.79 m
Made by the sisters of the Ursuline Convent
Quebec City, Quebec

In the early seventeenth century, Canada often acted like a magnet, pulling people from France to the new land. A small group of Ursuline nuns felt the call to mission and to teach in Canada so strongly that, in 1639, they left their cloisters in France. Under the indomitable leadership of Marie de l'Incarnation,[29] they set off on a 5,000 kilometre journey across a most unpleasant ocean to the colony of New France. It took them three months to reach their destination at Quebec, which at the time consisted of only about 250 people, perched precariously in the middle of a vast wilderness. After a brief flurry of welcome the sisters retired again into a cloister and set about fulfilling the teaching mission that had originally inspired them. In their small school they taught both French and Indian girls, and a letter written by Marie de l'Incarnation in 1640 gives us a picture of what the teaching was like. In speaking of a young Indian girl, she says "She has made a very great progress with us in the knowledge of the mysteries and, as well, in good manners, embroidery, reading, playing the viol, and a thousand other little skills."[30] At that time, any well-brought-up young lady in France would have been taught embroidery and, with the coming of the Ursulines, so it was in Canada. The sisters, having been well brought up themselves, were fully equipped to both teach and practice the art of fine embroidery and naturally the churches in the new country needed adorning. Along with all their other duties the Ursuline sisters managed to produce many beautiful ecclesiastical hangings and vestments and, as time went on, their embroidery became a way of making money to help provide for their support. A number of pieces made for their own foundation are still in the convent in Quebec. There was a disastrous fire in 1686, so none of these date before the latter part of the seventeenth century, and this beautiful altar frontal was probably made in the early years of the eighteenth century.

Silks and velvets were sometimes sent to the nuns from France, but such imports were not always available and this lovely piece is made of local materials. The ground is a fine wool blanket cloth (2/2 twill; see Diagram 3), that was probably spun and woven in the convent and, since the sisters had a farm, perhaps the wool came from their own sheep. The embroidery is almost all in woollen yarns and it is possible that these also were made by the nuns. The work is expert, even to a limited and very subtle use of gleaming silk mixed with pale blue wool, to give the shine of porcelain in the couched work of the blue-and-white vases. Quebec may have been a long way from France, but contacts remained close, and the sisters were not far behind in style. The impractical little shelves are reminiscent of the Berain designs that were popular in France at the end of Louis XIV's reign. The typical eighteenth-century bouquets of flowers are worked in satin stitch and French knots, in a

wide range of bright colours. The central medallion of the Virgin Mary is surrounded by a yellow glory, radiating out from it in the form of a cross.

In any surrounding, this embroidery would be impressive, but in early eighteenth-century Quebec, beset as it was by wars and pestilence, it must have appeared as a glorious affirmation of the faith. For us, it is moving, visual evidence of the courage of those women who brought to Canada some of the graces of France.

Monastère des Ursulines de Québec, Quebec City.

38 **Curtain**   early twentieth century

Tabby with knotted fringe, 1.45 x 0.99 m
Belœil County, Quebec

In the province of Quebec, flax and hemp were raised and processed from the early days of settlement, but in spite of official encouragement the production was on a small scale. During the nineteenth century, increasingly poor economic conditions made home production a necessity among the rural population. From then, until well into the twentieth century, flax and some hemp were raised, processed, spun, and woven on many farms. They were turned into plain household linens, sheets, towels, pillowcases, and even the farm sacks. This curtain is typical of much of the linen that was produced. The warp is good quality, strong linen thread. The weft, however, since it does not require the same strength, has been spun from the tow, which is low-grade fibre that is separated from longer fibres during the processing of flax. As with most of the simple linens, it is a tabby weave (see Diagram 2). It was probably put into use in an unbleached state, but was eventually bleached by repeated launderings with dryings in the sun.

Musée du Québec, Quebec City, Bilodeau Collection (89).

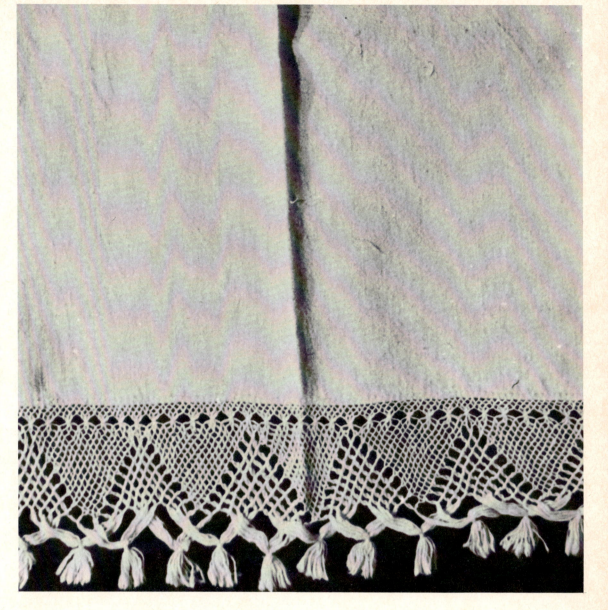

39 Bed covering late nineteenth century

Checked tabby, 2.24 x 1.74 m
Made by the sisters of the Ursuline Convent
Quebec City, Quebec

The sisters of the Ursuline convent not only produced beautiful ecclesiastical embroideries, they were also expert in the spinning and weaving of all kinds of simpler textiles, making whatever household fabrics that were needed for their own establishment. This activity continued until well into the present century. The whirr of spinning wheels and the thump of looms still lingers in the memory of some of the older sisters. This bed covering is a white cotton tabby, checked in a fine, handspun, indigo-blue wool. This type of fabric, with a cross-check in blue wool on either a cotton or a linen ground, was used in rural Quebec for tablecloths, as well as for bed coverings.

Monastère des Ursulines de Québec, Quebec City.

40 Length of carpet   mid-twentieth century

Tabby *catalogne*, 6.70 x 1.05 m
St Robert, Richelieu Country, Quebec

Probably the best-known type of Quebec weaving is the kind done with rag strips of cotton or wool cloth called *catalogne*. This length is tabby weave, striped in the warp and banded in the weft. The colouring is excellent and the weaver used designing skill to make the plain weave interesting. In the light stripes of alternately yellow and white cotton yarns the warp spacing is twice as close as in the rest of the warp, resulting in a variation of texture as well as colour. The weft is of fine cotton cloth strips, punctuated at intervals with a very simple patterning device, consisting of blue and white strips, twisted together. These are used in pairs, with one twisted S and the other twisted Z, making a sort of arrowpoint pattern. As this is a comparatively modern piece, it was probably intended for use as a carpet, but the early use for such weaving in all French areas was always for bed coverings, made from two joined lengths. None of these simple wool strip coverlets seem to have survived in Quebec, but they were undoubtedly made, and it is probable that they were fairly similar to those made in Acadia (cat. nos 42 and 43).

National Museum of Man, Centre for Folk Culture Studies, Ottawa, Ontario (77.604).

41 Coverlet 1915

Tabby *catalogne*, 1.88 x 1.78 m
St Boniface area, Manitoba

In spite of its appearance, this coverlet does
not come from Quebec but from an area in
Manitoba where Quebec weaving traditions
were continued among the French settlers.
Like earlier examples of *catalogne* weaving,
it is a bed covering made from two widths.
The warp is white cotton yarn, the rags are all
cotton, cut very finely, and are used in a
manner that is usually called "hit or miss."
Obviously, care has been taken in the
planning and weaving of this piece. The rags
have been very carefully selected from an
interesting range of materials, both plain and
printed, in shades of purples, pinks, and
blues. The way these colours have been
arranged on a white background is very
pleasing, and definitely "hit" rather than
"miss." The piece came from the collections
of the St Boniface Historical Society, with no
information beyond the fact that it was from
that area, and had been made in 1915. It
could equally well have been produced fifty
years earlier.

Musée de St Boniface, Collection de la Société
historique de Saint-Boniface, through Bishop Lapointe,
St Boniface, Manitoba (SH V 91).

42 Coverlet (half)   late nineteenth century

Tabby, *catalogne*, 1.88 x 0.83 m
Chéticamp, Cape Breton, Nova Scotia

Among the Acadians in Cape Breton the use of *catalogne* bed coverings survived until the middle of this century, when oil space-heaters were introduced and bedding no longer needed to be as heavy. Among the surviving coverlets from the area the rag strips, except for a limited use for patterning, are of woollen materials. The Acadian women were skilled in the art of varying and balancing the simple weft bands that were their usual form of patterning.

This half-coverlet from the west coast of Cape Breton is remarkable in both design and execution. Black wool rags from two different sources have been used. One is plain, and probably comes from either blanket or clothing material. The other is recognizable as coming from an old bed covering of black wool, banded with white cotton cloth strips. The decorative bands, combining white and pink cotton yarns and fine twisted strips, are very expert, but the unusual and subtle beauty of the piece comes from the use of three weft shots of a fine, blue cotton yarn between each weft strip of black wool cloth. The colour can hardly be seen unless the piece is moved, but it gives a life and sheen to the whole. This addition would have added considerably to the time required for the weaving, but it has produced a very firm, durable material. Whether the main reason for the extra work was practical or aesthetic, the result is a masterpiece of the weaver's art.

Museum of Cape Breton Heritage, Northeast Margaree, Nova Scotia (996.61).

43 Coverlet   late nineteenth century

Tabby *catalogne*, 1.97 x 1.64 m
Woven by Sabine Bourque
South River Bourgeois, Cape Breton, Nova
Scotia

A scarcity of raw materials, particularly wool, was a constant problem for the Acadian, as well as many other Canadian weavers. It was no doubt a major factor in the popularlity of *catalogne* bed coverings, with their thrifty re-use of every scrap of worn-out textile, inevitably causing the non-survival of any early material. This coverlet was woven at South River Bourgeois, an Acadian settlement on the east coast of Cape Breton Island. Sheep were a little more plentiful there than at Chéticamp, on the west coast, and this coverlet shows an unusually lavish use of new woollen yarn. In a reversal of the unsual Acadian weaving custom, the new yarn is used for the body of the weave, and the rag strips are introduced only for patterning. The colouring is very lovely. The pink and brown wool is acccented with black-and-white cotton strips, and there is also the characteristic Acadian "barber pole" twist in blue cotton rag with pink wool.

Museum of Cape Beton. Heritage, Northeast Magaree, Nova Scotia.

44 Coverlet   1825–1850

Tabby, weft-banded, 2.25 x 1.59 m
Tignish, Prince County, Prince Edward Island

This rare and beautiful Acadian coverlet is made entirely of handspun linen yarns. Its fine warp is regularly banded by four weft shots of fine linen, alternating with two weft shots of a heavy 3-ply linen, giving a beautiful weight and handle to the fabric. This texture, and the added cross-knotted side fringes, make it exceedingly handsome. In the Acadian communities of Prince Edward Island all-white coverlets were often made by a relative as a special wedding gift: a *couverture de mariage*, for either a bride or a groom. As in other Acadian coverlets, cloth strips are often used for the main weft, with the rag strips carefully saved from worn-out white materials, such as sheets, towels, and tablecloths. It usually took some years to accumulate enough white materials to make a *couverture de mariage*.

Musée acadien de Île-du-Prince Éduard, Miscouche, Prince Edward Island. Gift of Mlle Clothilde Arsenault.

Figure 10: This is a typical Acadian spinning wheel. It was made in Tracadie, Antigonish County, Nova Scotia, during the nineteenth century, and is 1.01 m high. The diameter of the driving wheel is 66.0 cm.

With this wheel, the spinner sits to her work, turning the wheel by means of the treadle. The yarn is spun off the tip of the straight spindle and then, with a separate motion, is rolled onto the spindle. Spinning traditions among the French of Quebec are different from the Acadian. There, the standard type of spinning wheel has a flyer attachment on the spindle, allowing for simultaneous spinning and winding of the yarn (see fig. 24). Royal Ontario Museum, Toronto. Gift of Mrs Edgar J. Stone (970.202.29).

Pattern Rod Weaving, Called à la planche

This is a way of extending the patterning possibilities of the simple two-shaft loom that is the basic loom of the French areas of Canada. Behind the shafts, a thin, smooth board of two or three inches (5 to 8 cm) width is inserted, passing over and under groups of warp threads. The ground of the fabric is woven in a normal way, varying the colours of the weft threads if banding is desired. At intervals, the board is turned on its side, to open a special pattern shed, and a pattern weft is used. For efficient pattern rod weaving, the heddles through which the warp threads pass cannot have the usual small eyes. They must have either long eyes, or be of a clasped form that opens up as the *planche* is turned on edge. As a rule, pattern wefts and ground wefts alternate (Diagram 52). If more than one pattern shed is required, the first pattern rod is pushed back on the loom after being used, and then a second rod is inserted. The second rod must be removed before the first can be used again. In many parts of the world, pattern rod weaving was used in quite a complex way, with many rods; but in Quebec, with *à la planche* weaving, there were never more than two rods and they were always in exact opposition to each other (Diagram 53).[31]

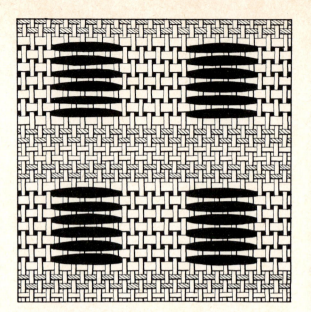

52 À la planche, *one block*

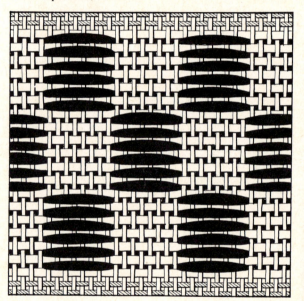

53 À la planche, *two blocks*

45 Coverlet 1875–1885

Tabby with *à la planche,* 1.99 x 1.70 m
Woven by Mme Germain-Hilaire Demeules
Île-aux-Coudres, Charlevoix County, Quebec

This coverlet had been kept stored away by the family of the weaver for many years. In 1933, the ethnographer, Marius Barbeau, found it, and was able to collect it for the National Gallery. It illustrates well *à la planche* patterning, using a single pattern rod. The warp is white cotton yarn, the ground weft is of *catalogne* strips, cut from various plain and printed cottons, many of them pink, and the banding and the *à la planche* patterning are in red, purple, maroon, and green woollen yarns. The centre seam of the coverlet has been beautifully matched, the test of a really expert weaver.

National Gallery of Canada, Ottawa, Ontario, Barbeau Collection (9615).

46 Coverlet   early twentieth century

Tabby with *à la planche,* 2 x 1.88 m
Woven by Ema Barnabé
St Pierre, Manitoba

All through history, the readily transportable quality of textiles has meant that they have been one of the great carriers of style, technique, and pattern motifs from one part of the world to another. Often, it was just the textile that moved and became an influence on a weaver in a far distant area. Sometimes weavers themselves migrated and their skills and techniques went with them. Ema Barnabé, the donor's grandmother, was born in Drummondville, Quebec and when she went west to Manitoba she took her knowledge of weaving with her. Her husband made her a loom, and this coverlet, which is indistinguishable from Quebec weaving, was made in St Pierre, Manitoba around 1900. The warp is white cotton yarn, the ground weft is of fine, evenly cut white cotton cloth strips, *catalogne,* and the patterning wefts are in blue, yellow, and pink wools.

Musée de St Boniface, Manitoba. Gift of Antoine Bérard (VC 192).

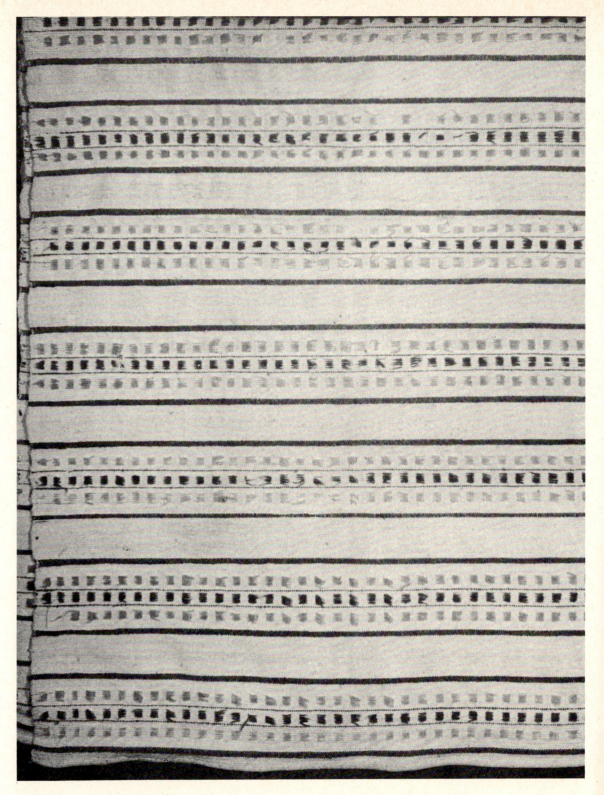

47 Coverlet   about 1850

Tabby with *à la planche,* 1.6 x 1.6 m
Woven by Priscilla Boudreau (née Godin)
Caraquet area, New Brunswick

When the woven coverlets that have survived in Quebec are compared with those that have survived in Acadia, it at first appears that the traditions were fairly distinct, with the plain ones from Acadia and the patterned ones from Quebec. This is actually more a matter of accident of survival than a division between the two areas. The main surviving Quebec material is that which was collected by Marius Barbeau in the 1930s. He was searching for the special, decorative weaving – and we are fortunate that he found it – and

that a number of pieces are now in our museums.[32] Unfortunately, however, little of simpler Quebec material has survived. From Acadia, it is the exact opposite. With their thrifty re-use of every scrap of woven material, those pieces that have come down are the utilitarian bed coverings that were still in use during this century, many of which may have been made in the latter part of the nineteenth century. The Acadian communities were always closer to the edge of survival than their Quebec counterparts. It is probable that the really decorative coverlets were not made there, but there was a limited use of the *à la planche* and *boutonné* techniques.

This piece is a rare survival of an early and unusually decorative Acadian coverlet. The warp is striped in different coloured cottons,

the ground weft is of exceptionally finely-cut white cotton strips, and the cross-banding is in beige, red, yellow, and dark-blue wool, with cleverly placed lines of *à la planche* that seem to give a scalloped edge to the weft bands. Its history is that it was woven in the area of Caraquet by the donor's grand-mother, Mme Michel Boudreau (Priscilla Godin). It is a happy chance that it was not cut up to make weft for a later coverlet.

Musée acadien, Caraquet, New Brunswick. Gift of M. Martin J. Legère (72.7.18).

Weft-Loop Weaving, Called boutonné *or* boutonnue

The second patterning technique that was commonly used in Quebec to ornament the plain tabby weaving was weft-loop weave. This had either a main or a supplementary weft, pulled up by hand to form loops on the face of the weave. It is a free and creative form of patterning and it was used in many varied and imaginative ways for the making of colourful designs on coverlets. This weft-loop weave was called *boutonnue* or *paresseuse boutonnue* (idly-twisted knots) in Quebec, but is more widely known by the name of *boutonné* outside that province.[33]

The simplest form is for the main weft to be pulled up into loops, so as to form a textured design all in the colour of the ground. Usually, the loops are made on only every third or fourth weft, which is heavier in weight that the intervening ones (Diagram 54). The more usual method is for the loops to be formed on an extra brocading weft that is inserted just where it is required by the pattern (Diagram 55). When this method was used for the coverlets, the brocading wefts were of brightly coloured woolen yarns and the ground was most frequently of *catalogne* strips, sometimes banded with cotton yarn. Frequently, *boutonné* was freely combined with bands of *à la planche*.

48 Coverlet   1865–1870

Tabby with *à la planche* and brocaded *boutonné*, 1.81 x 1.76 m
Île-aux-Coudres, Charlevoix County, Quebec

This coverlet combines the two Quebec patterning techniques *à la planche* and *boutonné* most effectively. Checkerboard lines, made by inserting two pattern rods behind the shafts to open two pattern sheds (see Diagram 53), separate the brocaded *boutonné* (Diagram 55) motifs of stars and trees that are used alternately down the length of the coverlet. The side borders exploit the *boutonné* technique to the full, and fairly vibrate with zigzag lines, working on different rhythms. The colours of the brocading wools, purple, yellow, green, red, and mauve are remarkably strong and bright. They are most exciting against the crisp, white cotton *catalogne* strips that form the ground.

National Gallery of Canada, Ottawa, Ontario, Barbeau Collection (9616).

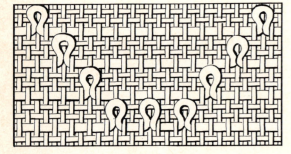

54 *Weft-loop weave with main weft*

55 *Weft-loop weave with brocading weft*

49 Coverlet   1875–1900

Tabby with brocaded *à la planche*,
1.79 x 1.69 m
La Baleine, Île-aux-Coudres, Charlevoix
County, Quebec

This is an unusual type of *à la planche* patterning. Two pattern rods have been used threaded through the warp at the back of the shafts, so that they raise opposite groups of warp threads right across the piece. On this checkerboard grid the pattern of diamonds, with zigzags in the borders, has been brocaded in red and pale green wool with the colours inserted into the sheds just where needed for the pattern. It is a well-designed and skilful piece of work. The warp is white cotton yarn, with the same yarn used in the weft, and every third shot of weft is a fine, white cotton *catalogne* strip. The order of the wefting is always the same: 2 cotton yarn, 1 brocading wool, 1 *catalogne* strip, 1 brocading wool, and repeat, making a very pleasantly textured ground. The second pattern rod had to be removed after it was used before the first one could be used again, a tedious process, but for one skilled in the technique not too difficult.

National Museum of Man, History Division, Ottawa, Ontario, Barbeau Collection (A 287).

50 Coverlet   about 1885

Tabby with *à la planche* and brocaded
boutonné, 2 x 1.66 m
Woven by Mérence Bradette
Baie-St-Paul area, Charlevoix County,
Quebec

The pattern of this coverlet is based on a
common motif, the eight-pointed star, and
the star has been turned into a comet by the
addition of a flaming tail. A little astronomi-
cal research turned up the fact that a comet
known as the "Great Comet" could have been
seen with the naked eye along the North
shore of the St Lawrence River for some time
during the month of September in 1882. This
must have been an event that created
considerable excitement, since Barbeau also
collected another coverlet with similar
pattern, made by a different weaver.[34] The
warp is of handspun linen. The ground weft of
white cotton cloth strips is patterned with *à
la planche* bands and brocaded *boutonné*
motifs in a combination of brightly coloured
woollen yarns and scarlet and purple
catalogne strips.

National Gallery of Canada, Ottawa, Ontario, Barbeau
Collection (9626).

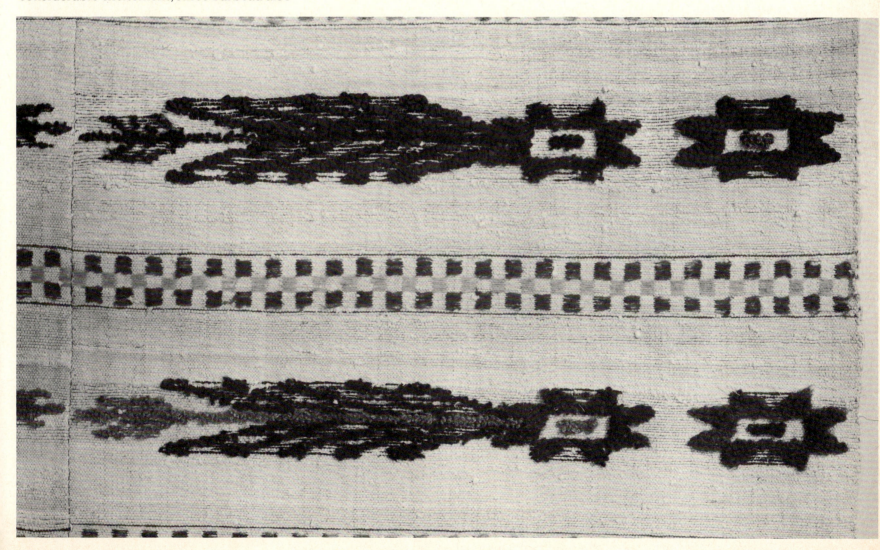

51 Coverlet early nineteenth century

Tabby with brocaded *boutonné*, 1.86 x 1.63 m
Île-aux-Coudres, Charlevoix County, Quebec

This is unusually plain for a decorative bed covering from Quebec. When it was collected on the Île-aux-Coudres in th 1930s it was said to be "very old – beyond the memory of living people." All elements of the piece do suggest an early date. The warp is handspun linen yarn. The ground weft is of *catalogne* strips, cut from plain white cotton tabby materials that could be of early origin and the brocading wefts are handspun wool dyed with the simplest and most basic of home dyes – indigo blue, an imported dye, but one that was readily available at an early date. The whole feeling of the piece is simple, almost classic, and it probably dates from a time before the fancy tastes of the mid-nineteenth century reached the north shore of the St Lawrence River. It is certainly from the period beyond the memory of people living fifty years ago, and could well be the oldest surviving coverlet from Quebec, made fairly early in the nineteenth century.

National Gallery of Canada, Ottawa, Ontario, Barbeau Collection (9617).

52 Coverlet   about 1870

Tabby with brocaded *boutonné*, 2.07 x 1.54 m
Woven by Nelsie Laforest
Île-aux-Coudres, Charlevoix County, Quebec

This is another piece that was collected by Marius Barbeau fifty years ago on the Île-aux-Coudres. At that time, it was said to have been woven about sixty years before, by Nelsie Laforest. A date of about 1870 seems quite possible. It has a bleached handspun linen warp which may be an indication of an earlier date, but might also be a frugal use of a homemade yarn, rather than a bought one. The linen gives a firm beautiful handle to the piece and the ground has an exceptionally pleasing texture. Five weft shots of white cotton yarn are closely packed together. They are followed by one white cotton *catalogne* strip that takes about the same space in the weave as the five shots of cotton yarn. The *boutonné* brocading wefts are always laid in with the *catalogne* strip, and the loops are regularly pulled up over every fourth warp, so that they come in straight rows (Diagram 56). The colours of the wools are soft, mainly in shades of brown with some crimson wool cloth strips.

National Gallery of Canada, Ottawa, Ontario, Barbeau Collection (9618).

56 Brocaded weft-loop weave

53 Coverlet   about 1860

Tabby with *boutonné,* 2.52 x 1.95 m
Woven by Alida Thiboutat
Ste-Anne-de-la-Pocatière, Kamouraska
County, Quebec

This coverlet comes from the south shore of the St Lawrence River and is an exceptionally beautiful example of linen spinning and weaving. Its history is that about 1863, at Ste-Anne-de-la-Pocatière, Alida Thiboutat grew and processed the flax, spun the linen thread, wove the coverlet, and won first prize with it at the Quebec Provincial Exhibition. The design and feeling of the piece are quite unlike the colourful coverlets shown in the previous examples. Some time before its making, white bedspreads had become the accepted thing in fashionable circles. A particularly popular type was made at Bolton in Lancashire, England, of heavy white cotton with *boutonné* patterning on the ground weft and many of these were exported to Canada. We can only imagine that Alida Thiboutat admired them so much that she decided to make one for herself. Her handloom was of the usual narrow width, so, unlike the imports, her coverlet is made in two widths, joined by a well-matched seam. Pattern and technique are as close to the original Bolton type as an expert craftswoman could make them, but the quality, sheen, and colour of the handspun linen lifts this coverlet away above the cotton one that inspired it.[35]

Royal Ontario Museum, Toronto. Gift of Mrs John David Eaton (970.90.6).

54 Coverlet   late nineteenth century

Tabby with *boutonné*, 2.2 x 1.74 m
Woven by Henriette Maillet
Ste Marie de Kent, New Brunswick

Colourful *boutonné* coverlets like the Quebec variety do not occur in Acadian areas. It seems likely that they were never made in the Atlantic provinces. Nevertheless, when the search was undertaken in New Brunswick to find bedding to use at the Acadian Village at Caraquet, a number of all-white cotton coverlets like this one, with *boutonné* patterns, somewhat similar to the Bolton imports, came to light. It seems most probable that they were made in response to a demand created by the pervasive nineteenth- to early twentieth-century fashion for all-white bedspreads. They have turned up in Acadian communities, so the Acadian weavers must have made some for their own home use, but they were probably also a readily saleable item. This one was made in an Acadian area north of Moncton. It is known that the weaver was expert, and made many coverlets, but there is no record as to whether they were all of this type.

Village historiqe acadien, Caraquet, New Brunswick (75.27.2).

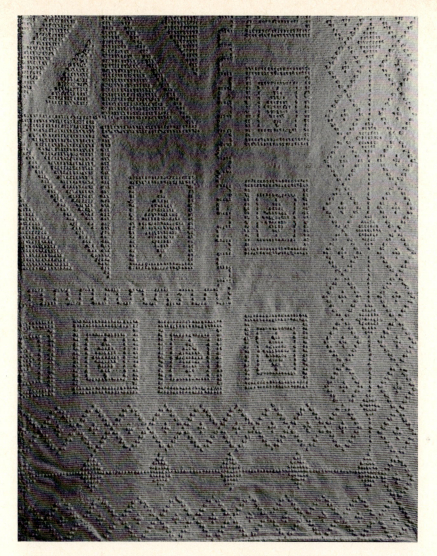

Figure 11: James Duncan (1806–1881), Market Scene. Selling Canadian Homespun Cloth, Montreal *(1859) Watercolour over pencil (23.2 x 33.3 cm). In the mid-nineteenth century census reports, bolts of handwoven woollen cloth are often listed along with other farm produce, such as pigs and chickens, turnips and potatoes. Royal Ontario Museum, Toronto (951.158.11).*

Costume

There is an exceedingly small store of actual material evidence on which to base any study of handwoven costume used in the French areas of Canada. For Quebec, there is a considerable body of pictorial evidence and documents are fairly numerous,[36] but the actual survival of garments is very, very scarce. We know that thousands of yards of heavy woollen materials were woven by the country people for use in their own garments and also as articles of trade that could be taken to market with other farm produce (see fig. 11). The only actual surviving garments made of this material are a man's suit and a hooded coat, or *capote*, both of the latter part of the nineteenth century, that are in the collections of the National Museum of Man, Human History Division.[37] The men in figs 11 and 12 are wearing garments of this type and their grey country cloth is brightened by a braided *ceinture*, tied firmly around the waist. Plain white linen was also woven in quantity and undoubtedly was used, as elsewhere, for underwear and for men's shirts and women's bodices, but survival of such garments from either Quebec or Acadia is nil. Some women's shawls have survived, but as far as is known there is only one skirt or petticoat that is surely of Quebec origin, and another that may be (cat. no 57). From the Acadian areas there are no men's costumes but there are the few precious surviving skirts (cat. nos 55 and 56). Pictorial and documentary evidence is not plentiful, but the evidence that does exist has been very carefully sifted, and sound re-creation of Acadian costume has been made for use at the Acadian Village, Caraquet, New Brunswick.[38]

Figure 12: John Crawford Young (active 1825–1838). Watercolour and pen and ink over pencil, inscribed Habitans Lower Canada *(18.7 x 13.3 cm). These men are wearing a common type of hooded winter garment that was called a* capote, *and was often made from the fulled grey woollen cloth that was produced on the farms of Quebec. Royal Ontario Museum, Toronto (957.63.5).*

55 Woman's skirt early nineteenth century

Banded weft-faced tabby, 0.91 x 2.6 m
Chezzetcook, Nova Scotia

This is the only complete early Acadian garment known to have survived. Probably, as with so much of their other weaving, the costumes perished because they could be re-used as wool strips for the weaving of coverlets. No male costume is known at all and, apart from this skirt, the only female costume pieces are two skirt lengths and a few fragments of skirt materials.[39] This beautifully spun and woven piece has a timeless elegance, to be expected more from a Paris model than from a peasant skirt on the Atlantic coast of Nova Scotia. The warp of mixed white cotton and linen yarns is completely covered by fine handspun wool in natural white and black. The material has been used sideways, with one selvage pleated into a linen waist band. The design of the banding is well worked out, with two white pin-stripes breaking each heavy black band. Much of the sewing has been done with handspun woollen thread, which is usually an early feature. Althoughs no similar skirts have survived in Quebec, pictorial evidence suggests that skirts fairly similar to the Acadian ones probably did exist there, too.

Nova Scotia Museum, Halifax (8031).

56 Woman's skirt length   about 1875

Weft-faced tabby with *à la planche,* 0.91 x
2.48 m
Traditionally woven by Mathilde Melanson
Scoudouc, New Brunswick

This skirt length has been taken off its
waist-band at some time in the past, but is
otherwise complete and a remarkably lovely
example of Acadian weaving. As with the
previous piece, it would have been made up
sideways, with the weft bands forming
flattering vertical stripes on the wearer. A
more subtle but equally important reason for
using the material in this way is that with the
weft-faced weave the weight is in the closely
packed wool wefts, rather than in the more
usual warp direction and, if used sideways,
the material would fall into loose pleats
easily and hang beautifully.

The bands repeat in regular mirror-image
in the typical Acadian way. The warp is
completely covered by fine wool wefts,
mainly in rust and blue-black, with medium
blue, green, and yellow, and a semi-bleached
linen. Rows of heavy weft, put in *à la planche*,
add to the design and an effective finishing
touch is a rust-coloured wool fringe, worked
in by needle above the hemline. Traditionally, this piece was woven at Scoudouc,
close to Moncton, about 1875. It is of a
timeless, classic type and could well have
been made considerably earlier, especially
since by that time many of the Acadian
women were starting to wear ordinary
clothing.

Musée acadien, Université de Moncton, Moncton, New
Brunswick. Gift of Mme M. Laplante (née Melanson)
(77.25.54).

57 Woman's petticoat   after 1865

Tabby with twill banding, 0.84 x 2 m
Scottish-French? Quebec?

Sometimes an interesting piece turns up in an unlikely place without documentation…a lost orphan. Occasionally one of these orphans is so unique that it is worthwhile to work through the evidence and try to come to some decision as to where it originated. This petticoat, found in British Columbia, fits in this category. The survival of any kind of early handspun, handwoven costume is so scanty that it makes every piece important, but gives little chance for comparison.

This petticoat is made from two widths of material, seamed together at the sides and with a wide, decorative border above the hemline. The material is pleated into a plain waist-band and most of the fullness has been placed at the back, suggesting a date no earlier than 1865. The weaver was expert, for the banding matches beautifully at the side seams. All yarns are wool (Z singles), with striped warp in beige and grey, and weft bands in red, pink, pale green, black, and yellow. The yarns are similar to others of known Canadian origin. The body of the weave is tabby, with the banding in 1:3 twill, indicating the use of a four-shaft loom. The style is unlike those of various ethnic groups who settled in the West, the piece is not similar to known Ontario material, and it is completely different from Acadian skirts. This leaves two areas of possible origin: rural Quebec, or Scottish communities in the Atlantic provinces. In both these settings, oral history and early illustrations indicate that short petticoats with banding similar to this one were worn under longer plain skirts, and that the skirts were often looped up, to show the decoration of the petticoat. The use of the four-shaft loom suggests that the Scottish history is the more likely. On the other hand, by the time the petticoat was made, four-shaft looms were also quite common in Quebec. One known petticoat with a sound Quebec history is similar in colour and cut, although simpler in weave.[40] There is also one fragment from a banded petticoat which survives in private hands (in a Scottish family in Cape Breton), making the scanty evidence almost even. French and Scottish customs and people often mixed quite happily in Quebec, and perhaps in this delightful piece we have a mingling of the two traditions. So, for the time being, the best we can do is to label it Scottish-French, followed by a question mark!

National Museum of Man, History Division, Ottawa, Ontario. Gift of Mr Ivan Sayers (F-4127; neg. no. 77-3787.)

58 Woman's shawl   about 1810

Twill (2/2), 1.75 x 1.75 m
Woven by Mme Gaumont
St Charles, Bellechasse County, Quebec

As far as is known, this is the earliest surviving piece of domestic weaving from the province of Quebec. It was spun and woven by the donor's great-great-grand-mother Gaumont at St Charles, south of Quebec City, about 1810. The yarns are natural white and indigo-blue wool (Z singles), made of very long staple fibres that have been combed rather than carded (see figs 20 and 21), and have been most expertly spun into a very fine, hard, worsted yarn. The weave is a 2/2 twill, with a tiny check that is surrounded by wide, dark borders, striped and banded with white. The shawl is in two widths, with a well-matched seam. It is finished with fringes of warp and weft threads, twisted in small groups, and each group is carefully tied off with a tiny overhand knot. Good shawls were expected to last a lifetime, and great care was always taken over the spinning of their yarns, as well as the designing and weaving. This shawl is a truly exceptional example.

Royal Ontario Museum, Toronto. Gift of Miss Ninette Lachance (961.112.1).

59 Woman's shawl early twentieth century

Tabby, colour and weave effect, 1.9 x 1.8 m
Probably Belœil County, Quebec

Shawls ceased to be an article of fashionable attire towards the end of the 1860s, when the bustle was coming into style and top garments started to fit the form of the wearer. For country wear, shawls held their place, and were spun and woven and worn by women all through the rural areas of eastern Canada throughout the nineteenth century and into this one. The shawl in cat. no 58 is exceptionally fine and light. This one is far more the type and weight of the usual Quebec shawl, and was intended for useful warmth rather than show. The yarns in black and shades of natural grey are heavy but well spun, and the piece is well woven in a simple colour and weave effect (Diagram 57).

Musée du Quebec, Quebec City.

57 Tabby, colour and weave effect

60 Man's work shirt   about 1900

Checked twill (2/2), 0.80 x 0.65 m
Quebec

Survival of handwoven clothing for men is even rarer than for women. This is a very unglamorous garment, but is nevertheless quite special. It was spun and woven in rural Quebec and is the type of warm, heavy work shirt that was worn by men for outdoor labour on the farm or in the woods. Shirts like this are the ancestors of the lumberjack shirts, popular for present-day camping. The garment may be rough, but the spinning of the wool is expert, and care has been taken in the dyeing of the yarns and the designing of the weave. The warp order is 2 pink, 10 blue, 2 pink, 10 brown, and this is crossed by a weft order that is 2 red, 8 beige, 2 red, and 10 pale green. It would have been far simpler to have knocked out a plain sheep's grey material for a utilitarian garment such as this, but that would have been very dull work and dull wearing. The making of this yardage probably gave the weaver considerable creative pleasure, and it may have even raised the spirits of the wearer, as well as keeping him warm.

National Museum of Man, Centre for Folk Culture Studies, Ottawa, Ontario (77.631).

61 Mat (Tapis à languette) early twentieth century

Twill with applied decoration, 0.99 x 0.68 m
Belœil County, Quebec

In different parts of the country, there were different fashions for the using up of scraps of materials. One of the oddest of these was the making of small mats, called *tapis à languette*. They consist of rows of over-lapping petals, or tongues, with each tongue carefully bound, and the whole piece decorated with appliqué, usually in the form of small rondels of different materials. The ground of this attractive piece is a handspun, handwoven, red woollen twill. Mats of this type were used on the floor in low traffic areas, such as beside the bed or in the parlour and sometimes to dress the top of a chest.

Musée du Québec, Quebec City, Bilodeau Collection (No. 82).

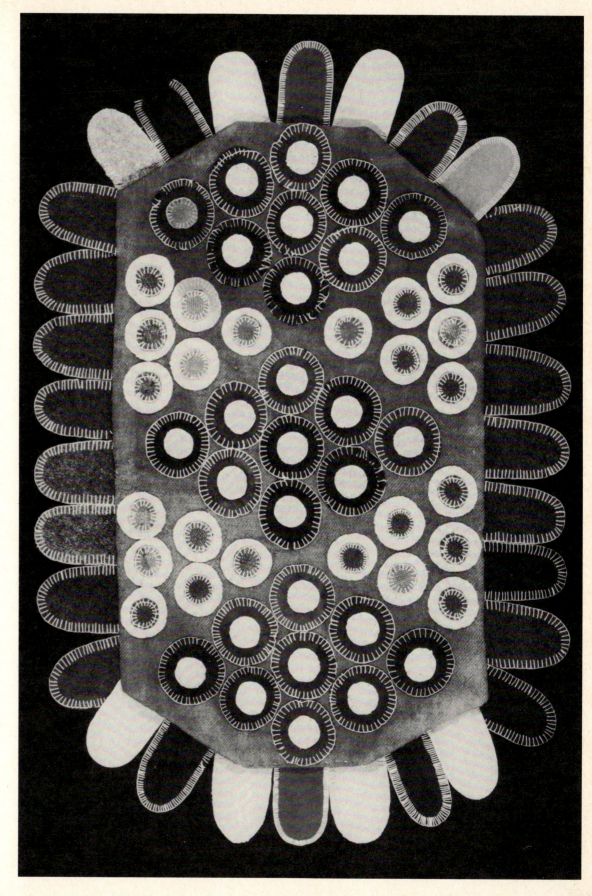

(Detail, cat. no. 67)

The Loyalist traditions came to Canada with the refugees who had to flee the newly-constituted United States because they had been on the losing side during the American Revolution. Those who managed to reach Nova Scotia and New Brunswick were able to travel by boat, and often brought some of their possessions with them. On the other hand, those who had to reach the borders of Canada along the shores of the St Lawrence River and Lakes Ontario and Erie by an overland route usually arrived completely destitute. Grants of land and some tools and supplies were issued to them, but the whole pioneering process, starting with the clearing of the land, had to be gone through again, just a generation or so after it had been completed south of the border. These "Americans" had the advantage over the newcomers who were to arrive later from Great Britain. They already possessed the necessary knowledge and the skills that allowed them to survive the first years, helping them to flourish eventually. Those who came as a result of real duress, between 1776 and 1783, are dignified by the name of the United Empire Loyalists. However, there were to be many others who followed that first wave of forced emigration, and who also brought "Loyalist" traditions from south of the border. Good, empty land exerts a powerful magnetic force, and the flow of immigration that had started with those who *had* to come continued with those who *chose* to come. Settlement of the American colonies had been of mixed ethnic origin, and this was also true of the people who decided to leave the new United States and move on to a new life, in a country which was still under the Crown.

Although the production of textiles had not been encouraged in the American Colonies it had nevertheless developed. In many areas, skilled specialists had produced quite complex weaving for a local clientele and, among those Loyalists who came to Canada, there were weavers skilled in the use of complex looms. As soon as day-to-day living passed from the earliest stages of hand-to-mouth existence, these weavers set up again in their old business. Summer and winter and double-weave coverlets, and fine linens were once more being produced on a professional basis in any neighbourhood where the weaver was located.

With anything as basic as the making of textiles, it is not possible to say that a given technique fits with one tradition and one tradition only. A type may be more characteristic of one certain tradition than it is of another, but as people moved and merged so did textile practices. In the following section, all examples of double weave, and the pieces illustrating the various ways of interlacing threads to make satisfactory use of linen are shown, not because they are exclusively within the Loyalist tradition, but because it was that particular wave of immigration which introduced them to Canada.

62 Coverlet ("bed rugg")   about 1800

Tabby with pile embroidery, 2.29 x 1.59 m
Miramichi, New Brunswick

This very effective piece is unique in Canada. It has a handwoven ground of natural wool tabby that has been entirely covered by embroidery stitches, with the embroidery yarn cut between the stitches to make a pile (Diagram 58). The embroidery is in quite heavy wool in dark green, rust, dark and light blue, yellow and brown, on a white ground. The white yarns have deteriorated badly, probably due to having been treated with some kind of bleach. The piece can be dated some time around 1800 and, according to its family history, it was made at Miramichi. It must have been a very special production, possibly for a marriage coverlet. The extravagant use of wool is quite unusual in pioneer surroundings.

It is similar to a rare group of embroidered bed-coverings that originated along the Atlantic seaboard, mostly in Connecticut and Massachusetts, between about 1720 and 1830. These are known in the United States as "bed ruggs."[41] There is a possibility that this one may have been brought up from the States when the settlers moved to New Brunswick, but the ground fabric is heavier than in the American versions. Also, the actual shape of the coverlet is much

58 Pile embroidery stitch

narrower than the square shape with rounded lower corners that is usual in the States and the embroidery stitch is quite different from the simple running stitch that is commonly used there. With all these points of difference, it seems most likely that the making of this piece followed the New England tradition for coverlets with embroidered pile, but it was actually produced in New Brunswick a generation after the Loyalists moved north.

The New Brunswick Museum, Saint John. Gift of the Misses Margaret and Janet Keay (61.42).

Summer and Winter Weave

The origin of the name of this weave is not known, but it may be because on one side the white ground predominates, making it the "summer" side, while the other is mainly dark, and is therefore the "winter" side. The name may sound rather vague and general, but the weave is a specific type that was brought to Canada by the Loyalists. It occurs only in areas of Nova Scotia, New Brunswick, the Eastern Townships of Quebec, and the older parts of Ontario, where the Loyalists first settled when they came from the United States. Coverlets in this technique are quite rare, and all seem to date from the early part of the nineteenth century. As far as is known, none were woven after about 1835. Summer and winter weave required a slightly more complex loom than the one needed for overshot weave, which produced a warmer coverlet using the same amount of wool. As a result, overshot weave seems to have replaced summer and winter weave in popularity by the time the first generation of Loyalist settlers died off. Summer and winter weave produces a very close and durable fabric. The ground is tabby, woven of white linen or cotton yarns and, after every ground weft, a pattern weft is used, moving over and under the ground fabric in three thread floats (Diagram 59).[42]

59 Summer and winter weave

63 Coverlet   1815–1820

Summer and winter weave, 2.09 x 1.73 m
South Crosby Township, Leeds County,
Ontario

This summer and winter weave coverlet
comes from a Loyalist family, the Singletons,
of South Crosby Township, just north of
Gananoque. The ground is of fine white
cotton and the pattern is dark, indigo-blue
wool. Another coverlet, very badly worn, and
from the same family, is also at Upper Canada
Village (60.6439.1). It is a very rare survival,
for it has a ground of homespun linen. Linen
was used in the very first coverlets woven in
Canada before imported cotton yarns were
available, but very few with a linen ground
still exist.

Upper Canada Village, Morrisburg, Ontario. Gift of Mrs
R.T. Tamblyn (60.6439.2).

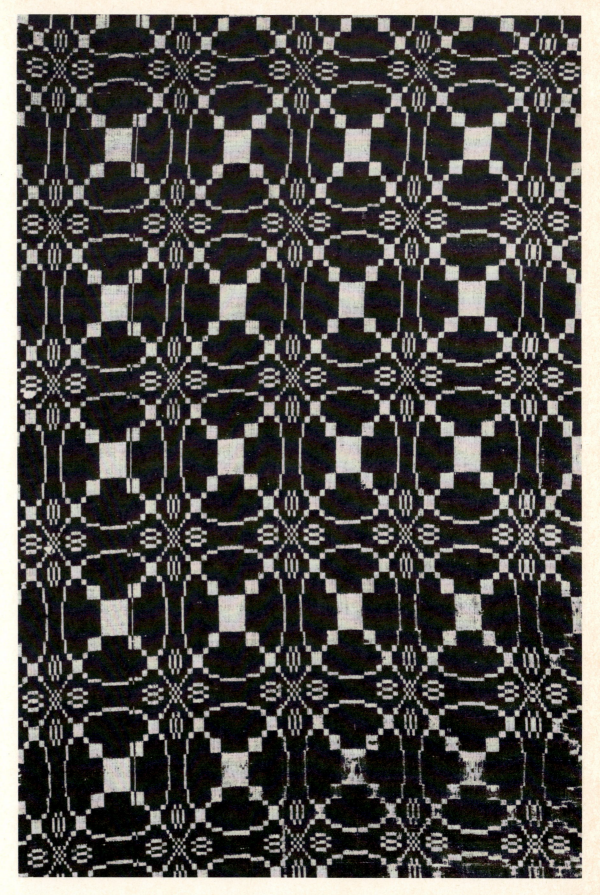

64 Coverlet   about 1820

Summer and winter weave, 2 x 1.78 m
Woven by Mary Anne Toole
Kars, Kings County, New Brunswick

This is a most expert piece of weaving, with a
centre seam that is so well matched that it
can hardly be seen. The design, with its
imaginative use of radiating leaf forms, that
vibrate and move as you look at them, is a
remarkable change from the usual static and
quite staid summer and winter weave
patterns. A member of the weaver's family
remembered that on the old property there
had been three looms, two of them for simple
things like blankets and yardage, and one
with the six shafts necessary for the weaving
of this type of coverlet.

The New Brunswick Museum, Saint John, Webster
Foundation (54.50).

65 Coverlet 1820–1830

Summer and winter weave, 2.26 x 1.98 m
Eastern Townships, Quebec

As with the other summer and winter weave coverlets, this has a white cotton ground with an indigo-blue wool pattern weft. The warp has been spaced rather close together, which has elongated the pattern. It is a very handsome coverlet and the wide ornamental fringes add greatly to the effect. The fringe at the bottom is an integral part of the weave, while those at the sides have been woven in two sections and sewn on. The fringes were made by weaving a narrow band of pattern, leaving a short length of warp bare, then repeating this process twice. After the weaving was finished, a heavy thread was run through, twisting the unwoven warp threads in groups. The corners have been left without fringe, so that they would fit neatly down around the posts of a four-poster bed.

Royal Ontario Museum, Toronto. Gift of Miss H. Norton (950.157.44).

Double Weave

Double weave is a technique that produces two textiles simultaneously, one above the other. The warp is in two series and each series works with its own weft. The two layers of textile are separate from each other, but can be made to exchange places in order to make a pattern (Diagram 60). This is a weave with a wide distribution in the world. It can even be accomplished on a very simple loom, if a lot of the work is done by hand. In North America, the patterning was always loom-controlled, and a complex loom with usually sixteen or twenty shafts was needed to produce it. In Germany and Switzerland the weave was used for the making of feather-bed covers and in Scotland for carpeting. Therefore, since trained weavers were among those who emigrated from those countries to North America, it is probable that the North American use of the technique for ornamental bed coverings developed through them.

It was certainly one of the specialized techniques brought by the Loyalist weavers when they moved on from the States to Canada. Double weave coverlets were extravagant in their use of the often scarce yarns, and they also required a weaver of very special skill, so they were never plentiful. On the other hand, their survival is fairly good, because they were treasured as a special possession. They often seem to have been made as a wedding coverlet, but once the jacquard attachment for the loom (see fig. 32) was introduced in the early 1830s the geometric patterning which was achievable with a shaft loom could not hold its appeal against the more realistic patterns of roses and lilies and birds that then became possible. Very few double weave coverlets with geometric designs were made after about 1840.[43]

60 Double weave

66 Coverlet about 1820

Double weave, 2.07 x 1.94 m
Probably woven by James Blaney
Woodhouse Township, Norfolk County,
Ontario

This coverlet comes from the Swayze family, who settled in Norfolk County about 1801. The daughter of the house, the donor's grandmother, was married about 1820 and it seems likely that the making of this coverlet is associated with her wedding. Family tradition has it that she made the coverlet. This is a history that families quite often attach, not only to simple weaving when the story is believable, but also to coverlets woven, as was this one, on a complex sixteen-shaft loom, or even to those that required a jacquard loom. The chances that great-grandmother was the weaver of this coverlet are nil, but undoubtedly she did do a great deal of the time-consuming work that went into its production. The customer always provided the yarns. The wool was usually from her own sheep, and she did both the spinning and the dyeing. The cotton yarn was bought, but as it was only available in the form of singles yarn it had to be doubled and plyed by hand on the spinning wheel, to make it suitable for the weaving of a doublecloth coverlet.

The customer then took the yarns to the local professional weaver, picked the pattern from his pattern book and left the skilled, but much less time-consuming, work of the actual weaving to him. With all this labour behind her, as well as the probable necessity of having to scrape together the ready cash to pay the weaver by some means, such as selling her eggs or butter, her family may be excused for passing the word down the generations that great-grandmother made the coverlet. In this case, the weaver was probably James Blayney, who had come from Ireland as a trained weaver and who doubled as the local school teacher in the area where the Swayzes lived.

Royal Ontario Museum, Toronto. Gift of Mrs F.A. Ballachey (960.18).

67 Coverlet   about 1840

Double weave, 2.15 x 1.78 m
Woven by Samuel Fry
Vineland area, Lincoln County, Ontario

This was woven by Samuel Fry, an expert professional weaver. The Fry family were Mennonites from Pennsylvania, who moved to Ontario after the American Revolution. They settled and farmed near Vineland, in the Niagara Peninsula, and Samuel was born there in 1812. At a young age he was sent to Pennsylvania to learn the craft of weaving. In 1836 he came home as a trained weaver, and sent out an advertising bill (see fig. 13) to, tell the neighbourhood that he was ready to serve them for all their weaving needs, which he did until his death in 1881. Due to the foresight of his granddaughter, Miss Annie Fry, a considerable amount of his weaving survives, as well as his pattern books and his account book. Through the generosity of her nephews and niece, the entire collection is now in the Royal Ontario Museum and is the most valuable archive concerning any weaver who worked in Canada. As with many weavers, Fry combined weaving with farming. As a result, our best-known professional Ontario weaver was never listed in the census reports as anything other than a farmer. He probably only wove when work on the farm was slack. He is known to have had two looms, one for simple work such as blankets and yardage, as well as a multiple shaft of the type needed for the more prestigious weaving of doublecloth and twill diaper coverlets.[44]

Royal Ontario Museum, Toronto. Gift of Mrs Zeta Haist Davis (967-286).

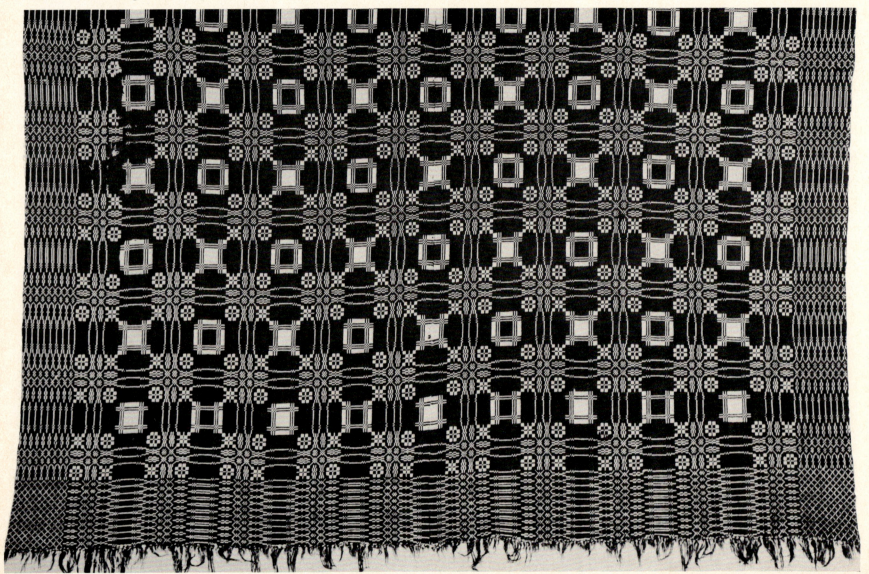

Figure 13: Advertising bill, Samuel Fry, 1836, from Lincoln County, Ontario. Royal Ontario Museum, Toronto. The Annie R. Fry Collection (L 965.11.62).

WEAVING.

SAM'L FREY, respectfully informs the inhabitants of the Niagara district, that he is prepared to WEAVE all kinds of PLAIN and FANCY

COVERLETS,

DIAPERS, &c. at reduced prices, in a workman-like manner, and on reasonable terms, at the house of Jacob Frey, about half a mile west of Ball's Mill, on the **20** mile creek.

SAMUEL FREY.

CLINTON, October 4, **1836.**

Figure 14: When Samuel Fry came back to Vineland, in Lincoln County Ontario, after serving his apprenticeship in Pennsylvania, he brought with him a number of patterns, drawn in ink, that would be suitable for the weaving of either double weave or twill diaper. This pattern sheet (37.0 x 30.6 cm) is signed and dated 1834. To weave this four-block pattern a loom with sixteen shafts would be required. Some of the designs are a little more complicated, having five blocks, and would need a loom with twenty shafts. As well as some other loose sheets, there is, in the Fry Collection, a book that has a whole series of numbered designs and a small notebook with the threading drafts for the same series of patterns.[45] Royal Ontario Museum Toronto. The Annie R. Fry Collection (L 965.11.66).

68 Coverlet   1825–1850

Double weave, 2.04 x 1.44 m
Waterloo County, Ontario

The addition of a cross-check in medium blue on the white cotton layer adds considerably to the interest of this design. Three colours are quite often used in double weave coverlets of American origin, but the use of anything other than white cotton and dark, indigo-blue wool is very rare in Canada. This pattern would have required a loom with twenty shafts. Double weaving requires four shafts on the loom to make each section or "block" of the pattern.[46] This design has five blocks. Three of them are combined to make the solid "snowball" motif, and two others are used to make the "stars" that occur in a group of four. All other elements in the design are repetitions of these five blocks. This coverlet comes from the German area of Waterloo County, and may have been woven by one of those settlers of German descent who came up from the States. Equally, it may well be the work of one of the many trained German weavers who came directly from Germany to that area in the next wave of immigration.

Royal Ontario Museum, Toronto (966.82.1).

69 Coverlet   about 1820

Double weave, 2.10 x 1.7 m
Nova Scotia

This double weave coverlet in indigo-blue wool and white cotton, and another similar one turned up at the same time. They are both said to have come from an old Halifax family, but are otherwise without traceable history. They are, however, the only double-cloth coverlets that have so far surfaced in Nova Scotia. Double weave is rare anywhere in Canada and, in spite of its extreme rarity, there seems no reason to doubt that the technique was used in Nova Scotia to a limited extent, as it was in other areas of early Loyalist settlement. It is somewhat surprising that a pattern as complex as this could be built up using only the five patterning elements possible with a twenty-shaft loom. "Pine tree" borders are common on coverlets of this type, but this is an exceptionally attractive version.

Nova Scotia Museum, Halifax (79.106.1).

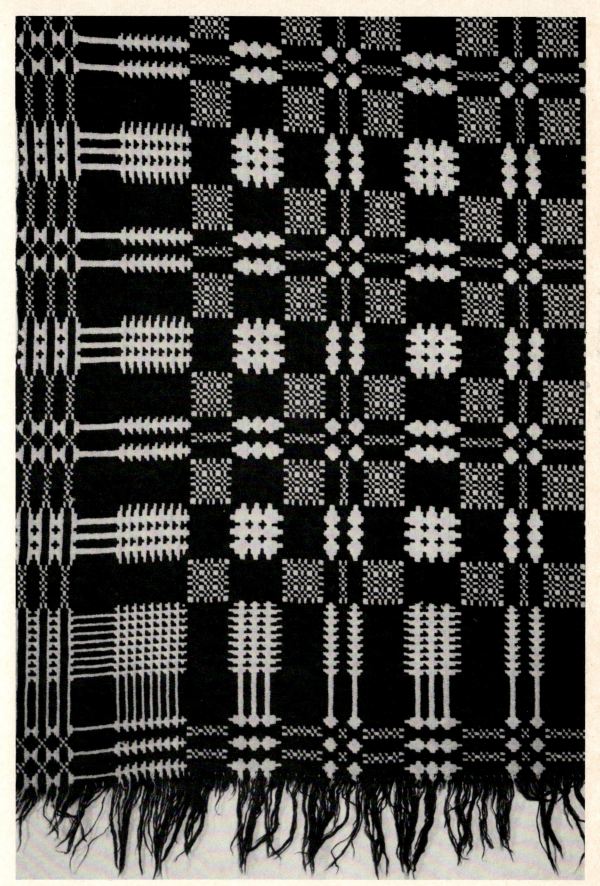

Linen Weaving

Flax had long been raised in Canada by the French settlers when it became one of the first crops to be planted by the Loyalists. It is the bast fibres in the stem of this plant that are useful for textile purposes. By a sequence of processes, starting with rotting the stems followed by beating, breaking, and combing (see figs 15, 16, and 17), these strong fibres are separated from the woody part of the stem and are rendered soft and pliable enough to be spun into a strong, fine thread.[47]

Linen is a very beautiful fibre but its preparation is very labour-intensive. As a result in those rural areas where weaving was done on either a domestic, or a small local professional basis, linen yarn was seldom sold, since only sufficient flax was raised and processed for the family's own needs. Survival of handwoven linens, particularly ones that are patterned in any way, is very scanty. Before the invention of the band-aid, old household linens were used for first-aid and, during the First World War, women's work parties gathered to tear and roll old linens for bandages to be sent overseas. We are fortunate that a few examples escaped that honourable end. Plain linen of differing qualities was made for sheets, pillow cases, and underwear. However, for such things as

towels and tablecloths there are simple ways of interlacing warp and weft threads that make them more absorbent, or thicker in texture, or just more attractive. A number of these are illustrated in the following pages.[48] Such techniques have their origin in the weaving traditions of Great Britain and Europe and were brought to this country either directly, or filtered through from the United States, arriving here with the Loyalists. It is hard, in this age of plenty, to realize just how scarce and expensive material was during the early period of settlement. In an account book that belonged to a man who carried on a complex barter business in the Niagara Peninsula in the 1790s are balancing items: one yard of linen cloth and one day's wages for a farm labourer, each listed at six shillings.[49]

Figure 15: The flax brake was a simple and often clumsily made implement, with two sets of hardwood blades hinged together at one end. Stalks of flax that had already been softened by rotting, or "retting" as it was called, were laid on the lower blades and the upper ones were brought down sharply and repeatedly as the stalks were moved backwards and forwards. This cracked the woody parts of the stems, releasing the bast fibres. This early nineteenth-century flax brake comes from Lunenburg County, Nova Scotia. It is 77.0 cm in height and the central blade is 1.10 cm in length. Royal Ontario Museum, Toronto. Gift of Mrs Edgar J. Stone (966.157.46).

Figure 16: After the brake was used to crack them, the stalks of the flax were laid over a block and were hit repeatedly with a dull-bladed wooden knife, using a scraping motion. This process was called "scutching" and it cleaned the broken parts of the stem away from the fibres. It also helped to separate the short tow fibres from the long, good quality ones. This photograph shows a woman scutching flax on a farm in Quebec in about 1900. National Museum of Man, Ottawa, Ontario (neg. no. 66-184).

Figure 17: After the stalks of flax have had the seeds removed, been softened by retting, broken on a brake, and cleaned by scutching, the fibres, in bunches, are pulled repeatedly through this type of a tool, called a hackle. Hackling completes the cleaning, as well as combing and separating the fibres. The coarse teeth of the hackle are used first, then the finishing is done with the finer teeth and the fibres are ready for spinning. This nineteenth-century, covered hackle (68.0 x 23.0 cm) comes from L'Îslet County, Quebec. Royal Ontario Museum, Toronto. Gift of Mrs Edgar J. Stone (966.157.30).

70 Width of linen 1830–1850

Checked tabby, 1.67 x 0.78 m
Sherkston area, Welland County, Ontario

Blue-and-white checked linen tabby, used for pillow cases and sheets, is to be seen in pictures painted by German artists as far back as the fifteenth century. The tradition continued in North America in areas of German settlement and this piece is from a Mennonite family that originally came from Alsace-Lorraine.

Royal Ontario Museum, Toronto. Gift of Mrs Verna Hall (975.136.5a).

71 Width of ticking mid-nineteenth century

Twill, 2.07 x 0.71 m
Sherkston area, Welland County, Ontario

During the nineteenth century, Ontario was an area of great contrasts. After the first few years, imported materials were available for those with the money to buy them, but there were areas where life had to be almost completely self-sufficient and even such a utilitarian fabric as this striped blue-and-white linen ticking was still made from home-grown linen fibre, processed, spun, and woven on the farm. The quality of this piece is superb, with a very closely set warp of heavy linen, woven in a 3/1 twill (see Diagram 4), making a very firm fabric that would be fairly feather-proof.

Royal Ontario Museum, Toronto. Gift of Mrs Verna Hall (975.136.4b).

72 Linen towel mid-nineteenth century

Bird's-eye twill, 0.93 x 0.58 m
Woven by Hester Young
Picton, Prince Edward County, Ontario

This linen towel, in a weave called a bird's-eye twill (Diagram 61), shows what simple linens looked like before they had been used. As a rule, they were woven of unbleached yarns in the natural shade of the fibre. With repeated washing, followed by drying in the sunshine, they gradually became white. An old-fashioned name for small, all-over patterns of this type was "diaper" and, as materials woven in this way are usually very absorbent, they are suitable for towels and also for baby wear, hence the name "diaper" for the basic baby garment. This towel was woven by the donor's mother, Hester Young who, with her sister Rosanna, wove professionally during the 1840s. Two pattern drafts that belonged to the Young sisters are shown in fig. 31.

Royal Ontario Museum, Toronto. Gift of Miss Annie Abercrombie (954.148.5).

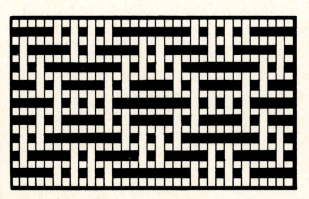

61 Bird's-eye twill

73 Napkin   late nineteenth century

Goose-eye twill, 0.40 x 0.40 m
Woven by Mrs McNutt.
Wittenburg area, near Stewiacke, Nova
Scotia.

This linen napkin is woven in a twill pattern
that is on a slightly larger scale than the
bird's-eye of the previous piece. When the
diamonds are large enough to form a lattice
of concentric lozenges, the weave is commonly called a goose-eye twill (Diagram 62).

Nova Scotia Museum, Halifax (32.149).

62 Goose-eye twill

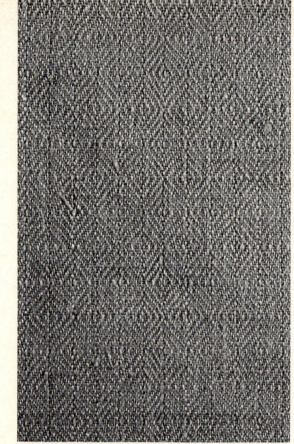

74 Width of linen   about 1825

Huckaback weave, 1.30 x 0.60 m
Woven by Susanna Sutton
Norwich, Oxford County, Ontario

This handspun, handwoven linen of beautiful
quality was woven by Susanna Sutton for the
use of her own family. The weave, a simple
one that can be done on a loom with four
shafts, is called "huckaback." It has small
floats of weft on one face and of warp on the
other, producing such an execellent texture
for towels that the term *huck* became almost
synonymous with linen towelling in the later
nineteenth century (Diagram 63).

Royal Ontario Museum, Toronto. Gift of Miss Alma
Clutton (950.55.3).

63 Huckaback 5-thread unit

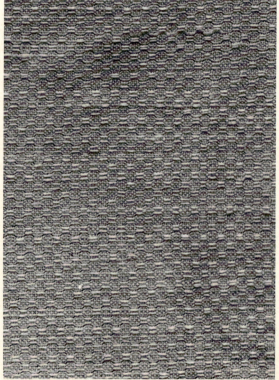

75 Small tablecloth   dated 1865

Spot weave, 1.45 x 0.99 m
Probably woven by Samuel Fry
Vineland area, Lincoln County, Ontario

If the same type of thread interlacing as that used to make the float in a huckaback weave is done on a slightly more complex loom, it is possible to space the floats so that they form a pattern. It is called a "spot" weave, or, in some books for modern handweavers, a "Bronson" weave (Diagram 64). This small tablecloth was woven by this method. It is dated 1865 and marked in fine red cross-stitch with the initials "E–M," for Elizabeth Moyer, the donor's grandmother. A spot weave pattern requires a loom with five shafts, one more than the normal household loom, which very likely means that the weaving was done by a professional. The Moyers were neighbours of the Frys, and Samuel Fry was most probably the weaver.

Royal Ontario Museum, Toronto. Gift of Mrs D.C. Wills (953.151).

64 Spot weave

76 Tablecloth   mid-nineteenth century

M's and O's weave, 1.86 x 1.6 m
Mahone Bay, Lunenburg County, Nova Scotia

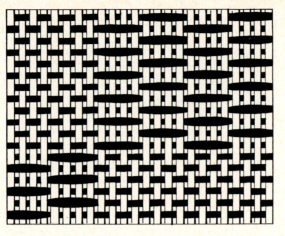

This fine linen tablecloth shows another technique of weaving that can be done on a loom with four shafts and is particularly suitable for use with linen yarns. For unknown reasons, the weave is traditionally called by the strange name of "M's and O's." Unlike huckaback and spot weave, with M's and O's the floats are always in the weft (Diagram 65). This piece was probably woven of unbleached yarns and simply bleached through use. It is rather formally marked in one corner "Mrs A S," in fine silk, which is now beige but was probably originally red.

65 M's and O's weave

Nova Scotia Museum, Halifax (59.20.3).

77 Width of towelling   1825–1850

M's and O's weave with twill, 1.87 x 0.78 m
Shinimecas, Cumberland County, Nova Scotia

This width, which has never been used, shows the M's and O's pattern very clearly, with the warp of white cotton and the weft of semi-bleached linen yarn providing quite a strong contrast. The weave is somewhat different from the previous piece, because parts of the pattern have been woven to produce a twill.

Nova Scotia Museum, Halifax (69.119.4).

78 Tablecloth   1825–1850

Overshot weave, 1.06 x 1.09 m
Bedeque, Prince County, Prince Edward
Island

This small tablecloth is an absolutely exquisite piece of weaving. The linen is of top
quality, the spinning is fine and even, the
warp is closely set and expertly woven in a
small, overshot pattern (for explanation of
overshot weave, see Diagrams 76 to 79).
Overshot weave is rather looked down on as
a way of weaving linen, and is even derisively
called "poor man's damask." Nevertheless,
the fineness and precision of the way the
technique has been used here produces a
fabric that even the most fastidious "rich
man" might covet. Some idea of the fine scale
of the weave can be gained from the fact that
the pattern repeat has 104 warp threads in it,
and a repeat only occupies 6 cm. The linen
fringe, now unfortunately quite worn, is also
on a fine, precise scale, with complex
cross-knotting.

Confederation Centre Art Gallery and Museum, Charlottetown, Prince Edward Island. Gift of Mrs R. Bell
(65.2.1.)

79 Width of towelling   late nineteenth century

Broken twill diaper, 1.09 x 0.42 m
Woven by August Ploethner
Preston, Waterloo County, Ontario

This length of towelling is very much in the German tradition, and almost identical pieces have been seen in a rural museum in southern Germany.[50] It has a white cotton warp and an unbleached linen weft and, since it has never been used, the linen is still quite dark in colour. It was woven by the donor's grandfather, August Ploethner, a well-known jacquard coverlet weaver. Besides the coverlets, he wove simpler things like this to sell in a small shop he had near the market in Kitchener. The weave is a two-block twill diaper (for twill diaper weave, see Diagram 81), that would have required an 8-shaft loom. It is a 3/1 twill, but instead of being woven with an unbroken diagonal line, as in most twills, the line of the diagonal has been broken, producing a rather rougher weave that would be more suitable for towelling (Diagram 66).

Royal Ontario Museum, Toronto. Gift of Mrs Robert Nix (968.142).

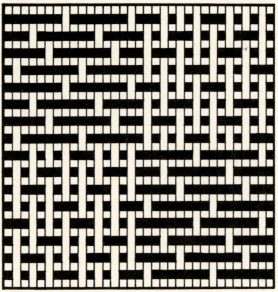

66 Broken twill diaper

80 Tablecloth about 1860

Twill diaper weave, 1.89 x 1.76 m
Woven by Samuel Fry
Vineland area, Lincoln County, Ontario

This beautiful tablecloth, made from two widths of fine bleached linen, was woven by Samuel Fry for one of his children. He is known to have woven one for each member of his family, but this is the only one that has survived. On their farm, the Fry's kept one field that was in a particularly favourable spot for raising flax. They only grew and processed enough for the family's own needs. When Fry wove linens for other people, the customer provided the yarn. The cloth is woven in a four-block twill diaper. The pattern is the same as the one used for his wool coverlet, illustrated in cat. no. 123, and it would have required sixteen shafts on the loom.

Royal Ontario Museum, Toronto. The Annie R. Fry Collection (L 965.11.5).

(Detail, cat. no. 113)

England, Ireland, and Scotland – these three names roll off the tongue with easy familiarity – but when considering the introduction of textile techniques to Canada they must be put in a less familiar order: Scotland, Ireland, and England. Scottish contributions to the development of Canadian textiles are, by a long way, the most important of the three. Older English traditions were undoubtedly among those filtered through several generations of residence in the United States and then brought on to Canada with the Loyalist immigration. By the time English settlers were coming to Canada directly from England – not as governors or administrators – but as simple people, looking for land, significant changes had taken place in their way of life. The Industrial Revolution came early in England, and it had already taken the textile skills out of the cottages and into the factories. As a result, the English who emigrated to Canada in the early nineteenth century had lost their knowledge of hand-spinning and handweaving at least a generation earlier, and so had no textile traditions to bring with them.

In Scotland, the situation was different. There, the effects of the Industrial Revolution were felt much later, by which time the big move to Canada was already well in motion. A number of Scottish regiments that had served in North America were disbanded on this side of the Atlantic during the latter part of the eighteenth century, and many of the soldiers settled in Canada and their families came out to join them. In a normal Scottish community, the women spun their own yarn and there was always at least one man who wove for the neighbourhood; these skills were continued, since they were as necessary for a pioneering life in Canada as for life in the Scottish glens. To these settlers were added many persons who had been forcibly displaced by the Highland Clearances, and they also brought their textile abilities with them as naturally as they would bring any other household or farming skill.

There was also another type of Scottish weaver who had a considerable – and more of a professional – effect on weaving in Canada. Handweaving was an important industry in southwest Scotland and, as the Industrial Revolution, with its increasing mechanization of all the processes, took hold of that area, many highly-trained muslin and shawl weavers were thrown out of work. Conditions became increasingly hopeless and no kind of a future seemed possible in Scotland. Emigration was the obvious answer. In many centres, benevolent societies were formed to help to raise money for passage to Canada. Along with many others, the desperate handweavers availed themselves of any help they could get and thus found their way across the Atlantic. To acquire land and to be independent was, of course, the overwhelming ambition, but often a weaver found that the craft he had spent years learning could be very useful. Combined with farming, it added a much needed source of money and it was even more of a back-up if it turned out that he did not like farming, or could not make a success of it. In the census reports of 1851 there are many, many people, mostly men, listed as professional weavers in the rural areas and smaller communities, and many of them have Scottish names.

Ireland was also a source of weavers, but it is very difficult to separate the traditions of Ireland from those of Scotland since most of these Irish came from Ulster and had traditions similar to those of the Scots.

The other group from the British Isles, the Welsh, had strong weaving traditions, but never came to Canada in sufficient numbers to effect the Canadian textile production in any significant way. The following pages show various textile techniques in a number of traditions that took root and flowered in Canada. Most were introduced by settlers who, following our "two founding nations" theory, are considered to be English, a description many of them would indignantly reject, especially those that spoke only their native Gaelic.[51]

Blankets

In the following pages, all the blankets have been grouped together, even though they are not all in the Scottish, Irish, and English tradition. The making of warm bed coverings was almost an obsession with the early settlers, and for very good reason. There were those who arrived well supplied with this world's comfortable goods, but there were many, many more who arrived with only the warmth of the clothing on their backs plus what they could carry. With hastily put up houses and fireplaces or, if lucky, a stove to heat them, the matter of keeping warm in bed was an urgent consideration. Blankets had been a staple of trade with the Indians. The famous Hudson's Bay point blankets, made in England, are as much a part of this country's history as beavers and beads. Blankets of that type were issued along with tools, and seed, and other necessary things to the Loyalist settlers. To many who came after, warm bedding had to be assembled through their own efforts and it was very difficult in those early days to establish a flock of sheep. With largely uncleared land, wolves were a constant threat. Even as late as 1843, Anne Langton complains of their flock having been visited twice by wolves during the winter.[52] Many of the earliest blankets made in Canada are a mixture of cotton and wool. Cotton yarn was available by trade and, even though imported, it was more readily available than the homegrown wool and was therefore used to eke it out. As time went on

and wool became more plentiful, blankets were produced by both home weavers and local professionals. Literally miles of handspun, handwoven, perfectly plain wool blanketing was woven on the looms of the countryside throughout the nineteenth century and, until a very few years ago, these sturdy reminders of our pioneering past, recognizable by the telltale centre seam, were still to be found in use. The standard homespun blanket was plain, but no matter how simple the surrounding, or how hard the life, there were always those creative souls who took the extra trouble to dye some of the yarns, or to thread the loom in a different way, so as to produce something that was attractive as well as warm. The artistic abilities of some of the blanket weavers are evident in the following examples.

Figure 18: Joseph Swift (active 1878–1889), Flock of Imported Cotswold Sheep, *watercolour (44.7 x 85.1 cm). We are told that these sheep won many prizes at the Toronto Industrial Exhibition in 1887. Certainly they were soft and pampered by comparison with those earlier pioneering sheep that had to rough it in the bush, but their importance is unmistakeable. What greater pride of ownership can there be than to have a portrait recorded for posterity? Royal Ontario Museum, Toronto (971.97.15).*

81 **Blanket**   dated 1829

Tabby, 2.08 x 1.76 m
Prince Edward County, Ontario.

Many a pioneer on winter nights slept
between ordinary blankets without benefit of
cool linen sheets, but often the finest wool
was put aside and made into really light, soft
blankets that were designed for use as winter
sheets. This example is on the borderline of
weight between a winter sheet and a blanket.
It probably served the dual purpose of being
a sheet in the winter and a blanket the rest of
the year. It is marked in dark grey silk, with
the owner's initials, "R+B," the date, "1829,"
and the number "6." Numbering sheets,
towels, and so on, was a usual custom in a
household, and this was the sixth blanket
that was made and put aside in preparation
for the marriage of Rebecca Barker, an
ancestress of the donor. Other blankets from
her trousseau are known, each marked with a
different year date. Rebecca probably did the
preparation of the wool and the spinning
herself, but very likely an older relative did
the weaving.

Royal Ontario Museum, Toronto. Gift of Miss H.M.
Armour (968.320).

82 Blanket   late nineteenth century

Twill, 1.98 x 1.42 m
Woven by Zella Oquinn
Codroy Valley, Newfoundland

While gathering material for this publication it has been a case of either feast or famine. From many areas, the choice has been agonizing, because of the large number of outstanding pieces which have had to be rejected for lack of space. On the famine side, this blanket is one of the very few pieces of Newfoundland weaving known that is truly traditional and not just made the day before yesterday in the craft revival that has swept the whole of Canada. The lack of traditional Newfoundland weaving is not surprising when one considers that the Newfoundland economy was based on the export of fish and the import of most other things, so there was little incentive for local craft industry. Sheep were raised in a small way and a lot of handspinning and knitting was done for simple, everyday garments. These things were so utilitarian that very few have survived (see cat. nos 106 and 107). Weaving was only done in one limited part of Newfoundland – the farming areas of the Codroy Valley on the west coast. Settlement there during the nineteenth century was from Cape Breton, and comprised a mixture of nationalities, with Irish, Scots, and Acadians predominating, all of whom possessed spinning and weaving skills. This red wool blanket, with its triple bands of light brown wool, was spun and woven in a 2/2 twill by the grandmother of the donor. Her name was Zella Oquinn (the same as the Acadian name, "Auquoin"), and she married an Irish settler named Downey, whose family had come into the Valley in 1841. These people made their living by farming. Sheep were kept for both meat and wool, and the women spun and wove the clothing materials and simple household goods needed by their own families.[53]

Newfoundland Museum, St John's. Gift of Mr Alan MacLellan, in memory of his sister, Miss Ann MacLellan.

83 Blanket about 1850

Checked twill, 2.22 x 1.77 m
Woven by Peter Fretz
Napanee area, Lennox and Addington Counties, Ontario

The care that was taken to make an object of utility into something that would also give the user pleasure is very evident in the everyday weaving done in Ontario throughout the nineteenth century. Checked, woollen blankets like this one are typical of eastern Ontario. The donor's great-grandfather, Peter Fretz, was a weaver and since this blanket survived in his family we can be almost certain that it is his work. It is of high professional quality, with excellent spinning. The red and green colouring of the check are very well proportioned, and the weaving expert, with the cross bands matching beautifully at the centre seam.

Royal Ontario Museum, Toronto. Gift of Mrs Archie Lamont (970.257.8).

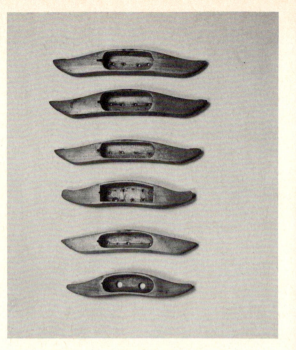

Figure 19: A weaver's shuttle was as personal a possession as a musical instrument. The beauty of the shapes of these nineteenth-century shuttles (lengths 27.0 to 34.0 cm) is evident – in the hand they are a delight. The weights vary, making them suitable for different yarns. Into the hollow of each one a rod was fitted to hold the bobbin of weft yarn which ran freely through a small hole at the side of the shuttle.

This set belonged to Peter Fretz, the professional weaver who made the blanket shown in cat. no. 83. He worked near Napanee in Lennox and Addington Counties, Ontario. Royal Ontario Museum, Toronto. Gift of Mrs Archie Lamont (970.257.19-24).

84 Blanket about 1855

Twill with side borders, 1.88 x 1.90 m
Tyendinaga, Hastings County, Ontario

This piece is in a very strong Scottish tradition. Instead of the end borders that are usual on blankets, it has two strong, indigo-blue stripes in a herringbone twill down either side. This placing of the decoration at the side of the blanket is found both in Scotland and in the Scottish areas of Canada. It probably stems from the fact that, in the very small Scottish cottages, the beds were usually built into the side of the room. If a blanket such as this was used as a top cover on the bed, the borders could hang over the side, adding a touch of colour to a simple interior.

An even stranger survival of Scottish tradition is that the herringbone pattern does not come to a point at the axes of the chevrons but the weave breaks (Diagram 67), making the lines of the twill alternate rather than meet. This is the way that herringbone twills had to be woven, given the technical restrictions of the ancient warp-weighted loom. These simple looms continued to be used in isolated parts of northern Europe, long after they had been replaced by more efficient loom types in other areas. The break in the herringbone of this Scottish-type blanket is a ghost-like reminder of the fact that traditions survive long after any technical reason for them is gone.[54]

Royal Ontario Museum, Toronto. Gift of Miss Grace Worts (969.246.1).

67 Broken herringbone twill

85 Blanket   1840–1860

Bird's-eye twill, 2.08 x 1.98 m
Woven by Samuel Fry
Vineland area, Lincoln County, Ontario

This beautiful wool bird's-eye twill blanket in dark indigo-blue and red, with pale blue overcheck is a well-known Pennsylvania German type. It was woven by Samuel Fry for himself and is marked with his initials. Fry's expert weaving is obvious in the well-matched centre seam, but the meticulous care taken with the designing is not so visible in the photograph. The bird's-eye twill threading has been drafted with doubled threads at the points of the diamonds (Diagram 68). In other examples of this type, the placing of the stripes is not necessarily related to the threading of the pattern. However, in this piece, Fry has carefully placed his colour changes in the warp, so that they fall neatly between the doubled threads, thus providing a crisp precision that no doubt gave pleasure to Samuel Fry, the expert weaver, when he climbed into bed under his own weaving.

Royal Ontario Museum, Toronto. The Annie R. Fry Collection (L965.11.16).

68 Bird's-eye twill

86 Blanket   mid-nineteenth century

Huckaback weave, 1.65 x 1.50 m
Probably Lincoln County, Ontario

This is a very strange but a very beautiful blanket. The yarns are all wool, with the warp in strong pink, striped with dark, indigo-blue. In the weft we find the same colours, but used in reverse proportions. The weave is a huckaback, with small floats of warp on one face and of weft on the other (Diagram 69), just as with the popular linen weave. It is a very unusual technique for a blanket, but has produced a most pleasant texture. With its rather loose weave it would trap air, as in a thermal blanket, giving good warmth in relation to the amount of wool used.

Royal Ontario Museum, Toronto. Gift of Mrs Edgar J. Stone (963.171).

69 Huckaback, 4-thread unit

87 Blanket or coverlet 1850–1860

Weft-faced tabby, 2.11 x 1.87 m
Woven by Hans Peter
Sherkston area, Welland County, Ontario

This coverlet, or blanket, belongs with a rare group — all of which have Mennonite connections. It was woven for Margaret Reeb, the donor's grandmother, by a professional weaver, Hans Peter, who lived near Sherkston. He is listed in the census of 1871 as being a Mennonite, born in 1810 in France, probably in Alsace. The technique is extravagant in its use of wool, for the weft is closely packed, covering the cotton warp entirely and making the coverlet very heavy. It would be slow weaving, but with only two shafts on the loom a fairly complex pattern was possible. Heavy and light warps are used alternately, except where a colour change is desired and then two heavy warps come side-by-side. The same thing is done with the wefts which, in this coverlet, are dark red and dark blue. They are used alternately until a colour change is wanted, then two darks are used, one following the other (Diagram 70).[55] This is a very simple version of what is known as a colour-and-weave effect.

Royal Ontario Museum, Toronto. Gift of Mrs Verna Hall (950.93-1).

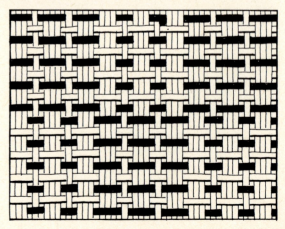

70 Patterned weft-faced tabby

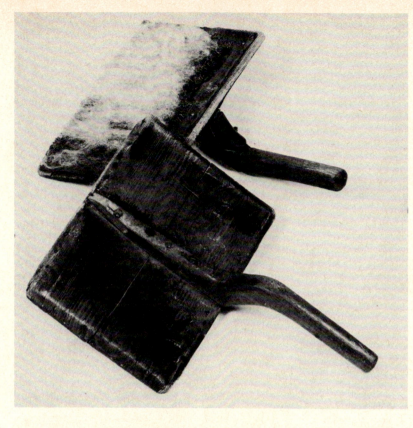

Figure 20: There is a great deal of hand work in the preparation of wool and a pair of implements such as these, called wool cards, were most commonly used to make the fibres ready for spinning. This early Ontario pair (39.0 x 26.0 cm) is homemade, with the sections of leather in which fine metal teeth have been set, placed on wooden handles. Washed woollen fibres were laid on one card that was held firmly against the knee, while the other was worked across it, combing and fluffing the fibres and making them into a loose roll, ready for spinning. Carding mills came quite early in many parts of the country, taking this time-consuming task out of the hands of the housewife. Royal Ontario Museum, Toronto. Gift of Mr and Mrs Harold B. Burnham (967.124).

Figure 21: Most of the woollen yarns that occur in the early weaving of eastern Canada are fairly soft and have been prepared by carding. Occasionally, and particularly in early pieces, one finds yarns that are too hard and smooth to have been prepared in this way. A much more ancient method of wool preparation has been used – they have been combed. Wool combs turn up rarely in eastern Canada and probably were never common. They have long metal tines, in two or sometimes more rows, that are set in horn on a wooden base with wooden handles. One comb was hung up and secured into position firmly and the wool was laid on it. Then the other comb was worked through the fibres with a swinging, chopping motion, gradually transferring the fibres from the rigid comb to the hand-held one. The process was repeated until the fibres could be drawn off in a long, smooth ribbon ready for spinning.[56] This pair of combs (34.0 x 15.0 cm) come from the Middleton area of Nova Scotia. They were probably made in England and brought out among the tools of a trained textile worker when he emigrated. Nova Scotia Museum, Halifax. Gift of Miss Dodge (58.24.1).

Figure 22: This "Great" or "Wool" spinning wheel was made in the Eastern Townships of Quebec, sometime between 1830 and 1850 (diameter of wheel 1.22 m). The owner's name, Sabra Anthony, is carved on the platform. With this very common type of wheel the spinning motion is simple. The carded wool is held in the left hand of the spinner so that it is connecting with already spun yarn on the spindle. The wheel is turned with the right hand, making the spindle revolve rapidly and putting a twist into the fibres as the spinner draws them out and back, away from the wheel. When sufficient twist has been put into that handful of wool to turn it into yarn she moves in beside the wheel and, turning it again, rolls the spun yarn up on the spindle. These two motions of twisting and winding are repeated, with the spinner stepping away from the wheel and back to it, sometimes covering many miles in the day. Spinning was the work of women, particularly young women, hence the designation "spinster" for an unmarried woman, but sometimes if there were no girls in the family a reluctant boy was pressed into service. *Royal Ontario Museum, Toronto. Gift of Miss Emily LeBaron (966.211.1).*

Figure 23: The large wool wheels were not very difficult to make, and were produced by many anonymous wood-workers all over the country. The smaller treadle wheels were a much more complex and valuable piece of equipment and the making was always the work of specialists. Many wheels were brought out from the old country, but there were a number of skilled craftsmen in this country who made their names as wheel-makers, among them the Youngs (Jungs) of Lunenburg County in Nova Scotia and this wheel, which dates from the middle of the nineteenth century, is typical of their work (diameter of wheel, 50.0 cm). The wood is finished in natural tones and is decorated by bands painted in red and black following the lines of the turning. The name "J. Young" is stamped along the inner edge of the stand. With this type of wheel the spinner sits to work and turns the wheel with a treadle. There is a flyer attachment on the spindle that makes it possible to spin and wind simultaneously, and the wheel is equally good for use with wool or with flax. The angled upright is a distaff for holding prepared flax fibres during the spinning.[57] *National Museum of Man, History Division, Ottawa, Ontario (D7051; neg. no. 77-746).*

Figure 24: Photograph of an old woman taken in 1946 by Marius Barbeau near Tadoussac, Quebec. She is spinning on a wheel that is the shape and proportion typical of Quebec spinning wheels made after about 1875. Regrettably, these wheels are usually found stripped down to plain wood, which changes their character from the original cheerful Frenchness of bright yellow, or red, or blue paint. *National Museum of Man, Ottawa, Ontario (neg. no. 100.200).*

Figure 25: There was always much winding and unwinding to be done as raw fibres were changed into woven cloth. This simple and ancient form of hand reel is traditionally called a "niddy-noddy." When in use, the worker holds it by the central bar, dipping it first one way and then the other, making it nid and nod as the yarn is laid on it to make a skein. This example comes from Cape Breton, Nova Scotia, dates from the middle of the nineteenth century, and is 50.0 cm in length. Royal Ontario Museum, Toronto. Gift of Mrs Edgar J. Stone (966.157.45).

Figure 26: Niddy-noddies were simple to make and widely used, but a much faster device for winding was a standing clock reel, such as this (height, 88.0 cm). It was commercially made, and has "Hailer Burckle 1868 Berlin C.W. Warranted" printed on the base (C.W. stood for Canada West and Berlin is the old name for Kitchener). It has a counting device that makes a click after forty revolutions of the reel. The circumference of the reel is 90 inches (2.29 m), so each click indicated that one hundred yards (91.44 m) had been laid on the skein. By knowing the circumference of a reel, or niddy-noddy, and keeping count of the rounds, yarn could be prepared in accurate quantity for a given purpose, such as the making of the warp for a pair of blankets. Royal Ontario Museum, Toronto. Gift of Mrs Edgar J. Stone (967.129.6).

Figure 27: Niddy-noddies and reels are for winding skeins. A different piece of equipment was needed for unwinding. These are called "swifts" and come in many forms, but all have a way of holding skeins of different sizes and all need to turn freely so that the yarn can be drawn off speedily and easily. This type is called a "barrel swift" because of the form of the small rotating cages that hold the skein. It was made in the nineteenth century, in Ontario, and the height of the stand is 90 inches (2.29 m). A more common type was the umbrella swift that had a frame of slats that opened out like an umbrella and could be adjusted to different sizes. Royal Ontario Museum, Toronto. Gift of Mr and Mrs John E. Langdon (971.393.1).

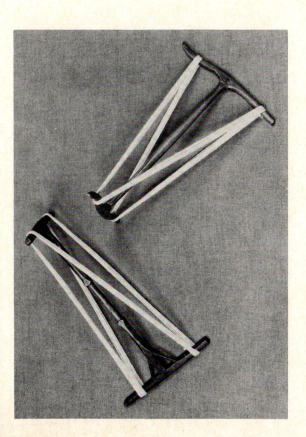

Figure 28: This loom belonged to Samuel Pentland, who came to Ontario from Northern Ireland in 1825. He settled first near Kingston and then, about 1845, moved on to the newly developing area on the shores of Lake Huron. He took up land at Nile, just north of Goderich, and there he combined farming with professional weaving. His loom is typical of those used by home weavers and by many local professional weavers in eastern Canada. It is 1.83 m high and has four shafts, which is to say that the arrangement for the making of the passages for the shuttle through the warp is in four parts. Each shaft consists of two bars of wood that have rows of string loops, or heddles, stretched between them with an eye in the middle of each heddle. A warp thread is carried through each heddle eye. Thus, by raising a shaft, the group of warp threads that it controls will also be raised. Tabby can be woven on a loom with just two shafts. Four shafts on a loom add the possibility of weaving all sorts of simple twills, some of the linen weaves, as well as fabrics with overshot patterns. Up to twenty shafts are needed for complex patterning techniques, such as double weave and twill diaper.[58] Royal Ontario Museum, Toronto. Gift of Mr and Mrs Harold B. Burnham (947.62.1).

Carpets

Carpets come well down the list of weaving priorities for a pioneer family. If wool was in short supply, clothing and bedding had first call on whatever supplies were available. Much pioneer carpet weaving depended on a supply of rags and if times were not good you went right on wearing your rags, instead of tearing them up to provide weft for a carpet. When life finally became a little easier, it was possible for the housewife to warm and brighten up her bare floors.

There are two main types of early carpeting.[59] The earliest has a handspun, striped wool warp, set very closely, so that it completely covers the weft, which may be either of nondescript cotton rag strips or of cotton yarn, used several ends together. The second type has a cotton warp, set so that the rag weft shows. It may be woven in a hit-or-miss fashion, or the colours of the rags may be used in carefully worked out bands. In Quebec, the cotton rag type, called *catalogne*, was first woven for bed coverings, but late in the nineteenth century it was produced by the mile for floor coverings. In the Atlantic provinces, the same two types were used. There were also carpets using wool in both warp and weft for plain checks, or overshot weave (see cat. nos. 101 to 103). All types of handwoven carpets were woven in the narrow width of the usual hand loom and the widths were then joined by sewing, to make wall-to-wall floor coverings. The housewife prepared the yarns for warp, and cut and joined the rag strips to be used for the weft, but as a rule the weaving was done by the local professional weaver.

(Detail, cat. no. 92)

88 Width of carpet   about 1875

Warp-faced tabby, 66.0 x 86.0 cm
Ridgetown, Kent County, Ontario

This is a very handsome width of the striped wool tabby carpeting that was the most popular handwoven floor covering during the middle part of the nineteenth century in all the rural parts of Ontario and also in Nova Scotia and New Brunswick. The yarns for the warp were spun and dyed by Miss Elizabeth Green, but the weaving was undoubtedly done by a professional. The striping is in very bright colours: yellow, mauve, purple, red, and blue, with a little black and white. The "ikat" type patterning of the wide stripes was simply done by tying the skeins of yarn with rags to form a resist against the dye. For one "ikat" stripe, white skeins were tied and then dyed red, for the other, the skeins were first dyed yellow, then tied and dyed green. The designing of the stripes in this type of carpeting was usually very clever, since the weaver could only use the wools brought to him by the customer, in the colours and quantities the customer supplied. He had to come up with a pleasantly balanced layout, and the stripes had to be arranged so that the various widths for a room-sized piece could be sewn together without the seams showing.

Royal Ontario Museum, Toronto. Gift of Mrs H.E. Fries (949.228).

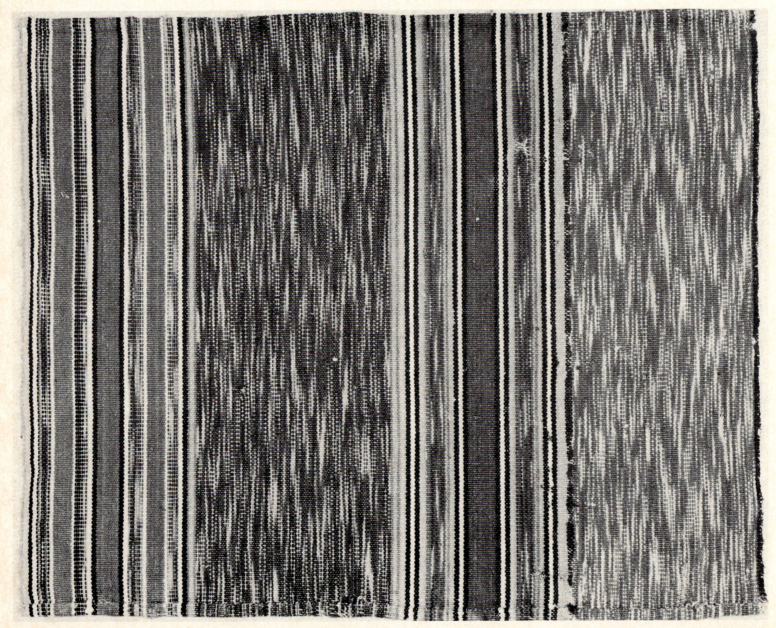

89 Length of carpet early twentieth century

Tabby rag, 3.37 x 0.87 m
Woven by Addie Mick
Warminster, Simcoe County, Ontario

The simplest textiles often survive in the smallest quantities and the poorest condition. Special productions were treasured, but the everyday utilitarian pieces were used, battered, and finally worn out completely. As a result, with rag carpeting, practically nothing of any age survives. This length is the work of a Simcoe County weaver, Addie Mick, who started to weave rag carpets about 1880, and continued to do so for some seventy years. This piece of carpet, and one other, also in the Royal Ontario Museum, are probably the only examples of her work that are still in existence. Her mother was a weaver who came from Ireland as a young woman and Mrs Mick learned the art from her and wove professionally all her life. In her time, and in the area where she lived, there was demand for only one type of hand-weaving – the making of rag rugs, so that is what she wove. This is a common story. As industrialization took over most textile production from the local weavers they could still strip their looms down to two shafts and make a living weaving rag rugs. Mrs Mick was no ordinary rug weaver, turning out miles of yardage with haphazard bands. Within the limits of this very simple medium she was an artist. Her pattern box contained samples of changes of warp settings, combinations of rag strips and yarns, colour and weave effects, and all sorts of subtle things that could be done to make the pattern and the texture of a rag rug interesting. This piece is sadly worn, with the rag wefts now grey and faded pink and the warp of alternately green and pink cotton yarns also faded. Nevertheless, there remains some feeling of the weaver's artistry in the way the warp has been varied by stripes of closely set yarns and in how the weft bandings of brown cotton yarns were used alternately with beige cloth strips, to provide colour and textural interest.

Royal Ontario Museum, Toronto. Gift of Mr and Mrs Harold B. Burnham (947.80.2).

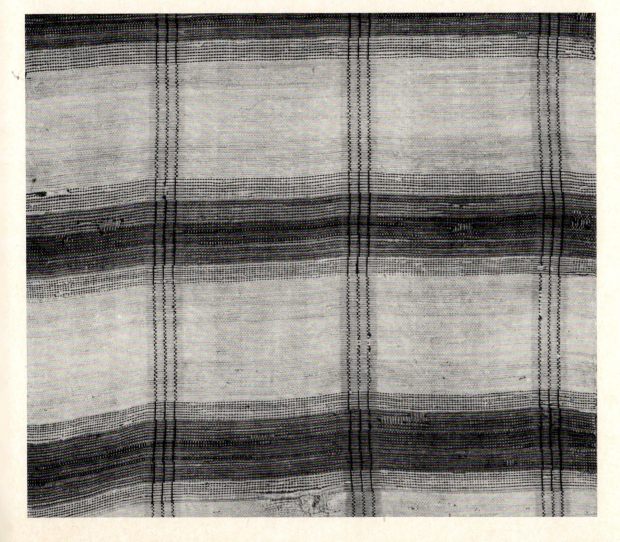

90 Length of carpet   1840–1860

Checked tabby, 3.5 x 0.89 m
East Cape, King's County, Prince Edward
Island

This all-wool tabby carpeting was found in an
abandoned farm house. It was still in place,
covering the floor of the parlour from wall to
wall.[60] While the two previous pieces are of
types that were made in very considerable
quantity and a number of examples exist,
particularly of the warp-faced woollen
striped variety, this is a type that has been
found only in Prince Edward Island, and only
a few pieces have survived. We have no way
of knowing whether it was ever common
there, or whether it was ever made at all in
other areas. Being entirely of woollen yarns it
was dependent on a fairly plentiful supply of
wool – so very likely was always rare. The
wool used in this piece is smooth and hard,
and appears to have been combed rather
than carded (see fig. 21). This probably
indicates a comparatively early date, and
also accounts for the carpet still being in
good condition. The combed yarns would
wear far better than softer, carded ones. The
colours are pleasing, with warp of yellowish
brown, red, and two shades of green
repeated in the same order in the weft, and
then cross-checked in black.

Confederation Centre Art Gallery and Museum, Charlottetown, Prince Edward Island. Gift of Mrs Alton
Robertson (68.17.3).

91 Length of carpet late nineteenth century

Checked broken twill, 4 x 0.91 m
Prince Edward Island

Another example of all-wool carpeting from Prince Edward Island. The warp has wide beige stripes, broken by narrower ones of purple, yellow, and blue. In the weft the purple, yellow, and blue are used in the same proportions, and the beige is replaced by black which makes the broken twill weave show quite strongly. The weave is unusual and interesting. It has been threaded as a plain twill but, in the process of weaving, a change from the normal treadling has resulted in a fabric which has a little, broken-up pattern. The texture is firm and reversible and eminently suited to its use as a carpet (Diagram 71).

Prince Edward Island Heritage Foundation, Charlottetown. Gift of Miss Amy Burroughs.

71 Broken twill

92 Carpet of two widths   about 1900

Overshot weave, 2.39 x 1.6 m
Prince Edward Island

Overshot weave has a tabby ground and an extra weft that moves over and under the ground to form a pattern. It is best known in coverlets (see cat. nos 110 to 118), but the weave was also quite extensively used for carpets. It produced decorative but not very durable carpets and surviving examples are fairly rare, particularly in Ontario. In the Atlantic provinces, where handweaving traditions persisted longer, more of these carpets are to be found. Some have woollen patterns on a heavy cotton ground, but the best are, like this one, all in wool. As with the striped wool carpets, care was taken in the designing to make the joining of the narrow widths as unobtrusive as possible. In this piece, the pattern starts in the centre of one of the square "table" motifs and finishes at the same point and, with even beating of the weft, the sign of a good professional weaver, the motifs come together neatly where the lengths are joined. It is a striking piece, with pattern in black wool on a strong, red wool ground.

Prince Edward Island Heritage Foundation, Charlottetown.

Costume

As in the French areas, the survival of actual costume from other groups in eastern Canada, Loyalist, Scottish-Irish-English, and German, is extremely rare. The dress of these settlers of different origins does not differ greatly, so they have been grouped together in the following pages and a sampling is given of those pieces that have found their way into our museums. In some cases the piece is unique: the child's dress, cat. no. 94, the kerchief, cat. no. 95, and the knitted underwear from Newfoundland, cat. no. 107. In other cases, the choice has been made from a very few existing pieces: the woman's dress, cat. no. 93, the man's coat, cat. no. 101, and the wedding shirt, cat. no. 104. With the shawls and petticoats, there are a number of examples to choose from. When the whole existing body of handwoven costume items from the nineteenth century – from all parts of eastern Canada – is put together, it is a pitifully small group. Nevertheless, it is quite impressive as far as the practical use of available resources, suitability to purpose,

and the quality of material. Our knowledge of what was worn here in pioneer times does not have to be limited by the seeming narrowness of this evidence. We can take what actually remains, add to it what can be learned about cut and style from the much greater body of surviving fashion costume, and complete the picture from archival records and illustrations. Last, but not least, we can refer to the vital evidence of the handwoven materials that have survived as patches in many a Canadian quilt. From all of these sources emerges a very fair and accurate idea of what our ancestors looked like as they went about their business of settling this country.

(Detail, fig. 30)

Figure 29: As a rule, people dressed in their best to have their pictures taken, so in early photographs they are usually wearing store-bought materials and often, by the time photographs were taken, store-bought clothes. This early photograph, taken some time between 1865 and 1870, gives us a rare view of handwoven garments in use, and we can only assume that these were the family's best clothes. Mr and Mrs Johann Schultz (Anna Catherina Schenk) and their two children, lived near Mannheim in Waterloo County, Ontario. They were Lutherans from Germany. It is known that the Schenk family came to Canada in 1848, so the marriage probably took place in this country.

Anna Catherina's skirt and her husband's pants are certainly local handweaving. In Waterloo County of that period it is highly likely that Schultz's jacket was also of handwoven material and tailored by a female relative. Unfortunately, the children did not stay still and are rather fuzzy, but the one on the right may also be wearing homemade material. From the picture file of Doon Pioneer Village, Kitchener, Ontario. Gift of Mr Alfred Schenk.

93 Woman's dress 1865–1870

Checked tabby, 1.4 m
Welland County, Ontario

Survival of handspun and handwoven dresses is extremely rare. In spite of its plain, utilitarian appearance this is a very special piece. It belonged to the donor's grandmother and by some lucky chance escaped the fate that overtook most such garments – it was not cut up for quilt patches. Handwoven costume was always expected to last indefinitely, so was never made in the extreme ways of fashion. This bodice is of the basic, fitted form of mid-nineteenth-century dresses, and the skirt is made of three straight lengths, seamed together and pleated into the waist with most of the fullness placed at the back.[61] The material, which is checked in black, green, and pink is of wool tabby of a type called "flannel" in the old reports. Thousands of yards of flannels, either all wool, or wool combined with cotton, were woven during the nineteenth century by home weavers and local professionals. It was a sufficiently important production that the amounts were listed for any farm where it was made with their other produce in the census returns, during the middle of that century.

Royal Ontario Museum, Toronto. Gift of Mrs W.E.P. DeRoche (967.7).

94 Child's dress   mid-nineteenth century

Tabby, 0.78 m
Antigonish area, Nova Scotia

Children are notoriously hard on their clothes and, in the large families of the nineteenth century, garments were handed down from one member to the other – so the survival of any kind of children's clothing is fairly unexpected. There are many christening robes, and lots of other baby clothes, but children's garments of all kinds – and for all ages and both sexes – are rare. Adding to that is the overall rarity of handwoven clothing and, as far as is known, this is the *only* early handspun, handwoven child's garment that has survived in Canada. It is very difficult to date any dress as plain and basic as this, but judging from the yarns used, the sewing thread, and the cut, it was probably made between 1840 and 1860. It is plain tabby, with a beige cotton warp and a brown wool weft. This type of material is rather romantically called "linsey-woolsey." By the time this piece was woven, imported cotton yarn had replaced the earlier use of handspun linen for the warp, but the name remained.

Nova Scotia Museum, Halifax. Gift of Miss Mary Black (55.23).

72 Gauze weave

Figure 30: Even though, until the advent of the Industrial Revolution, all the beautiful silks and velvets of earlier times were woven entirely by hand, the term "handwoven" automatically brings up a vision of comparatively coarse and simple weaves. That is quite accurate for all handwoven garments made during the pioneering period in Ontario, except for this one dress. It is a wedding dress, 1.39 metres in length and in a gauze weave (Diagram 72), of the finest possible grey and blue wool, with a little silk on a fine cotton warp. It was woven in 1863 for the wedding dress of Helen Forsythe Bell, the donor's grandmother, by the bride's father. It is known that he was a weaver who came to Canada from Scotland and settled in the Perth area of Lanark County, Ontario.

Gauze weaving was an important trade in southwest Scotland, and he must have learned his weaving there. As far as is known, this is the only example of this special kind of fine weaving that he did in this country. He must have been both a proud craftsman and a proud father on that wedding day in 1863. Royal Ontario Museum, Toronto. Gift of Mrs H.J. Gibson (969.161).

95 Kerchief   early nineteenth century

Checked tabby, 0.75 x 0.73 m
Port Hope, Durham County, Ontario

This fine square is checked in blue, brown, and bleached white linen. It comes from the Choate family, who moved into the Port Hope area at an early date and this piece is probably from about 1880. It is the only example of this kind that seems to have survived in Canada, but almost identical pieces are known in Pennsylvania, where they are part of the Pennsylvania German woman's costume. They were worn as a neckerchief, folded diagonally, covering the plain neck of the simple bodices, and were pinned in a special way to form a "V" neckline.[62]

Royal Ontario Museum, Toronto. Gift of Mrs. Doris Wardenier (969.277.4).

96 Woman's shawl   about 1845

Checked twill, 1.74 x 1.74 m
Smith's Creek, King's County, New Brunswick

Shawls were both the fashionable and the utility top garment for women through much of the nineteenth century. For fashionable wear, the imports, such as the Kashmir and Paisley shawls, came in different sizes and shapes at different periods. The handspun, handwoven shawls, however, were always square and made from two widths, woven on the narrow handlooms. They had fringes on four sides and were large enough to envelop the woman comfortably, and could be pulled up over the head for extra protection. This shawl is of fine wool, quite hard to the touch, and has been prepared for spinning by combing (see fig. 21) rather than carding. It is in black, with triple cross-check in natural white. The black appears to be wool from a black sheep, top dyed, probably with indigo, to make it darker. The shawl belonged to the donor's grandmother. The wool came from their own sheep and she is believed to have done the spinning and weaving herself. It is a sombre piece, but the quality of the wool and the texture of the weaving would have made it very pleasant to wear.

The New Brunswick Museum, Saint John. Gift of Mrs. Irvine E. Murray (50.142).

97 Woman's shawl
mid-nineteenth century

Tabby with colour and weave effect, 1.75 x
1.75 m
Winchester Township, Dundas County,
Ontario

This beautifully spun and woven shawl is in
natural white and black wool, and is woven
with a simple colour and weave effect in a
"log cabin" pattern, which was a popular one
for shawls. It is a plain tabby weave, with dark
and light warp threads used alternately, in
this case for 35 threads the width of one of
the checks. Each check is threaded in the
same order: black and then white alternately.
This means that where the checks meet two
dark threads come together. When the weft is
put in, using the same order, the result is an
overall pattern of squares with alternately
horizontal lines and vertical lines (Diagram
73). It is a very clever pattern that is simple
but quite fussy to weave. It has to be done
carefully to look well, but care was always
taken in the making of shawls. This one has
very handsome warp, and weft fringes that
have been very carefully twisted.

Royal Ontario Museum, Toronto. Gift of Mr Herbert Ide
(967.69).

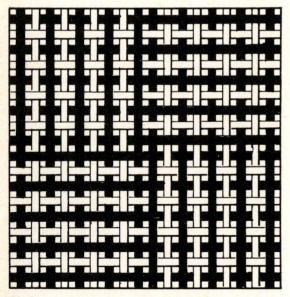

73 One-and-one colour and weave effect

98 Woman's petticoat   about 1876

Checked twill, 0.99 m
Perth, Lanark County, Ontario

This warm winter petticoat has a fine, black cotton warp, with narrow stripes in white and a weft of fine wool, banded in red and black, making a neat, small check. Handwoven garments are seldom cut in the height of style, but this piece reflects the change that was taking place at the end of the 1860s, when the wide skirts that went with the crinoline style were definitely out, and bustles were coming in. This petticoat has been cut from five pieces that are straight in front and slanting at the back, making quite a smart garment with fitted hips, straight front, and considerable fullness at the back. It would have been a very practical garment for wear in an underheated house in the country, but it may also reflect the fact that women were beginning to take more part in active sports. It would certainly have been excellent wear for skating or snowshoeing, or tobogganing, all popular Canadian winter sports at that time.

Royal Ontario Museum, Toronto. Gift of Mrs. J.H. Stewart (969.10.1).

99 Woman's skirt or petticoat
1870–1880

Banded tabby, 0.94 m
Mountain Township, Dundas County, Ontario

This petticoat is from the same area of
eastern Ontario as the previous one, and was
made at approximately the same time.
Traditionally, the donor's great-grandmother
was the spinner, weaver, and first wearer of
the garment. It has a natural white cotton
warp, covered by a handspun wool weft,
banded in black, beige, brown, and orange-
red. The skirt has been made up with the
material on the horizontal, with the coloured
wools producing vertical stripes. The cut is
somewhat like the previous one, but is
simpler and has been made from a surpris-
ingly short length of material (Diagram 74).
As with the previous piece, this would have
been a petticoat when it was first made, but it
was also to have a second incarnation. The
donor's mother took it west, and wore it as a
skirt while homesteading in the Vawn area,
near North Battleford, Saskatchewan, about
1911. If proof is needed of the durability of
Ontario handspun materials, the wearing of
one garment by two generations of pioneering women certainly provides the evidence.

Western Development Museum, North Battleford,
Saskatchewan. Gift of Mrs McDonald (73 NB 6069).

Gauged into waist band

RIGHT BACK	LEFT SIDE	FRONT	RIGHT SIDE	LEFT BACK

WEAVING WIDTH 94cm

74 Cut of skirt

100 Pair of woman's drawers
about 1900

Tabby, 0.89 m
Prince Edward Island

A fairly self-sufficient life style was still possible on the farms of Prince Edward Island at the end of the nineteenth and even into the beginning of the twentieth century. If an article could be made, money did not have to be put out to buy it. It was possible, with the farmer's own sheep, and the spinning and weaving skills of the women, to produce most of the family clothing, including unmentionable garments such as this. This style, with the two legs separate except at the waist, was usual until about 1910. These are white, with a cotton warp and wool weft, and are quite scratchy. The length would reach to about mid-calf, and the red embroidered, scallopped frills are a nice finishing touch that may well have been visible when being "swung on the corner."

Prince Edward Island Heritage Foundation, Charlotte-town (78.131.720).

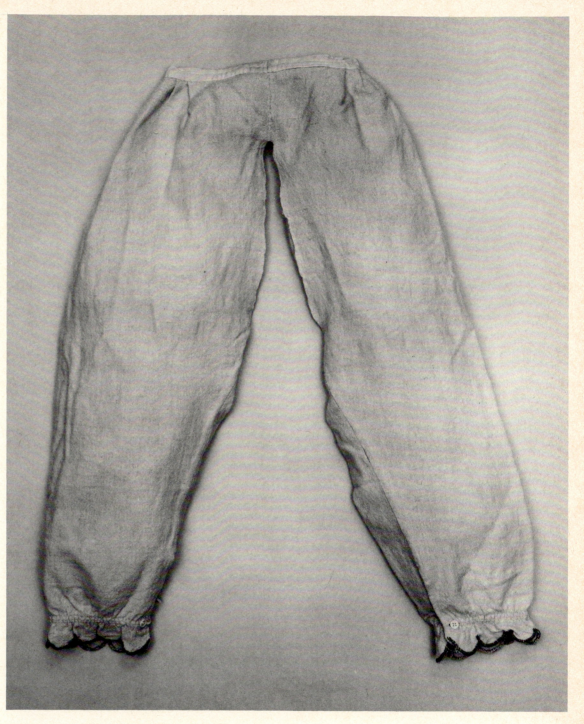

101 Man's coat   1840–1850

Fulled broadcloth, 0.98 m
Ontario

Not all Canadian handwoven materials were rough and comparatively coarse. A considerable amount of "fulled cloth" is listed as part of the produce of many farms during the middle of the nineteenth century. These fulled cloths were woollen materials that were woven locally of handspun yarns, either on the farm, or by professional weavers. They were then sent to fulling mills, to be professionally shrunk and napped to make fine, firm broadcloth. Mills for the professional shrinking and finishing of cloth are known to have been established in many parts of eastern Canada fairly early in the nineteenth century. This coat was worn in Ontario and, with close examination of the tabby material, it seems likely that, in spite of its sophisticated appearance, it was also woven in Ontario, rather than imported. The brown broadcloth has been well cut and tailored in a fairly conservative style.[63]

Royal Ontario Museum, Toronto. Gift of Mr Sidney Holmes (947.94).

102 Length of cloth   about 1875

Fulled twill, 1.83 x 0.72 m
Woven by Florence (MacLean) MacInnis
East Bay, Cape Breton, Nova Scotia

This length was woven by the donor's grandmother. It is a plain 2/2 wool twill that was woven in the natural colour of the sheep's wool and, after weaving, it was sent to the Glen Dyer Woollen Mill where it was dyed black, fulled, and the surface napped to make a heavy, firm, and very handsome coating material. The Glen Dyer woollen mills were a great feature of Cape Breton life for many years, giving service to a wide area and employing many people. They were established by Donald MacDonald, who was born in Pictou, Nova Scotia in 1825 and trained by his grandfather to be a fuller and dyer. He went to Cape Breton and found a suitable mill site near Mabou, on the west coast and, by 1849, he had established a mill for dyeing and finishing cloth and this was followed by carding and weaving mills. Cloth was sent to Glen Dyer for finishing from as far away as the Codroy Valley in Newfoundland and, after the introduction of chemical dyes, the mill supplied the women of Cape Breton with a range of fast dyes in vivid colours for their knitting and weaving yarns.[64] Not all the materials woven in Cape Breton were professionally finished. The old Scottish tradition, that hung on in many areas of the island, almost to the present day, was to shrink the cloth by hand. When a person completed the weaving of a length the neighbours were called in for a "milling frolic." In Ontario, such a working party would be called a "bee" but in Cape Breton they were "frolics" – and they were. With the accompaniment of the proper songs, the wet length of cloth was thumped and squeezed, and passed from hand to hand, around a table until shrunk to the desired width. The milling is no longer done in this fashion, but there are still a few people who know how and also know the proper songs to go with the work.

Museum of Cape Breton Heritage, Northeast Margaree, Nova Scotia. Gift of Miss Irene MacInnis.

---

103 Pair of man's trousers   1843

Striped tabby, 1.01 m
Probably woven by Samuel Fry
Vineland area, Lincoln County, Ontario

These trousers probably survived for the same reasons of sentiment that have led to the preservation of more wedding dresses than of any other kind of dress. They were worn by David Housser in 1843, on the occasion of his marriage. The material is a tabby weave with fine cotton warp striped in white, red, and blue, with a weft of bleached, handspun linen. It is probable that the weaving was done by Samuel Fry, who was a close neighbour of the Houssers. In the Fry collection at the Royal Ontario Museum there is a tiny seed-bag, made from a scrap of rather similar material, so presumably it was a type of weaving that Fry did for his customers. The cutting and tailoring of the trousers is expert, but with the sewing skills that the women had at that time they are probably homemade rather than profession-ally tailored. The fall front and brass buttons were stylish touches of the period. Here we find a smart garment – locally made from locally woven cloth.[65]

Royal Ontario Museum, Toronto. Gift of Mr Norman Macdonald (966.192.1).

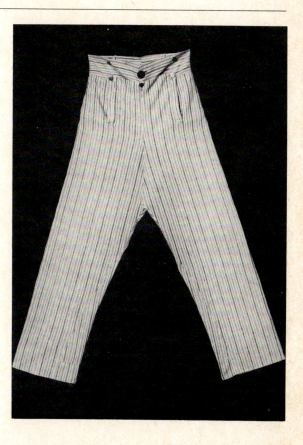

104 Man's shirt   about 1825

Tabby with lace trimming, 0.89 m
Woven by the Barkers
Picton, Prince Edward County, Ontario

The plain linen of this shirt is as fine and even as any top-quality imported material, but it is known that it was grown, processed, spun, and woven by the same Barker family who made the blanket in cat. no. 81. Several other linen shifts and undergarments survive, all of which have histories of Ontario making, but most are of a heavier, more utilitarian weight. This was probably a very special production. It is marked with the name "David Barker." He is known to have married about 1825. The cut of the shirt is of about that time, and probably we can again thank sentiment for survival of a special wedding garment. The sewing of the shirt is exquisite. The full width of the linen has been used for the body, with the selvages forming the side seams, top-sewn together with almost invisible stitches. Fine back-stitch outlines the front placket and the tiny gussets that ease the fit at either side of the neck. The front frill is of fine muslin, edged with lace, adding a touch of imported elegance to this beautiful home-grown, homespun, homewoven, and home-made garment.[66]

Royal Ontario Museum, Toronto. Gift of Miss Maisie Tyrell (948.180).

105 Man's shawl 1840–1850

Twill with colour and weave effect,
3.52 x 0.89 m
New Brunswick

During the early and middle parts of the nineteenth century, many men relied on shawls as a top winter garment. Men's shawls are quite distinctive in shape from those worn by women. They are made from a single width of handwoven material and are always long: three-and-a-half metres or even more. Worn wrapped around the body and over the shoulders in different ways, they made a garment that was equally practical for walking, riding, or driving and they were used in all areas except among the French people. They are closely related to the Scottish plaids that are still a colourful part of the full-dress uniform of the kilted Highland regiments. As with the women, a man's shawl was a lifetime investment and so was always carefully made of top quality wool, expertly spun and woven. In this one, two shades of natural wools, white and a brownish black, have been used alternately, two and two, in both warp and weft which, combined with the 2/2 twill weave, makes a nice little pattern (Diagram 75). As a further decorative touch, an effective banding of the darker wool and a knotted fringe is used at either end.

King's Landing Historical Settlement, Prince William, New Brunswick (M71.319.1).

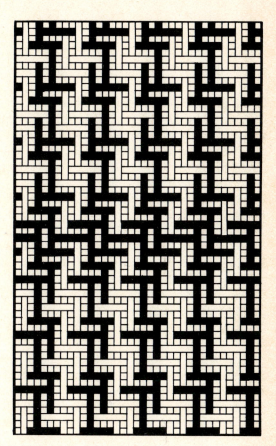

75 *Twill colour and weave effect*

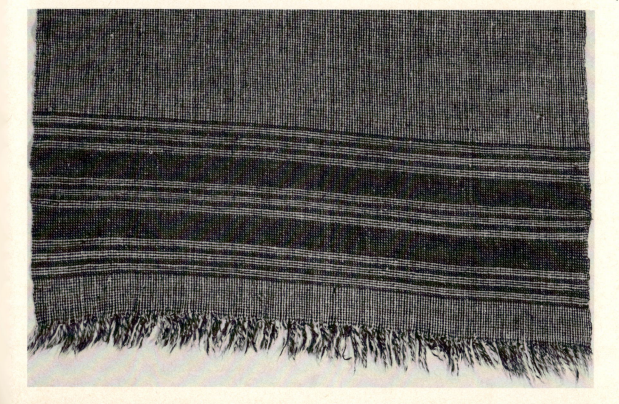

106 Pair of man's gloves
mid-twentieth century

Pattern knitted, 25.0 cm
Hibbs Cove, Conception Bay, Newfoundland

Weaving was not done in any part of
Newfoundland except in the farming communities of the Codroy Valley on the west
coast (see cat. no. 82), but sheep were raised
in many parts of the island. This was usually
on a small scale, to provide meat and wool
for the farm family. Using their own sheep's
wool, the women spun and then knitted
garments for their families and these "cuffs,"
as they were called, were a big production.
They are a cross between a mitt and a glove,
and the form is traditional in Newfoundland.
They are particularly useful to men when
fishing or sealing, because they give much of
the warmth of a mitt with almost the
movement of a glove. A man would wear out
many a pair in a single winter, so the
possibility of any early ones surviving is
practically nil. This pair was collected in
1960, and had probably been knitted shortly
before that. Many mitts were knitted with a
double layer of wool, for warmth, and
sometimes had unspun wool twisted in as
the stitches were formed, to make a small
spot pattern on the outside and a fleece
lining on the inside. This example has been
knitted of two homespun yarns in natural
white and natural brown wool, with the
stitches made alternately of one colour and
then the other, carrying the unwanted yarn
on the inside. On the backs, the two yarns
have been used to make a simple geometric
pattern.[67]

National Museum of Man, History Division, Ottawa,
Ontario (Z III N 93 a and b).

107 Pair of man's underdrawers
about 1900

Knitted, 1.03 x 0.41 m
Hibbs Cove, Conception Bay, Newfoundland

It may seem odd to include a pair of worn and darned "Long Johns" in an exhibition that has the word "ART" in its title. Even if this garment is not, strictly speaking, a work of art it is certainly a rare example of skilled craftsmanship and a unique survival. Probably Canada would not have been as successfully settled if it had not been for textile skills that kept the pioneers warm while they worked at making this country habitable. This long underwear was handspun and handknitted about the beginning of this century in a Newfoundland outport. Wool from the sheep of the farm was used, and it is a very happy chance that this garment has escaped the destruction of most such mundane clothing. It may not be quite from pioneer times, but many similar ones must have been made in earlier stages of settlement. The wool is of excellent quality, the spinning is even and soft, especially suited to the purpose. Care has also been taken to shape the garment well, with careful attention to detail, and the knitting is expert. An appreciation of the value of such a garment to its owner is made evident by the careful and repeated mending with which its usefulness was extended.

National Museum of Man, History Division, Ottawa, Ontario. Gift of Mrs Ernest Lear (Z III N 19).

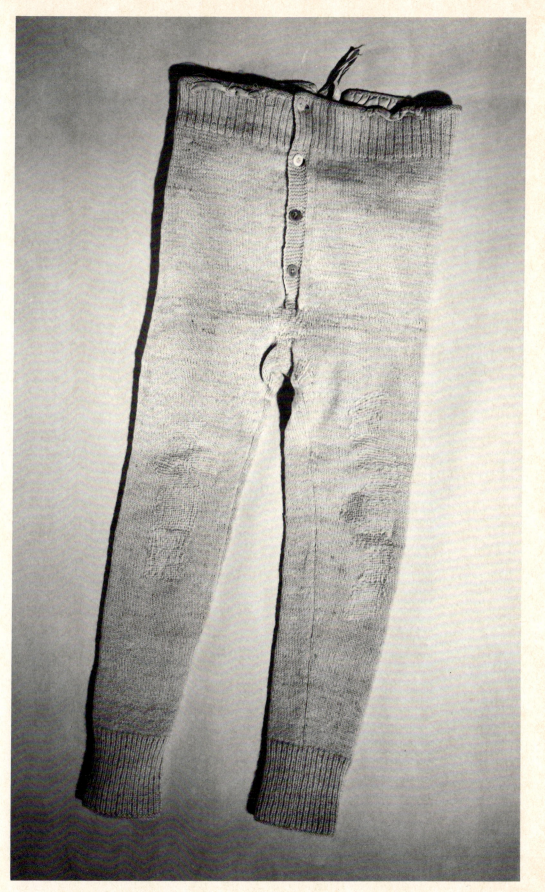

108 Pieced quilt   about 1820

Homespun tabby patches, 2.16 x 1.68 m
Coverdale, New Brunswick

Pioneering societies were not affluent, and textiles were usually in very short supply, so it was natural that any material with a little strength and warmth left in it was recycled. In the French areas, this meant cutting the fabric into strips, and reweaving them. In other parts of the country, the strips were often hooked into rugs, an equally effective way for a textile to lose its identity. We are fortunate that one recycling method has helped to preserve, rather than to destroy, the record of early weaving. Warm quilts made of handwoven patches were very popular. A number have survived, and their patches provide almost an album record of the materials used in the early days for the clothes of men and women in much of the countryside. As we examine these quilts, we can only marvel at the variety of the simple tabbies and twills, the range of colours, and the care that was taken to make a stripe effective, or a check well balanced. In this quilt, the patches, all tabby weave, are early in date. The colours are basically yellow, with some blue and brown. The backing is a grey homespun length and the batt is wool. The pattern is a simple four-patch, and many of the little patches have been pieced. One feature that confirms the early date is that the simple quilting was done with a hand-spun blue woollen thread. It is not likely this would have been used if bought thread had been available, and much of the piecing has also been done with wool thread.[68]

The New Brunswick Museum, Saint John. Gift of Mrs Frances McPherson (976.54).

109 Pieced quilt
late nineteenth century

Homespun and commercial patches, 1.91 x
1.51 m
Enterprise, Lennox and Addington Counties,
Ontario

Most of the wool quilts using handwoven
patches are pieced in the simplest of
patterns, and often with no pattern at all.
This one is unusually well-organized and
effective, with its strong pattern of eight-
pointed stars. The stars are made from a
number of different homespun materials that
are fairly similar in appearance. All of them
are tabby weave with cotton warps that are
striped in yellow, and have wool wefts
banded in blue and orange-red. The dark
backgrounds of the stars are also homespun. The bright red set is a commercial
material in cotton and wool.[69]

National Museum of Man, Centre for Folk Culture
Studies, McKendry Collection, Ottawa, Ontario
(79.292).

Overshot Weaving

Overshot weave is just that. It is a plain tabby weave that is shot over by an additional weft to form a pattern. It is a simple weave that can be produced with equally simple equipment: a loom with only four shafts, yet the patterns that are possible with this method of weaving appear to be quite complex. It is a technique which occurs fairly widely in Europe. Examples are known, in a rather scattered way, from Spain to Scandinavia, and from Scotland to the Ukraine. However, there are no known prototypes from France, and very few from Germany. In the older American craft books, the weave has been called *"Colonial Overshot,"* but there is no evidence that it was used in North America as early as the colonial period. Its appearance on this continent coincides with the arrival of the Scots in the latter part of the eighteenth century. Since the overshot weave was used by the country weavers of Scotland, and since it flourishes, in all its variations, in any area of eastern Canada settled by the Scots and the Irish, the timing fits perfectly. It seems certain that this useful, flexible, and beautiful weave found its way to Canada with those hardy settlers who came by the thousands from the Lowlands, the Highlands, the Isles, and Northern Ireland.

The technique of overshot weaving is very ingenious. With a four-shaft loom, if the shafts are used in pairs, there are six different combinations possible. Two are reserved for the weaving of the tabby ground, leaving the other four combinations of shafts to be used for opening pattern sheds. If the designs are analysed it is obvious that the repertoire of motifs is very limited: a square form called a "table," a smaller square form called a "star." If the "table" is surrounded by "stars," almost miraculously a circle is formed, and if the whole thing is repeated, the circles interlock and other motifs come into being beside them. Another basic motif is the diagonal "cross." If it is repeated a lattice forms, if it is elongated, the whole design starts moving and vibrating in an overall mix of undulating diagonal lines. All these variations, and many more, come from a simple order of threading the warp on the four shafts, and through the opening of the pattern sheds in the four different ways made possible by combining pairs of shafts.

Overshot coverlets have a pattern weft that is almost always of handspun woollen yarn, and is most frequently dyed with indigo. Indigo was imported, but it was available early, and was comparatively cheap, easy to use, producing a very fast, strong colour of blue. The second most usual colour was also an imported dye, madder, and it provided the strong brick red that is often combined with the indigo blue. Another, and much more expensive imported dye, cochineal, also occurs in the coverlets, and there were also many dyes, particularly browns and yellows, that could readily be obtained from local sources.[70] The colour range was limited but effective. Colour was also used for the tabby ground weave when it was of wool, but much more frequently the ground was white and, in the very earliest overshot coverlets, was of handspun linen (cat. no. 110). Cotton yarn was imported at an early date, and was the standard fibre for use in the grounds of overshot coverlets. At first it was available only in the form of a light singles yarn, and was plied by hand on a spinning wheel, to make it strong enough for warp, but that was used in its singles form for the ground weft. This imbalance of the yarns gives a quality to the early coverlets lacking in later examples, which were woven of machine-spun yarns of the same weight in warp and weft.

Overshot coverlets undoubtedly owed much of their popularity to the fact that an attractive pattern could be produced with simple equipment. In the small, early houses the bed often occupied the main room, and a bed covering that was colourful would do much to brighten the home. Overshot weave has another and a more practical advantage. It is a very warm weave for the amount of wool it requires. A single layer of wool, floating fairly loosely over and under a cotton ground makes a texture like a thermal blanket, with air trapped between the wool and the ground, Thus, with half the amount of wool usually required for a blanket, a warmer cover could be made.

The following diagrams illustrate the look of four different ways of weaving overshot:

Diagram 76: With its clean-cut pattern blocks, this type is called "on opposites." Just two sheds have been used for the pattern weft, making only partial use of the possibilities of the overshot technique. These two-block patterns are commonly called "Monk's Belt." They occur in Scandinavia, and are also found in Scotland. A few coverlets woven in this way have turned up in Canada, but seem not to have been made here. Rather, they were probably brought by Scottish settlers.

Diagram 77: This is a four-block weave "on opposites." The pattern weft floats cleanly, over and under the ground, to form the main motifs, but if a pattern like this, with four blocks, is woven on a loom with only four shafts, the background is automatically covered with one- and two-thread interlacings. This can be very effective (cat. no. 118), but it does limit the design possibilities.

Diagram 78: This is by far the most common way of weaving an overshot pattern. The four ways of opening the pattern sheds overlap each other, giving great flexibility. As a result, a wide variety of patterns can be formed against a plain tabby ground, with single thread interlacings framing the motifs. This type of overshot pattern is called "as drawn in," because the order of using the treadles to make the pattern sheds is the same as the order of threading the warp threads through the heddles. The old way of giving instruction to weave in this manner was "tromp as writ." The method produces connected diagonals running across the pattern.

Diagram 79: This shows a less common method of using the four pattern sheds. It is usually called weaving "rose fashion." The two pattern sheds that form a motif are simply used in reverse order – resulting in motifs that stand isolated, with no connection between each other (cat. no. 117).

In Diagrams 78 and 79 it is obvious that the right and left sides of the individual motifs are unbalanced. This is not a mistake. It is the natural result of the old method of writing the drafts that were used for threading up the looms. This imbalance actually enhances the design of many of the old coverlets, particularly in patterns like cat. no. 115. It is another subtle factor, like the different weights of yarns that are used together in the cotton grounds, and the slight unevenness of texture in even the best of handspun yarns, that contributes to the life and sparkle of the old overshot coverlets.[71]

76 Overshot, 2-block "on opposites"

77 Overshot, 4-block "on opposites"

78 Overshot, "as drawn in"

79 Overshot, "rose fashion"

110 Coverlet   about 1800

Overshot weave "as drawn in," 1.81 x 1.54 m
Possibly Colchester County, Nova Scotia

While doing rural research on textiles in Canada, the hope of finding a rare and early example is always there. Among the many other early types of material that are sought are coverlets with linen grounds. Cotton is just as good for this purpose, so as soon as cotton yarn was available by trade it released the limited supplies of homegrown linen yarns for the many other purposes for which they were urgently required. This means that linen in the ground of a coverlet is a good indication of a date very soon after settlement. Researchers are for ever being told that the coverlet just around the corner and over the hill has linen in the ground. After going around the corner and over many hills it almost always turns out that the coverlet in question has a normal cotton ground that has become hard with dirt and age, making it feel like linen, and once more the hoped-for early example has eluded the chase. This coverlet *has a linen ground*, a beautiful handspun, bleached linen ground, and the piece probably dates back to at least 1800. The wool is the usual homespun and a local natural dye has been used to colour it dark brown. This coverlet, in all its parts, has been local production, drawing only on the skills and materials available on the farm. The pattern is the most common of overshot patterns, "*Monmouth*." It combines two of the basic motifs of overshot weaving, the block called a "table," and the "cross" which, in Monmouth, is extended, so that it forms a diamond pattern between the "tables."

Nova Scotia Museum, Halifax. Gift of Mrs S.E. Cosman (73.154.1).

Figure 31: Survival of weavers' pattern drafts is rare. They were usually written on any old scrap of paper that the weaver could find. As a result, they did not look very important, and were usually thrown out when the weaver died. Another reason for their rarity is, that while being used, they were pinned up on the loom, as a guide for threading the heddles and later for the order in which the treadles were to be used. Weavers kept track of where they were by inserting a pin in the pattern and moving it along, block by block, as work progressed. Patterns that were used frequently were destroyed by repeated pinholes.

There are two main collections of pattern drafts: the first, which is in the Royal Ontario Museum, is a large group that belonged to Hester and Rosanna Young, two sisters who lived and wove in Prince Edward County in the early 1840s, two of which are illustrated here. The second group is in the Museum of Cape Breton, where can be found many that were used by the old weavers of that area.[72] All of these provide valuable information as to the method of notation. Also, since many of the drafts have the name of the design written on them, they are a source of Canadian pattern names. The two shown here are "Freemason's Felicity" (see cat. no. 111) and "Chariot Wheels and Church Windows," both names that also occur on the Cape Breton drafts. The notation is different from the modern type, but is not hard to read. The first number 1 indicates the shaft on which the threading starts, the second number, whatever it may be, indicates the number of warps to be threaded alternately on the two shafts on which the numbers are placed. Each measures 40.0 cm in width. Royal Ontario Museum, Toronto. Gift of Miss Annie Abercrombie (954.148.15; 954.148.12).

111 Coverlet   1850–1875

Overshot weave, "as drawn in," 2.20 x 1.59 m
Whitechurch, Bruce County, Ontario

This very effective coverlet from near Lake
Huron, is in the same pattern as the draft
shown in fig. 31. The design is called
"Freemason's Felicity," a fairly unlikely name,
that surely could not have been thought up
twice. Yet the same name is used for the
same rather complicated pattern in Cape
Breton, which surely argues a common
origin. Taking into consideration the areas of
settlement where the name and pattern
occur, that common origin must be Scotland.
This coverlet is woven in deep indigo-blue
and rust-red wool on a white ground. The
border, as can be seen in the corner, has been
threaded in a small diaper pattern. It is
woven in the corner as a diaper, but, as that
threading follows the treadling of the main
design, it becomes something quite complex. The result is a very effectively framed
design.

Royal Ontario Museum, Toronto. Gift of Mrs J.H. Crang
(969.32.2).

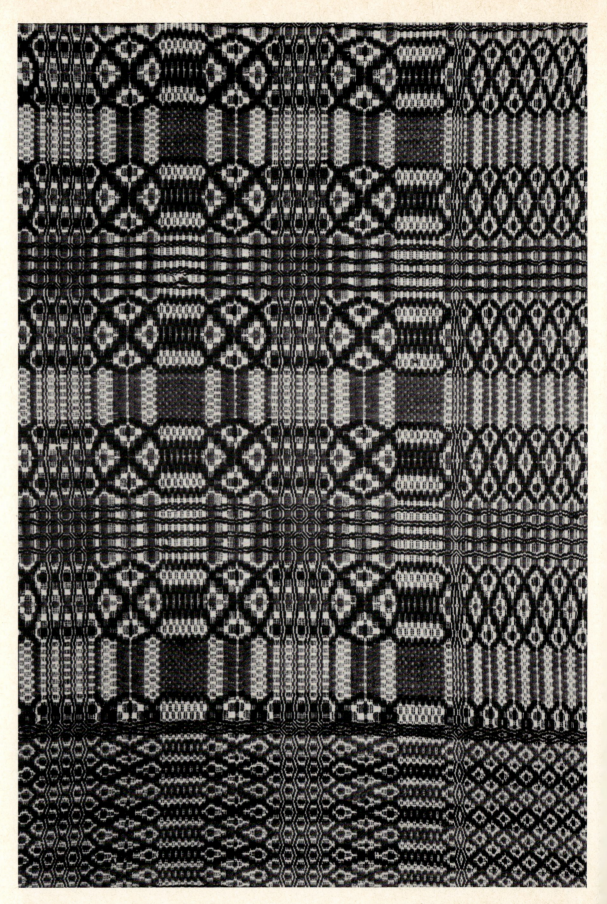

112 Coverlet   about 1860

Overshot weave "as drawn in," 2 x 1.78 m
Traditionally woven by Mrs John C. Calhoun
Fredericton, New Brunswick

This all-wool coverlet was woven by Mrs John C. Calhoun, a great-grandmother of the donor. Survival of coverlets with wool grounds is rare, compared with those with cotton grounds, but it seems likely that the number made was greater than their survival suggests. In areas of the Maritime Provinces they are called "storm blankets" and they were used in sleighs and buggies to cover the passengers until the destination was reached. Then they were put over the horse as it waited for the return journey – a fairly rugged use that did not allow for much chance of survival. This one has a blue wool ground and pattern in pink, white, black, and golden brown. It is a pattern with many names. The small motifs, in five rows of five, are known as "stars," and the Prince Edward County version *"MS Morning Star"* reflects that concept. Similar patterns from New Brunswick and Cape Breton were given the more romantic names of *"Ladies Delight"* and *"Bachelor among the Girls."*

York-Sunbury Museum, Fredericton, New Brunswick.
Gift of Gladys P. Baxter (71.14.7).

113 Coverlet   early twentieth century

Overshot weave "as drawn in," 1.96 x 1.64 m
Woven by Mrs Campbell
S.W. Margaree, Cape Breton, Nova Scotia

The weaving of overshot coverlets lasted until about the middle of this century in Cape Breton, long after industrialization had rendered it obsolete in other parts of the country. At the time this beautiful coverlet was woven there were still a number of professional coverlet weavers operating in Cape Breton, but this is not professional work. It is an excellent example of the spinning and weaving skills of many women of Scottish background. It was made by the owner's mother-in-law, for her own family, on a remote farm in the the hills of the central part of Cape Breton. It is heavy in weight with the ground of brown wool and the pattern in red with a little pale green used to emphasize the centres of the pattern and is a version of the popular "Monmouth" design.

Owned by Mrs Hector Campbell, Sydney, Nova Scotia.

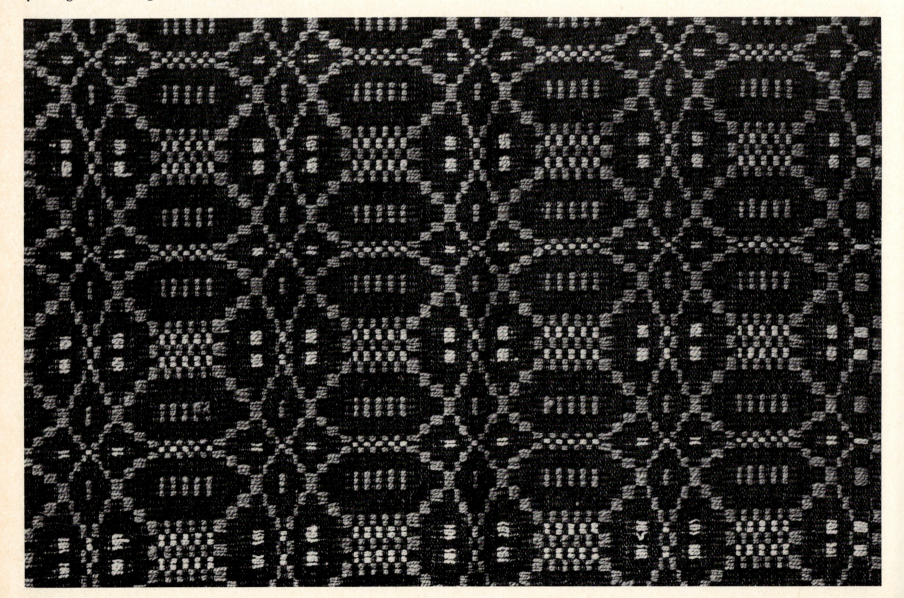

114 Coverlet 1966

Overshot weave "as drawn in," 1.83 x 1.26 m
Woven by Mrs John Munro
Margaree Harbour, Cape Breton, Nova Scotia

This coverlet was woven by the last surviving traditional professional coverlet weaver in Canada, Mrs John Munro, of Margaree Harbour, and she wove it when she was ninety-two. Mrs Munro learned to weave as a young girl at home, and wove professionally after she married. When she was interviewed in 1966 tapping her store of weaving lore was somewhat like being allowed to step back in history. She was able to answer all sorts of practical little questions, such as explaining that the customer always provided the yarn spun and dyed ready for the weaving; that if the cotton for the ground was in the form of singles yarn, the customer plied enough for a strong warp; the pattern draft was pinned to a strip of cloth that was stretched between the cords from which the front shaft of the loom was hung; and a black-headed pin was always used to mark the progress on the draft. She finished her professional career when she was over ninety. This is one of the last few pieces she made. Typical of Mrs Munro's attitude to life and weaving, this pattern, *"Four Spears,"* was a new one to her, and she just thought she would like to try it out! The colour is bright red, the most favoured colour for overshot coverlets in Cape Breton.[73]

Museum of Cape Breton Heritage, North East Margaree, Nova Scotia.

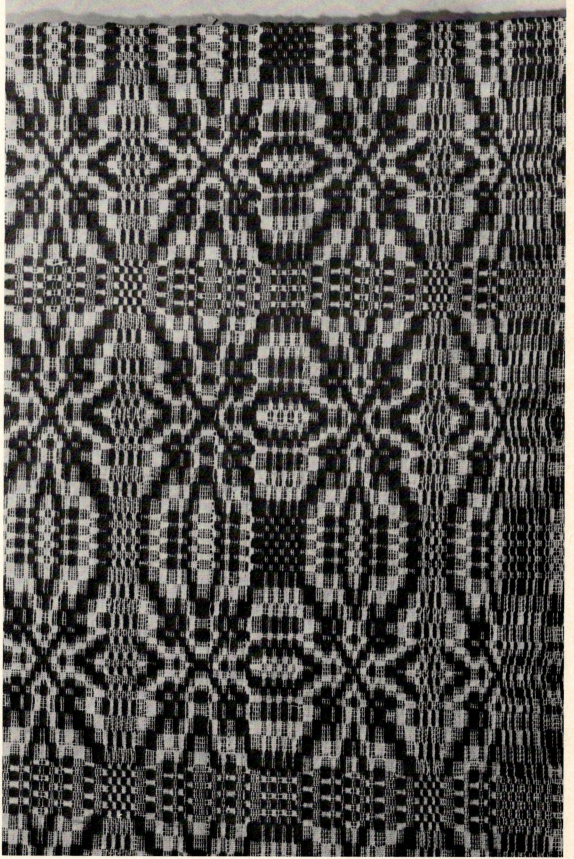

115 Coverlet early twentieth century

Overshot weave "as drawn in," 1.88 x 1.54 m
Woven by a weaver named MacPherson
Bellevue area, Prince Edward Island

This bright red coverlet has one of the most
effective forms of overshot patterning. If the
four pattern blocks are graduated in size, and
are repeated, vibrating lines like this build
up. The result would do credit to any "Op"
artist! As in Cape Breton, overshot coverlet
weaving survived as a living art in Prince
Edward Island until well into this century,
and this piece is fairly late in date. It can take
a lot of figuring to make sure that a coverlet
pattern works out satisfactorily with a given
width of material. Most of the old weavers
were not skilled at figuring, but if they knew
the tricks of their trade they did not need to
be. The drafts were drawn so that the pattern
started and finished at the centre of one of
the main motifs, usually a "table." In this
case, it is at the break between the parts of
the "table." The warp threads required to
make the desired width were set up on the
loom. Threading of the pattern started at the
right of the loom, at the point that would
become the centre seam of the coverlet.
Then threading could just continue until the
warp ran out, resulting in a coverlet that
matched at the centre, but with the outside
edge occurring wherever it happened to end.
This could be quite satisfactory, but a better
effect was gained by threading two or three
repeats of the pattern, and then putting the
leftover warp threads into one of the small
border patterns. On this coverlet, the four
pattern blocks have simply been threaded in
sequence, producing twill lines. On cat. nos
111 and 117 they have been threaded in a
reversing sequence, with a more complex
result. In this way, the pattern is finished
effectively, without resort to mathematics.

Prince Edward Island Heritage Foundation, Charlottetown. Gift of Christine Garnham (78.43.1).

116 Coverlet   mid-nineteenth century

Overshot weave "as drawn in," 2.20 x 1.76 m
Woven by Charles Irvin
Peel County, Ontario

This handsome coverlet, with its brownish
red pattern was woven by Charles Irvin who
had a weaving business during the middle of
the nineteenth century. He lived near the
junction of Derry and Dixie Roads, not far
north and west of Toronto.[74] A draft for this
pattern, but with one less repeat of the small
motif, comes from Prince Edward County
(R.O.M. Abercrombie Collection), and is
inscribed "January 7 1844 The Nine Roses to
Miss Young." Patterns were often given from
one weaver to another, and possibly this was
a belated New Year's gift for one of the Young
sisters (see fig. 31). Coverlets of this same
pattern, with nine, sixteen, or twenty-five
"roses," are of widespread occurrence in all
areas where overshot coverlets were woven,
and the same, rather strange "table motif" is
always used with the "roses." As there was
little opportunity for patterns to spread from
the Maritimes to western Ontario, during the
period when coverlet weaving was being
done, this seems to be further evidence of a
common origin for the designs.

Black Creek Pioneer Village, Downsview, Ontario
(73.9.5).

117 Coverlet   mid-nineteenth century

Overshot weave "rose fashion," 1.93 x 1.88 m
Leeds County, Ontario

The previous patterns were all woven in the
most common way of overshot weaving "as
drawn in," with block following block,
forming diagonal lines running across the
material. If the order of the blocks is changed
(See Diagram 79) a different type of pattern
results, and this beautifully organized coverlet is a striking example of another form, the
"rose fashion," a type that is rare in
Canada.[75] Instead of having rows of attached
"stars," as in cat. no. 112, the two groups of
blocks that form the motif are treadled in
reverse order, making the motifs rounded
and separate. The way that the colours, dark
blue and bright red, have been organized
against the white cotton ground, enhancing
the form of the pattern, is masterly. The
centre seam is beautifully matched, the
borders are effective and well-proportioned,
and the whole coverlet is a satisfying
creation of professional quality.

National Museum of Man, History Division, Ottawa,
Ontario (D555).

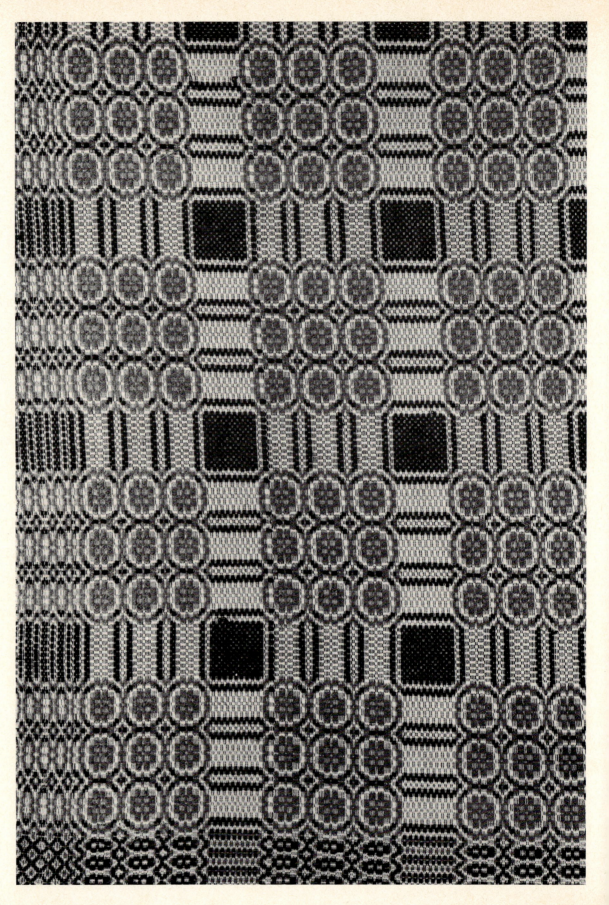

118 Coverlet 1875–1900

Overshot weave "on opposites," 2.40 x 1.88 m
Merrickville area, Lanark or Grenville
County, Ontario

This coverlet is woven in another way of
using the overshot weave (see Diagram 77)
called weaving "on opposites." If the design
is examined, it will be seen that the motifs
are woven so that the blocks are completely
opposite to each other with a series of one-
and two-thread interlacings in between the
motifs. This provides a half-tone and a
completely different effect from the over-
lapping blocks of the more usual way of
weaving overshot. It is a method which
occurs quite rarely, and is most frequently to
be found in pieces of early date. The present
example is a beautiful coverlet, with a very
effective use of the two most common
colours found in Ontario in overshot coverlets: a dark, indigo-blue and a rust-red, that
commonly comes from madder. The cotton
ground is a little heavier than the usual, with
a Z3S yarn used for the warp, instead of a Z2S.
Also two, rather than one, Z singles yarns are
used together for the ground weft. This
slightly heavier weight adds to the boldness
of the pattern.

Upper Canada Village, Morrisburg, Ontario. Gift of Miss
K. Pearson (60 H 6648.2).

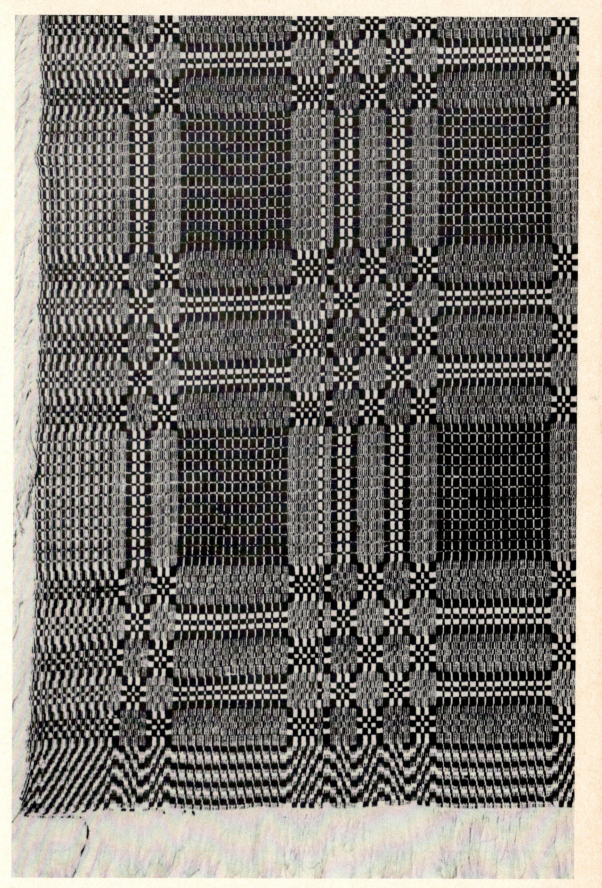

119 Coverlet   1860–1880

Overshot weave, eight-shaft, 2.16 x 1.86 m
Guelph area, Wellington County, Ontario

Overshot weave occurs in a wide variety of traditional patterns that were possible with four-shaft looms, wherever people of Scottish and Irish origin settled. A comparatively rare group of overshot coverlets, with a slightly different look to them, were woven on looms with eight or ten shafts. They come from western Ontario, particularly Waterloo and Wellington Counties, and were probably produced by weavers of German origin, who were trained in the use of more complex looms. They simply adapted their training and their looms to produce a type of coverlet that was in demand by their customers. This very beautifully designed and expertly woven coverlet required a loom with eight shafts for its weaving. The pattern is in dark green and brick-red wool on a white cotton ground.

Royal Ontario Museum, Toronto. Gift of Miss Adelaide Lash Miller (962.67.69).

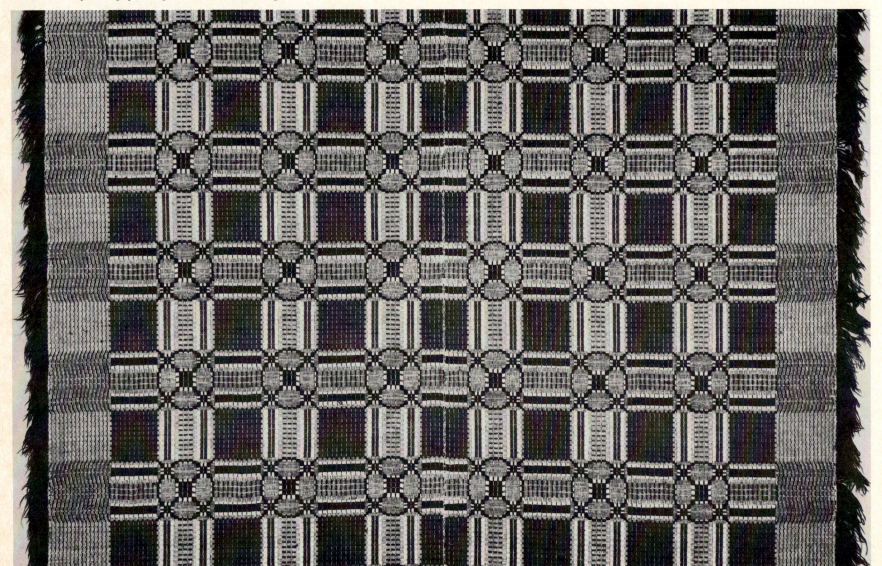

120 Horse blanket
late nineteenth century

Overshot weave, "as drawn in," 1.13 x 0.84 m
Quebec

Overshot weave is not an old traditional weave of Quebec. The early loom in Quebec had only two shafts, and relied on hand techniques, such as *boutonné*, for patterning. But many Scottish people settled in Quebec and many of the early Scottish settlers married Quebec women. As a result, the two nationalities got thoroughly mixed together as did their weaving traditions. Quite early in the nineteenth century we find evidence for the use of looms with four shafts (see cat. no. 58). With the limited adoption of the four-shaft loom came the ability to weave overshot patterns. This delightful horse-blanket turns an originally Scottish weave into something very French. The black wool ground is most effectively patterned in bright red wool finished off with bright red braid and a wool pompon on the tip of each ear, making a French *couturier* costume for a horse!

Royal Ontario Museum, Toronto (972.504).

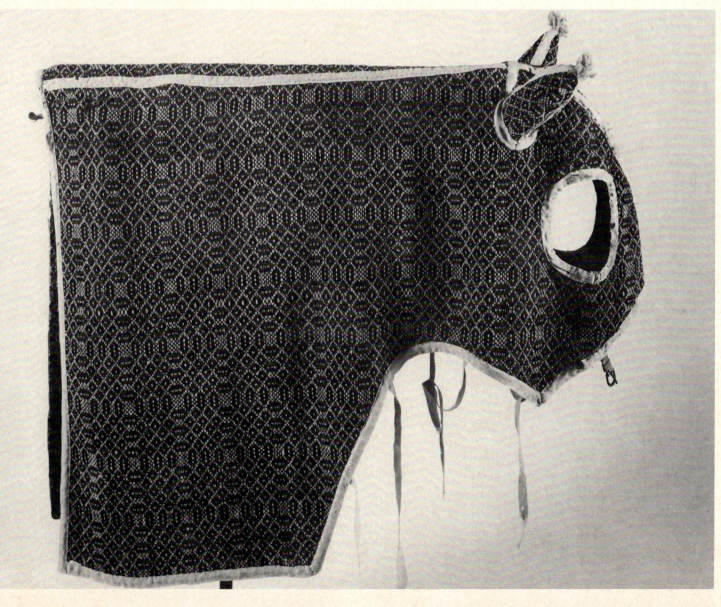

(Detail, cat. no. 129)

Although there was German settlement dating back to the middle of the eighteenth century in Nova Scotia, no memory of German textiles seems to have survived in that area. It is only in Ontario that the German weaving traditions took root and flourished at an early date. The influence came from two different directions. First, from the United States, with those United Empire Loyalists who had German roots, as well as others of German or Swiss origin who followed them, including many Mennonites.[76] These settlers brought their Pennsylvania German weaving traditions with them. We know that young Samuel Fry was sent back to Pennsylvania to learn the weaver's craft. He may well have been not the only young Canadian to have such training, because, in spite of the difficulties of travel, these people kept close touch with those relatives and friends who had stayed behind. Many from Pennsylvania moved up into the wilderness of Waterloo County and established settlements there. The second wave of German influence came with those immigrants who arrived directly from Germany, and who naturally gravitated to the area of Ontario where there already were German-speaking people. Following the Napoleonic wars, there was serious depression in Europe and with increasing industrialization many trained artisans were thrown out of work. The lure of land brought them across the ocean, and among them were many expert weavers who found their way to Waterloo County, and then beyond. As a result, concentrated in that one area of Ontario, there were weaving techniques being used which were not found elsewhere in Canada. Also, with the conservative clientele provided by the Mennonites, the handweavers, most of whom were Lutheran, were able to make a living from handweaving long after fashions had changed and such work had become uneconomic elsewhere.

Multiple-Shaft Weaving

As with other ethnic groups, it is impossible to place the weaving traditions of the peoples of German origin in any really separate category. There was always exchange of ideas between groups and a similarity in the basic techniques used by all peoples. In Waterloo County, as elsewhere, many miles of linens, blankets, yardage for clothing and carpeting were woven on simple looms with two and four shafts. However, the unique contribution that the German weavers made to Canadian weaving was the production of decorative bed coverings and horse blankets. These were made in the complex twill weaves and star and diamond designs that not only required the use of looms with many shafts, but the skill of weavers who had served years of apprenticeship in learning their craft. Cat. nos 121 to 126 give some idea of the variety of the designs and the skill required for this kind of weaving.

80 Multiple-shaft twill

121 Horse blanket   dated 1844

Multiple-shaft twill, 2.11 x 1.82 m
Waterloo County, Ontario

This blanket, made on a loom with sixteen shafts threaded in a point twill, is an excellent example of highly-skilled, professional weaving from the German area of Waterloo County in Ontario (Diagram 80). It is known that the type was woven for use as horse blankets—at that time, and in that area, nothing was too good for a good horse. The blankets must have been very popular, as a surprising number of similar pieces have survived. The Noll brothers, the jacquard weavers, kept one loom for weaving them through much of their period of production, which stretched from the late 1860s until into this century. Examples are found in all wool, or in a mixture of wool and cotton yarns. This one is in rust-red and indigo-blue wool, checked with white cotton. It is difficult to date such pieces, because the weave does not vary and, as the woollen yarns are hand-spun and home-dyed, they do not change. It is only the cotton yarns that may give some clue as to the date of a piece. When this one was found, with the embroidered initials "E M" and the date "1844" in very small letters, near the top beside the centre seam, it was greeted with jubilation. For once, it provided evidence of a definite and fairly early date for at least one of these rather undateable pieces. The embroidery is in the same wool as the warp and weft, and there seems no reason to doubt that it was done at the time of the making of the blanket.[77]

Royal Ontario Museum, Toronto. Gift of Mr and Mrs Harold B. Burnham (970.118.8).

122 Horse blanket 1850–1875

Twill diaper, 2.28 x 1.90 m
Waterloo County, Ontario

From the heavy weight of the woollen yarns used in this piece it is certain that it is a horse blanket. The colouring is very striking, with dark blue, green, and brick red used in both warp and weft. The warp order is 76 blue, 20 red, 36 green, and 20 red. In the weft the order is slightly different, with 76 blue, 20 green, 36 red and 20 green making a much more interesting effect than if warp and weft orders had been the same. This weave is called "twill diaper" or, by the more descriptive name, "reverse twill," since the pattern is due to the contrast of the reverse faces of a 3/1 twill (Diagram 81). Four shafts are required on the loom to make one block of pattern. So this four-block pattern must have required a loom with sixteen shafts.[78] Traditionally, the blanket was made on the farm of Solomon Brubaker, the donor's father. There is no reason to doubt that the sheep were raised, the wool was processed, spun, and dyed on the Brubaker farm – but not the weaving itself. There is no question that it was the work of one of the many skilled German professional weavers operating in all areas of Waterloo County at the time that this blanket was woven.

Doon Pioneer Village, Kitchener, Ontario. Gift of Mr and Mrs Marshall B. Brubaker (69.91.5).

81 Twill diaper

123 Coverlet about 1860

Twill diaper, 2.07 x 1.88 m
Woven by Samuel Fry
Vineland area, Lincoln County, Ontario

Twill diaper weave was used in Europe for the weaving of table linens. The technique was well-known to the highly-skilled German weavers who were coming out to Canada and settling in Waterloo County from the 1840s through the middle of the century. It was also popular with those people of German connection who came to Canada earlier, via the United States. There, the weave had been used for linens and bed coverings, and it was one of the techniques that Samuel Fry learned when he went to Pennsylvania to study his craft. This very beautiful all-wool coverlet in dark and light blue, and a strong, clear red, was woven by Samuel Fry. It is thought that it was made for his daughter Mary (Fry) Moyer at the time of her marriage about 1860. The pattern is in Fry's pattern book, and is the same one that he used for the tablecloth in cat. no. 80.

Royal Ontario Museum, Toronto. Gift of Mr and Mrs Harold B. Burnham (955.80.1).

124 Coverlet 1850–1875

Twill diaper, 2.05 x 1.72 m
Woven by Johan and Henry Lippert
Petersburg, Waterloo County, Ontario

It is a very happy chance when, as in this case, a piece of what would otherwise be unidentifiable weaving comes down through the family of a weaver, so it can be known for sure who the weaver was. This twill diaper coverlet is the expert and beautiful work of the Lipperts of Petersburg, the great-grandfather and grandfather of the donor. The elder Lippert, Johan, was born in Germany. He presumably came to Canada as a trained weaver, and his son, Henry, who worked with him, was born in this country. They had a well-known weaving business in Petersburg, where they wove decorative coverlets on a loom with jacquard attachment (see cat. no. 135). However, to be economically sound, a weaving business had to be diversified. The Lipperts therefore had other looms, on which they wove other types of material, including the popular wool twill diaper coverlets. The colour scheme of this one is simple but effective, with a warp of dark indigo blue, striped at the edges with green, and woven with a terracotta-coloured weft.

Royal Ontario Museum, Toronto. Gift of Miss Kathryn Lippert (974.384.4).

125 Coverlet 1850–1875

Point twill, 2.25 x 1.89 m
Waterloo County, Ontario

This is another type of professional weaving, requiring a loom with many shafts. Coverlets woven by this method are rare, and turn up only occasionally in the German areas of Waterloo County and Pennsylvania. They have a tabby ground, with extra pattern weft used alternately with the ground weft, floating over and under the ground in the same manner as overshot, but following the much more complex twill threading. The known patterns in this technique vary only slightly, and are all very attractive. This coverlet is in dark and light indigo-blue, and deep rust-red wool, on a white cotton tabby ground.

Royal Ontario Museum, Toronto. Gift of Mrs J.H. Crang (970.230).

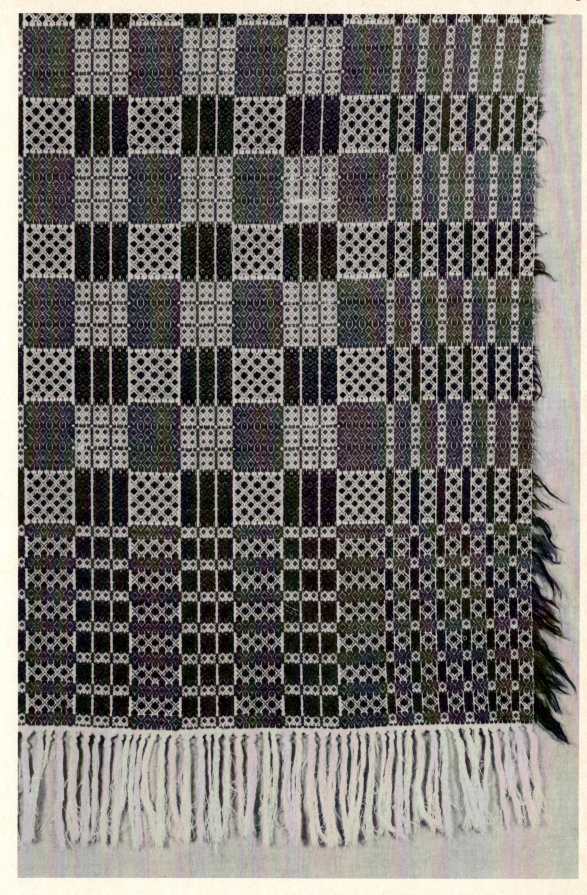

126 Coverlet   1850–1870

Star and diamond weave, 1.80 x 1.57 m
Kitchener-Waterloo area, Waterloo County,
Ontario

This is an example of a coverlet type that is
quite common among the German weavers
of Waterloo County. Its name is descriptive:
the *"Star and Diamond"* weave. Although
there is considerable variation in the patterns, they all follow similar layouts of
eight-pointed stars in rows, separated by
diamonds in some form or other. The
technique has similarity to overshot weaving
with a tabby ground and heavier pattern weft
moving over and under it, to form the design.
However, a loom with fifteen or more shafts is
required for this kind of weaving, and it was
always the work of trained professional
weavers. The present example has an
indigo-blue wool pattern on a white cotton
tabby ground.[79]

Royal Ontario Museum, Toronto. Gift of Mr and Mrs
Harold B. Burnham (957.98).

Jacquard Weaving

The pattern weaving that has been described so far has been made possible by passing the warp threads, in different sequences, through heddles held on the shafts of a loom. There is a physical limit to the number of shafts that can be mounted on a normal handloom and, in Canada, twenty was the usual top number. Patterns of considerable complexity can be made in this way, but all are geometric. The fine materials, with naturalistic patterns that were woven in Europe from early times, were made on a different type of pattern loom, called a "drawloom." With this equipment, it is theoretically possible to control the warp threads individually, but the drawloom is a very complicated piece of equipment, requiring at least two workers to operate it. Such looms were never used by the local, professional weavers in Canada. During the eighteenth century, the period of the great textile inventions of the Industrial Revolution, many men worked towards a simplification of the drawloom. Finally, Joseph-Marie Jacquard, a silk weaver in Lyon, France, developed a mechanism for that purpose, and by 1806 he had made it practical. This invention was the earliest form of the use of the punched cards that have come to dominate our present-day lives. Each card controlled the opening of one pattern shed. On the cards there were rows of spaces that either had a hole punched through them or were left blank, and each space controlled a single warp thread. A series of these cards were moved, one by one, over a revolving metal block that had holes punched in its four sides, which matched the rows of holes on the cards. Wherever there were holes on a card, a sequence of simple movements took place, so that while the threads corresponding to the holes were lifted, the other threads remained in place, and a pattern shed was formed. The invention first came into use in the silk-weaving industry in France, not without the violent opposition that usually greeted the invention of labour-saving devices. Slowly, however, the use of this attachment, called a "jacquard," after its inventor, became accepted, and was added to many of the handlooms that were being used in various sections of the textile industry at that time. The jacquard attachment reached North America in 1824, introduced by a Philadelphia merchant, William Horstmann. The attachment could be mounted on any sturdy handloom frame, was not very cumbersome, and was not even very difficult to make. Thus, it was ideally suited to the use of local professional coverlet weavers, and soon it was being used widely among that group of American artisans. Between the date of its introduction and the time of the Civil War, which virtually ended the production of hand-weaving in the States, the production of jacquard coverlets was enormous in the northern states. In Canada, the jacquard loom was never used by local professional weavers except in southern Ontario, and there it was employed by only a small number of men of German or Scottish background, who had come to this country as fully-trained weavers. The first weaver to use the equipment in Ontario was Wilhelm Armbrust, and the date of his first coverlet is 1834. From that time, until the early years of the twentieth century, when the production finally died out, probably not more than thirty weavers ever made these coverlets. But in spite of the limited number of jacquard weavers, the production was quite large, and since a jacquard coverlet was always a prized possession, the once-in-a-lifetime acquisition, they were much treasured, and their survival is considerable.

A number of different weave constructions were used by the jacquard coverlet weavers in Ontario, and diagrams of most of these are given with the following catalogue entries.[80]

Figure 32: This shows the only early loom with jacquard attachment for pattern weaving that is known to have survived in North America. The jacquard head was made by James Lightbody of Jersey City, New Jersey and the loom belonged to John Campbell, a Scot, born in Paisley and trained as a weaver there. He emigrated to the United States in 1832, and then moved on to Canada in 1859, bringing his jacquard equipment with him. He set up as a weaver in the little village of Komoka, in Middlesex County, near London, Ontario. There he wove jacquard coverlets and simpler things, like blankets, yardage, and carpets, until the time of his death in about 1885. His account book, which gives a fascinating insight into the business of a local handweaver and his two looms, are now at the Ontario Science Centre. The jacquard loom has been put into working condition. It measures 3 x 2 x 2.5 m. When in operation, it makes a fascinating exhibit, as it shows how complex, patterned coverlets could be produced by one man in a small workshop in rural Ontario.[81] Ontario Science Centre, Don Mills.

Figure 33: Early looms with jacquard attachment, such as John Campbell's, were hand-powered, like the simpler hand looms. However, the opening of the pattern sheds was performed automatically by the sets of cards into which the sequence of shed openings, required for particular patterns, were punched. The cards shown here are some of Campbell's original ones and he used them in Komoka, Middlesex County, Ontario, around 1860 to 1880. This particular set controlled the spelling out of the name "Nancy Carmichael" (Diagram 83), a customer who was willing to pay fifty cents extra to have Campbell weave her name into the border of her coverlet. Campbell's jacquard was a particular type, with a double lift mechanism. It required the cards to be set up in pairs that were identical, but that performed two different functions in the opening of the sheds. These cards measure 31.8 x 6.7 cm. Ontario Science Centre, Don Mills.

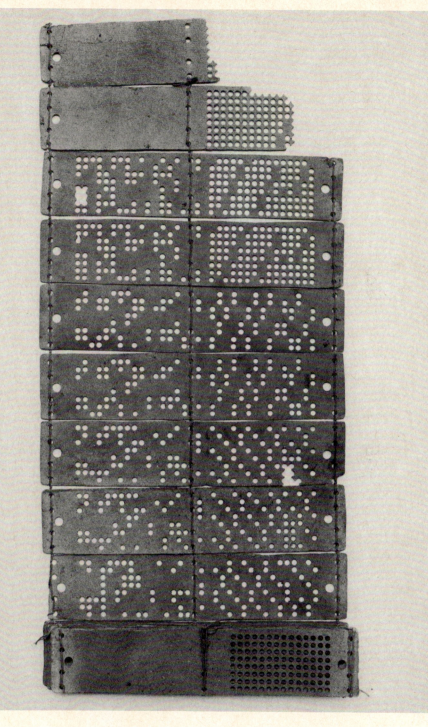

82 Jacquard pattern for name

127 Coverlet   dated 1842

Jacquard, free double weave, 2.12 x 1.84 m
Woven by Wilhelm Armbrust
Jordan area, Lincoln County, Ontario

This coverlet was woven by Wilhelm Armbrust, who was born in Germany in 1807 and settled near Jordan, in the Niagara Peninsula, in 1830. He is the first weaver in Canada known to have had a loom with a jacquard mechanism. In 1834 he advertised in a St Catherines newspaper that he was prepared to weave "Fancy Coverlets on the New Improved Loom" and it is known that he wove two dated coverlets that year. This is one of a pair he made for William and Ann Miller of Niagara-on-the-Lake in 1842, the year of their marriage. In the corner cartouche, with their initials and the date, Armbrust has put a device that he often used to mark bridal coverlets: two hearts hanging from a balance. This pattern with four roses is one that occurs over and over again, in different versions woven by many weavers. It seems to be the most popular pattern for coverlets that were especially ordered for a wedding. The weave of this coverlet is a free doubleweave (Diagram 83), like that used in the geometric patterns (cat. nos 66 to 69). It is the most common construction used for early jacquard coverlets. One layer is in dark, indigo-blue wool and the other is white cotton. The two layers have identical spacing, 1:1, and change places to form the pattern. The form of the pattern has what is called a *decoupure* of 2, that is, the outline of the pattern moves in steps of two threads at a time in both warp and weft directions.

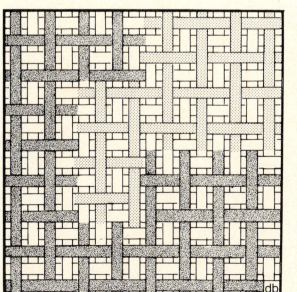

83 Jacquard, free double weave, 1:1

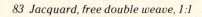

128 Coverlet   dated 1857

Jacquard free double weave, 2.17 x 1.89 m
Woven by Moses Grobb
Beamsville area, Lincoln County, Ontario

The weaver of this coverlet was Moses Grobb, who was a connection of the Fry family and worked in the same area of the Niagara Peninsula. Like Samuel Fry, he was a Mennonite and was basically a farmer who wove in the wintertime. It is not known where he received his training, but he must have been well trained, for the coverlets he is known to have woven prove that he was an expert weaver and could handle the complex equipment of the jacquard loom most skilfully. As with other early coverlets, this one was woven in two widths and seamed down the centre and with the evenness of the weaving the seam is almost invisible. His workshop produced much simple weaving and it is thought that he may have had other weavers working for him during at least part of his period of production. His coverlets are always dated, with the first known one in 1853 and the last in 1873. The construction is the same as the previous coverlet, free doublecloth with a *decoupure* of two, with one layer of white cotton and the other of indigo-blue wool.

Stone Shop Museum, Grimsby, Ontario. Gift of Mrs C.T. Terryberry (No. 1037).

129 Coverlet   about 1880

Jacquard, free double weave, 2.17 x 2.09 m
Woven by John Campbell
Komoka near London, Middlesex County,
Ontario

This is the work of John Campbell the weaver
who owned the loom that is now at the
Ontario Science Centre (fig. 32). It is another
version of the popular four roses pattern that
is called *"Rose and Stars"* in the Campbell
account book. Here the roses have been
combined with weeping willows and a row of
small American eagles. Campbell came from
Scotland, but he worked in the United States
for some years before moving on to Canada
and this is a design that he brought with him
from the States. Presumably, his Canadian
customers did not mind having American
eagles surrounding their beds, because it is
the most frequently found of his four known
patterns. The construction is a free doubleweave, with one layer of white cotton and
the other of dark, indigo-blue wool, but is
different from the previous examples. In
Campbell's work the warp proportions of the
two layers of the weave are 4:1 (Diagram 84).
The white cotton layer is a balanced tabby
weave, but the other layer has a heavy wool
weft weaving with a widely-spaced and quite
unobtrusive cotton warp that only occurs
between four of the warps from the other
layer.

London Centennial Museum, Ontario. Estate of Sarah
Ann McBain (972.62.2).

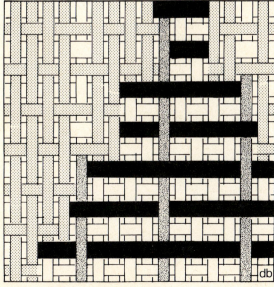

84 Jacquard, free double weave, 4:1

130 Coverlet   dated 1868

Jacquard weft-patterned tabby, 2.18 x 1.93 m
Woven by "J. Noll and Brothers"
Petersburg, Waterloo County, Ontario

This coverlet was woven, as it says in the corner, by J. Noll and Brothers for Mary Deichert in 1868. It must be one of the first coverlets the Nolls wove, for at that time John was seventeen and his brother, William, was nineteen. The Nolls usually put their own name on with their customer's name, making life easy for the textile researcher. This was usual practise in the United States but not in Canada, possibly we were not good at advertising, even at that date. The early Noll coverlets are in patterns that are identical with those woven by Aaron Zelner, the first jacquard coverlet weaver in Waterloo County. Zelner came to Canada from Pennsylvania and wove in Waterloo County from about 1855 until sometime in the late 1860s, when his patterns start appearing with the Noll name in the corner. It seems most likely that they apprenticed with him and then took over his loom and pattern cards just about the time this coverlet was woven. They had a workshop in Petersburg where they produced all sorts of weaving, including jacquard coverlets in a variety of patterns. Some of these were Zelner's designs, but many were their own. The construction used by Zelner and the Nolls is a weft-patterned tabby. It has a tabby ground and used, alternately with the ground weft, a heavy pattern weft. Every third warp is used to tie down the pattern weft but the tying warps alternate on successive rows, so that the basic float of pattern weft is over five warp threads (Diagram 85). The result is a texture that is slightly ribbed. This coverlet has a white cotton ground and the pattern weft is banded in indigo blue, green, and bright red.

Doon Pioneer Village, Kitchener, Ontario.

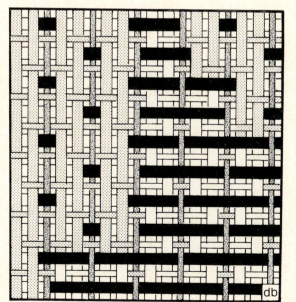

85 Jacquard, weft-patterned tabby, 5-thread float

131 Coverlet   dated 1891

Jacquard, weft-patterned tabby, 2.17 x 1.88 m
Woven by John Noll
Petersburg, Waterloo County, Ontario

This is a beautiful example of the Noll's later work, using the same construction as the previous piece and with the pattern banded in black and rust-red wool on a white cotton ground. The corner cartouche reads "W & J Noll Petersburg Ont. M. Rosenberger 1891." If the coverlet was ordered, the customer's name usually went on the cartouche and the customer provided the yarn but a number of the Noll coverlets have just their own name or no name at all. These were probably made for whoever wished to buy them, spreading the work out more evenly throughout the year. If the coverlets are signed, usually the names or initials of both brothers are used but it is known that John was the weaver of jacquards while William specialized in multiple-shaft weaving, making the popular twill horse blankets. Both brothers did simple weaving of yardage for clothing, blankets, and rag carpets. John Noll did not die until 1905 but no jacquard coverlets of his are known of as late a date as that.

McCord Museum, Montreal, Quebec (M965.22).

132 Coverlet   dated 1840

Jacquard, weft-patterned tabby, 2.18 x 1.73 m
Woven by Wilhelm Armbrust
Jordan area, Lincoln County, Ontario

This coverlet was woven by the same man
that wove cat. no. 127, Wilhelm Armbrust,
and is also in white cotton with indigo-blue
wool but has a completely different construction. Most of the jacquard weavers used
only one construction but Armbrust and a
few others used two. With free doublecloth
one layer was entirely of wool and each
coverlet would require a considerable
amount of that sometimes rare commodity.
With this construction the warp is entirely of
cotton and, as in overshot weave, the wool is
only used for one of two wefts, a much more
economic way of using it. An all-cotton warp
could be set up in a much greater length at
one time than the mixed wool and cotton
warp, providing quite a saving of time, so
Armbrust may have found it worth his while
to have two looms, one for free doubleweave
and the other for this construction, a
weft-patterned tabby. This is similar to the
Nolls construction, but every fifth warp is
used to tie down the pattern weft. The tying
warps alternate on successive rows, producing floats of nine threads in the pattern weft
(Diagram 86). Armbrust has used his device
of a single heart hanging between two pillars
so this was probably not a bridal coverlet. He
designed his own patterns and cut the cards
for them himself. Armbrust's production
period was short, 1834 to 1848, when he
became a full-time farmer, but considering
the number of his coverlets that are still in
existence that must have been a busy
fourteen years.

National Gallery of Canada, Ottawa, Ontario (9628).

86 Jacquard, weft-patterned tabby, 9-thread float

133 Coverlet   dated 1852

Jacquard, weft-patterned tabby, 2.03 x 1.72 m
Probably Welland County, Ontario

These coverlets come from such a recent period of history that it should be easy to find plenty of information regarding the different weavers, but that is not the case. They were skilled artisans but were not "important," and so were not newsworthy. Also, they, themselves, were not learned, and sometimes not literate, so they left no record of their lives beyond their work. Account books are exceedingly rare. There is the odd advertisement in a newspaper and there are the census reports. In these, occupations are listed, so a weaver's name and place of residence can be found, but there is nothing to indicate whether he is a master weaver or just someone who wove rag rugs. It is very frustrating, and one group of jacquard weavers that have so far defied identification are several men who wove at an early period in Welland County. This handsome coverlet in indigo-blue wool and white cotton is the work of one of these unknowns. The border is of a type that occurs in a number of versions, and has been popularly called "rose and crow." The bird, however, is much more special than a crow. It is a *Distelfink* (thistle finch), a popular motif in Swiss folk art, and one that is frequently found in Mennonite design in this country. The weave construction is the same as in Diagram 86, but instead of the normal *decoupure* of two threads, the pattern moves just one thread at a time. This *decoupure* of one gives a more rounded outline that is very apparent in the drawing of the birds.

Royal Ontario Museum, Toronto (969.71).

134 Coverlet   1855–1865

Jacquard, free double weave with tied areas,
2.08 x 1.85 m
Woven by William Withers
Stouffville, York County, Ontario

This coverlet was woven by a Scot, William Withers, who came to Canada about 1850 and settled near Stouffville. Here he wove professionally until his death, which occurred sometime between 1861 and 1871. He had one of the first wide looms with jacquard attachment in Ontario and could therefore weave coverlets in a single piece, without the necessity for a seam down the centre. It seems likely that Withers received his training in the carpet industry in Scotland, since his patterns have many elements that are strongly reminiscent of Scotch "ingrain" carpets. However, he was obviously aware of the designs of other Ontario coverlet weavers – the popular four roses motif has been lifted wholesale, and inserted into the middle of his carpet-like pattern. The four roses also occur in the corner, but there they must represent the rose for England, since they are surrounded by a wreath which includes thistles for Scotland, shamrocks for Ireland, and maple leaves for Canada. Withers may well have originated this design at the time of the visit of the Prince of Wales in 1860. Maple leaves were much to the fore during that period of patriotic fervor.

The construction Withers used was a double weave, with the layers free in part, and tied in part (Diagram 87). A white cotton warp weaves in tabby with a fine white cotton weft. For the other layer, a heavy wool weft, banded in dark indigo-blue and raspberry-red weaves with a fine cotton warp that is spaced between two of the other warps (proportion 2:1).

Black Creek Pioneer Village, Downsview, Ontario (59.151).

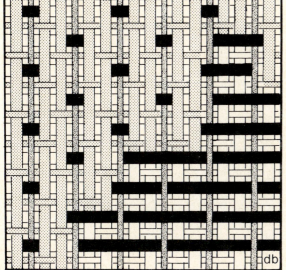

87 Jacquard, free double weave with tied areas, 2:1

135 Coverlet   about 1875

Jacquard, free double weave with tied areas,
2.20 x 2.03 m
Woven by Johan and Henry Lippert
Petersburg, Waterloo County, Ontario

This coverlet was woven by the Lipperts of
Petersburg, the same father and son who
wove cat. no. 124. It is known that in 1870
they imported a wide loom with jacquard
attachment from the United States. By that
time, industrialization, coupled with the
disruptions of the American Civil War, had
led to the end of the handweaving of
coverlets in the States. A number of weavers
in the very conservative area of Waterloo
County, where there was still a large demand
for handweaving, acquired looms that had
become obsolete south of the border. With
these looms came sets of jacquard pattern
cards. Usually, each weaver was able to offer
his customers a choice of four patterns. The
patterns that came from the States were not
changed as they moved north into Canada
and so, suddenly, bold and effective patterns,
many of them with aggressively American
themes, became available in Waterloo
County, such as this very un-Canadian eagle
in bright red wool on a white cotton ground.
It took skill to weave coverlets of this type,
but allowed for absolutely no originality. The
construction is the same as that used by
Withers (see Diagram 87), with the slight
difference that the cotton warp that ties the
pattern is blue, making it slightly less
noticeable than a white one.

Royal Ontario Museum, Toronto (968.210).

136 Coverlet   about 1875

Jacquard, free double weave with tied areas,
2.13 x 1.90 m
Woven by Edward Graf
Gasline, near Port Colborne, Welland County,
Ontario

This charming coverlet in green wool on a
white cotton ground is the work of Edward
Graf, who was born in Prussia in 1826. His
parents emigrated to the United States
during the 1840s. They settled in Buffalo, but
most of Edward Graf's life was spent near
Port Colborne. By 1852 he was married, living
on half an acre of land at Gasline and was
weaving professionally. It is not known where
he received his training, perhaps in northern
New York State, or he may have apprenticed
with one of the skilled weavers in Welland
County. It has been speculated that he may
have taken over Armbrust's loom, since his
beginnings as a jacquard weaver coincide
fairly closely with Armbrust's retirement. In
1868 he acquired a wide jacquard loom and
proceeded to put out an enormous volume of
work with the help of his son, Albert. The
coverlets from this period are marked, as this
one is, by the pattern name written so that it
faces upside down and rightside up on both
faces of the coverlet. He had a number of
patterns in this series including *"Morning
Glory," "Bird's Nest," "Bird of Paradise,"
"Flower Pot,"* and this *"Cherubim."* He
designed his own patterns, but made use of
motifs both old and new from the work of
other weavers. The construction he used was
a free doubleweave, with tied areas, like
Withers (see Diagram 87) but his designs
were drawn with a *decoupure* of 1 (Diagram
88), giving a more realistic outline to the
motifs.

Royal Ontario Museum, Toronto. Gift of Mrs Harold B.
Burnham (975.399).

88 Jacquard, free double weave with tied areas, decoupure 1

137 Coverlet 1885–1900

Jacquard, free double weave with tied areas,
2.03 x 1.95 m
Woven by Daniel Knechtel
Roseville, Waterloo County, Ontario

Coverlets of this pattern are known to have
been woven by Daniel Knechtel, who was
born in Pennsylvania and came to Waterloo
County about the time of the American Civil
War. In the 1871 census he is listed as a
weaver in Roseville, aged 28, married and
with one small child, and not much else is
known about him. His loom was obviously
one of the wide jacquards that were going
out of use in the States at that time. Knechtel
probably wove other patterns, as it was
customary to have four different ones, but as
the construction he used and the capacity of
his loom were the same as those used by two
other jacquard weavers in the area, August
Ploethner and Wilhelm Magnus Werlich, it is
very difficult to tell who wove which patterns.
As all their patterns were the ready-made
type, purchased as sets of jacquard cards
from the United States, it does not seem very
important to try to separate their work. It is
interesting that even with weaving as late as
this, the wool was often homespun and
home-dyed by the customer. This coverlet
has a very striking colour scheme, with the
pattern in blue, red, old-gold, and brown-
black wool on white cotton. The construction used is a free doubleweave with tied
areas, similar to Diagram 87, but the
proportion of the warps is 4:1, not 2:1, giving
a stronger ridging in the tied areas (Diagram
89).

Doon Pioneer Village, Kitchener, Ontario. Gift of Mrs
Elsie Brezina.

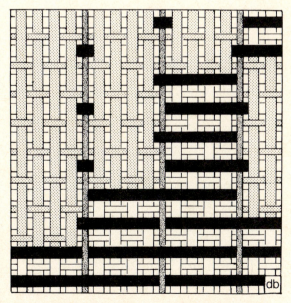

89 Jacquard, free double weave with tied areas, 4:1

138 Coverlet   1875–1900

Jacquard, fully-tied double weave,
1.90 x 1.70 m
Woven by Christopher Armstrong
Stouffville, York County, Ontario

This coverlet uses Withers's patriotic wreath pattern but the weaving was not done by Withers. The story can only be pieced together by comparing two census reports. In 1861, William Withers is listed as a weaver, aged thirty-six, living in Stouffville, married and with four children, the eldest of whom was a daughter. In 1871, the same household consisted of no parents, four Withers children, two under the age of ten and the eldest a boy of seventeen listed as a weaver. Living with this family group was Christopher Armstrong, aged twenty-nine, a widower and a weaver. Those are the bare bones of what must have been a considerable tragedy. Nothing else is known, but it seems likely that Armstrong had married the Withers' eldest daughter and had gone into partnership on the weaving with his father-in-law. Probably an epidemic, and there were plenty of them, carried off the parents and several of the children, including the eldest daughter, leaving four orphans and the widower in his twenties, Christopher Armstrong, to look after both them and the weaving business. Armstrong continued weaving until about 1910. At some time the set-up of the loom was changed because all the late work is in a construction different from the one Withers used. It is a minor change, but gives a slightly different look to the material. The same 2:1 proportion is used in the warp but the doublecloth is completely tied and the way it is done gives the look of a 4:1 warp proportion (Diagram 90). This coverlet is in the later construction, with the pattern banded in raspberry-red, blue, and old-gold wool on white cotton.

Black Creek Pioneer Village, Downsview, Ontario (75.22.1).

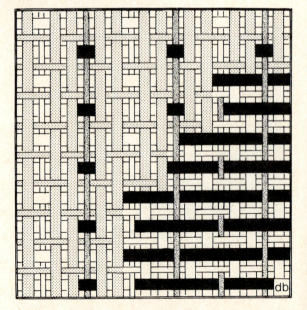

90 Jacquard, fully-tied double weave

139 Coverlet   1870–1880

Jacquard, damask, 2.27 x 1.90 m
Woven by the "Damask Weaver," probably
Moses Cherry
Purple Hill, Durham County, Ontario

Just as Withers' designs suggest that he was trained in the carpet weaving industry in Scotland, the weaver of this coverlet must surely have served his apprenticeship as a weaver of linen damasks, and it is likely that it was in either Ireland or Scotland, both of which countries were noted for their linen weaving during the nineteenth century. His patterns are reminiscent of those used for linen tablecloths and the construction is the same as a linen damask, with the pattern being formed by the exchanging of the two faces of a satin weave (Diagram 91). It would have been quite possible for a trained linen weaver to adapt his experience with this construction to the coarser weaving of a woollen weft on a cotton warp in response to the good market that there was in Ontario for warm bedding. His coverlets were woven on a wide loom and this grape pattern, which in this piece is in dark, blue-black wool with white cotton, was one of his most popular patterns. His production, which seems to date between about 1850 and 1880, must have been very large, judging from the quantity of his work that turns up in quite a wide area north of Whitby. Until recently the weaver of this unique group of coverlets has been thought to be a man who was known as "Weaver Joe," who lived between Whitby and Brooklin, but evidence now suggests that he was Moses Cherry, who lived and wove a little further east, in Purple Hill, just south of Lake Scugog in Durham County.[82]

Royal Ontario Museum, Toronto (968.70).

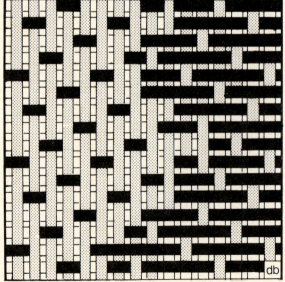

91 Jacquard, damask

(Detail, cat. no. 149)

As we move west in Canada, tracing the development of the basic skills of spinning and weaving, we move into another time zone, not only literally, but also as far as textile production is concerned. In eastern Canada, except for isolated pockets, local production of textiles was finished by about 1900. In western Canada, the pioneering period was just getting started at that time. In eastern Canada, although the population is now multi-cultured, during the early period the influences broke down to a few basic ones. In western Canada, the possible influences on textile production are as varied as the many groups that moved in to fill up that vast space.

The following items, illustrating textile production in the early years of western Canada seem to be both sparse and uneven, but until further research is done this is the best group that it has been possible to gather. There seems to be a very low rate of survival, probably explained by the fact that most of the spinning and weaving was completely utilitarian. Many spinning wheels and a number of looms used in the early days are in existence, but the evidence is that spinning was done to provide knitting yarns for plain garments and looms were mostly used for the weaving of rag rugs. Plain knitting was worn – and worn out, and rag rugs were put on the floor, walked on with muddy boots, eventually landing up under the dog on the back porch, and when badly worn were certainly not preserved for posterity.

The picture of textile production in the West is hazy, but if all the scattered information is put together things start to take form. We know that when an immigrant group was mostly male, as was sometimes the case, textiles were not made. We know that those who moved west from Ontario or came from the British Isles had already lost their ability to spin and weave. It appears that those who came to Canada from Europe, with a stay in the United States on the way, had usually dropped their weaving skills but not their spinning skills before reaching this country. The mail-order catalogues were a fact of life that effected all production on the prairies. You could even order a house from Eaton's catalogue, and certainly anything that was needed to furnish it or to dress the inhabitants. For that, money was needed so, in spite of the availability of bought goods, home production still had its appeal.

An interesting preliminary study of hand-spinning in Alberta has been made,[83] the results of which suggest that a great deal more handspinning was done than had been realized. It was found that Ukrainians, Germans, Austrians, Poles, Romanians, Russians, Scandinavians, and French spun particularly for knitting yarns and the same was true among the Hutterite, Doukhobor, and Mennonite settlements. The same study indicates that, although there was considerable use of spinning wheels, many simpler methods were used including hand spindles and also makeshift equipment, such as a dowel or even a wooden spoon held and twirled in the hand. It seems when all the evidence is added up that spinning was very widely practised among western settlers, except those of English-speaking origin, and there was plain utilitarian weaving done in a scattered way but weaving of a high order occurred among two groups, the Ukrainians and the Doukhobors.

140 Length of carpet
mid-twentieth century

Tabby, rag, 2.67 x 0.97 m
Alberta

Rag rugs were made wherever there were looms to make them and, when there were no looms they were often made, as this one undoubtedly was, on a frame with rag strips held firmly for warp, and other rag strips simply worked over and under them by hand for weft. This piece has no history except that it was made in Alberta. The colour scheme is well worked out from rags of very mixed origin. They are in cotton, silk, and rayon and are from both woven and knitted materials. The predominance of beiges, browns, and a little black probably indicates that many of the knitted rags are from stockings.

Glenbow-Alberta Institute, Calgary. Gift of Mrs Betty O'Donnell (17407).

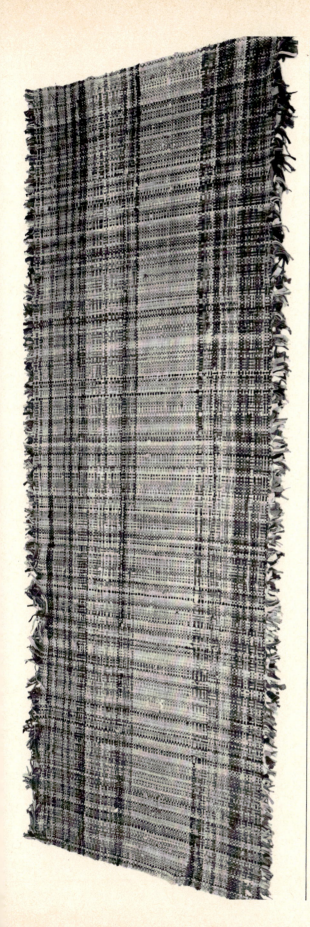

141 Length of carpet   about 1940

Braided rag, 2 x 0.73 m
Made by Alice Cockriell
Killarney area, Manitoba

Another way of making rag rugs without a
loom was by braiding and this is a very
impressive example of the type. Some
simpler ones are known that were braided in
narrow widths, joined by sewing, a technique
that was used among Swedish settlers.[84] This
one was made by Mrs Alice Cockriell (née
Pinkerton), around 1940. The method may
have come to the maker from Swedish
neighbours, or it is quite likely that she
learned it from the craft section of a farm
magazine. The colours of the rags – black,
browns, white, and a little bright yellow and
orange – have been carefully arranged to
form a strong diagonal check with a rather
mixed 1-and-1 colour and weave effect in the
background.

Glenbow-Alberta Institute, Calgary (C14217).

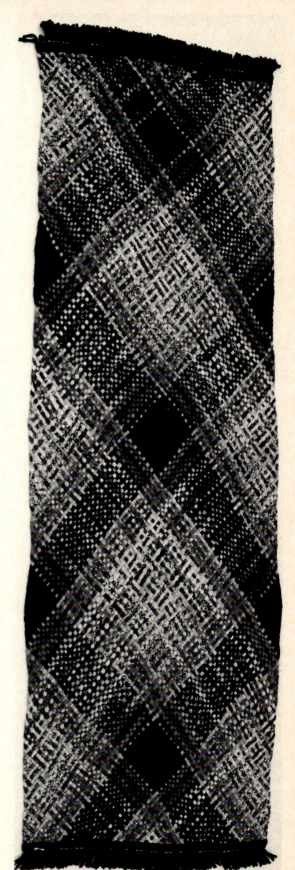

142 Sweater and bonnet   about 1935

Knitted, sweater 51.0 cm; bonnet 30.0 cm
Madey by Mr and Mrs D.A. McEachern
Sangudo, Alberta

In this publication we are describing textile productions that grew out of the needs of people as they moved in and settled down and lived off this land; we are not concerned with hobby work. Perhaps these two garments in a way fit into the hobby category, but the reason behind their production is far more basic than that. The Depression years of the 1930s were hard all over Canada, but the prairies not only had a Depression but also a drought that seemed to last for ever, and in many areas nothing grew and nothing survived, including sheep. Around Edmonton it was another Depression problem – no sale for a product. A letter written by the donor of the sweater and bonnet to the museum tells its own story. " ... During the 1930s wool would barely pay the cost of getting it to market. Those of us on farms, who had sheep, tried to make use of some of it at home. We had a spinning wheel brought from Scotland to Ontario by my husband's relatives. More as a hobby than from necessity he learned to spin. Radio was at its best then, and it entertained us in winter evenings, as he spun, I knit, and any relatives present helped with the carding .... " With Depression there was a return to the self-sufficiency of an earlier pioneer time, but with the radio replacing the traditional singing or reading aloud.

Provincial Museum of Alberta, Edmonton, Alberta. Gift of Mrs D.A. McEachern.

Icelandic Traditions

The first permanent Icelandic settlement in Canada was established at Gimli on the shores of Lake Winnipeg in 1875. If any handweaving ever was done in the Icelandic communities of that area of Manitoba it has vanished without leaving a trace. There are a couple of references that suggest that at least a few looms did exist and were used for household weaving, but so far that is the extent of our information on handweaving in New Iceland. For spinning and knitting the story is different. There is mention of sheep as early as 1877 and one account tells of a family herding over a hundred sheep all the way from North Dakota in the early 1890s.[85] Women seem to have spent every moment

they could spare spinning wool and knitting it into garments for their families' use: underwear, sweaters, scarves, socks and, as in Newfoundland, for the fishermen, mitts and more mitts, and many a family's income was supplemented by the sale of knitting. As elsewhere, such utilitarian garments have perished, but some of the spinning wheels remain. They were an important item in the Icelandic home. Some were brought from the old country, but there were skilled craftsmen in the various communities who could make them, as is shown in fig. 34.

Figure 34: This upright spinning wheel and small bobbin holder are the work of Trausti Eigfusson of Arborg, Manitoba. They were made in the early twentieth century. The spinning wheel is 0.97 m high, with a wheel diameter of 44.5 cm. National Museum of Man, Centre for Folk Culture Studies, Ottawa (69.49).

Hutterite Traditions

The Hutterites are a German-speaking sect that practise communal living and strongly believe in non-violence. They originated in central Europe at the time of the Reformation, and their wanderings, while seeking a peaceful place to live, took them through many countries before they emigrated to Dakota in the 1870s. From there, many have moved on to Canada during this century and there are now a number of colonies, particularly in Alberta and Manitoba. As they live a segregated life and are very self-sufficient, they seemed to be a likely group to be still weaving, but that is not the case. Probably the weaving skills were dropped during their sojourn in the States and only vestiges of them remain. They still weave a very coarse type of carpet, using a frame and very thick rags, held by binder twine, and they make various types of cords.

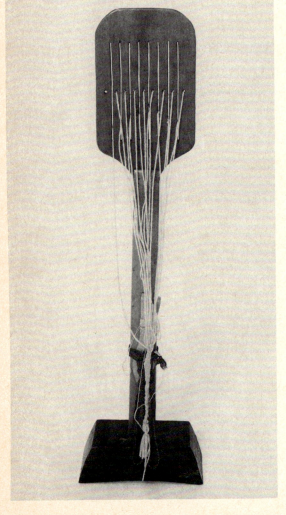

Figure 35: Baby-binding cords were often woven on a rigid heddle (see Diagram 27), such as this one, which is conveniently set on a stand, and is made of varnished hardwood. It measures 0.95 x 0.20 m. Glenbow-Alberta Institute, Calgary (C5403).

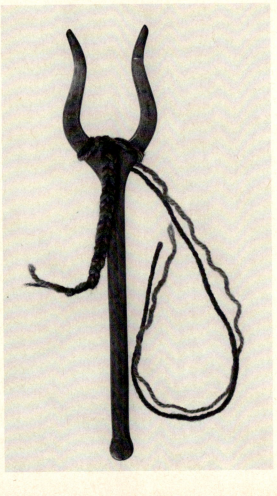

Figure 36: Another way of making the baby binding cords, and probably cords for other purposes as well, was a looping technique, rather like a double crochet, that was done on the two prongs of a braiding fork like this one. It is of carved wood, was made some time during the mid-twentieth century, and is 20.4 cm long. Glenbow-Alberta Institute, Calgary (C10252).

Figure 37: Spinning to produce knitting yarns was of sufficient importance in the Hutterite communities that among the craftsmen there were a number who were skilled in the making of spinning wheels. This wheel, which is dated 1912, is of a strongly German form and it is interesting that in the National Museum collection there are two Hutterite wheels, both from Alberta, that are similar in size and shape to this one, which is Manitoban in origin. They are dated 1894 and 1952, showing how enduring this type was among the Hutterites. Apparently it is a form that is particularly suited to producing soft, low twist singles that make excellent knitting yarns when they are plied.[86] This wheel is graceful and well-proportioned, measuring 0.68 x 0.78 m. The wood is very nicely turned and has a simple oil finish. Manitoba Museum of Man and Nature, Winnipeg.

143 Tape for tying a baby   1929

Rigid heddle weaving, 2.40 x 0.01 m
Rockyford Colony, Alberta

The old European tradition of baby care required that they should be wrapped in a tight bundle. As can be seen in some early European paintings, the babies almost look as though they are gift-wrapped, with criss-crossing coloured bindings firming the whole package up, so the baby could not move a muscle. The baby binding cords continued in Hutterite tradition, almost regarded as a fertility symbol, and were passed from one girl to another as a wedding present.

   This tape, to be used as a baby binding cord, was given to a Hutterite bride when she was married in 1929. It is a warp-faced tabby weave in grey, yellow, orange, green, and purple wool, and was woven on a rigid heddle, as illustrated in fig. 35.

Glenbow-Alberta Institute, Calgary (C13714).

144 **Pair of man's socks**   1933

Knitted, leg 43.0 cm; foot 28.0 cm
Pine Hill Colony, Red Deer, Alberta

Handspun purple wool has been used for this pair of man's socks and the initials "H.J." and the date "1933" have been knitted in to the top of each sock in purl stitches (Diagram 92). Living a completely communal life as the Hutterites did, no one owned anything and the only way a gift could be given was by the special making of something. With the initialling and dating these are probably not everyday work socks, but were spun and knitted by some loving woman as a special present.

Glenbow-Alberta Institute, Calgary (C2205 a & b).

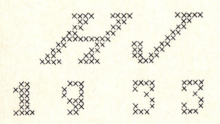

92 Knitted initials and date

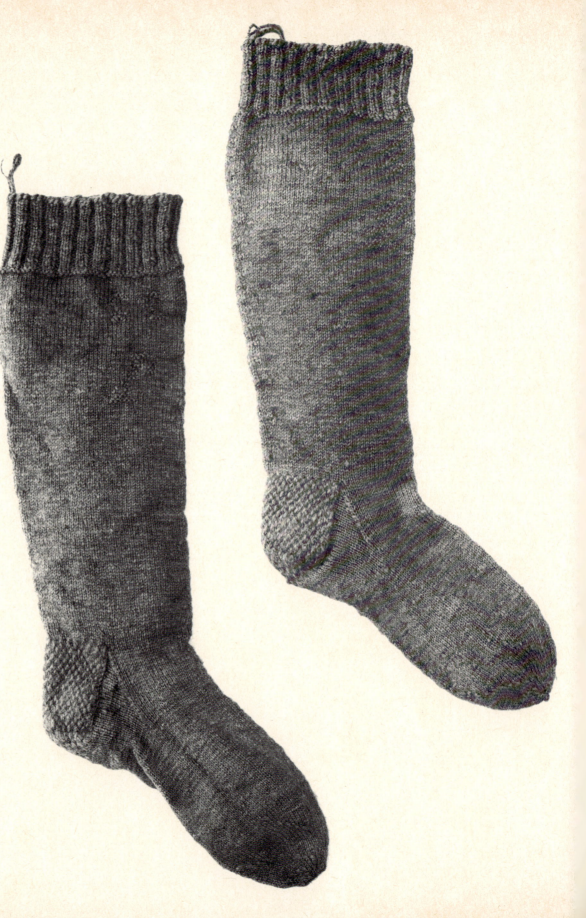

Ukrainian Traditions

From the time of their first small settlement in 1891 at Star, Alberta, Ukrainians, under all sorts of names, Galicians, Ruthenians, Bessarabians etc., came to Canada, took up land, and set to work to break it and farm it. Their scattered homesteads spread in a great wave from one end of the prairies to the other. Thousands had come when the stream was temporarily interrupted by the First World War. They came from rural areas in the Old Country, where textile making was an accepted part of farm work. They were accustomed to growing flax and hemp, to raising sheep and processing the fibres and, as soon as possible, on many a new farm seeds were planted, sheep were gathered, and the women were spinning and weaving, again providing textiles for their household needs. The Ukrainians were undoubtedly the largest group of textile makers in western Canada, but finding the weaving they did here in the early days of settlement is not easy. With the modern obsession for a search for identity, the emphasis in gathering for the collections that specialize in Ukrainian culture has been to record what was done and made and worn in the various areas from which these people came. Beautiful costumes display the traditions of different parts of the Ukraine, but in most cases these costumes also come from the Old Country. Connection was maintained with those who stayed behind and Ukrainian culture in Canada has been frequently renewed by imports and by newer comers. If by any chance a piece of textile made here has been preserved, usually the area of the maker's origin in the Ukraine is recorded, rather than the time and place of making in Canada. It is important that memory of the rich peasant culture from which the Ukrainian people came should be kept but, in the keeping of it, the record of its transplanting to a new land should not be ignored, for that also should be a great story. Little could be brought in the way of this world's goods but with the people came their wealth of tradition, their skills and their urge to create, and even with the almost impossible conditions of pioneer life in a harsh land, as soon as possible hand spindles were made, looms were improvised, and textiles of quality and beauty were produced. The following pieces are from the limited number that seem to have survived with the history that they were made in Canada. It is a small group, but the quality is impressive and hopefully with future research the picture of what must have been a large and important production will be filled out.

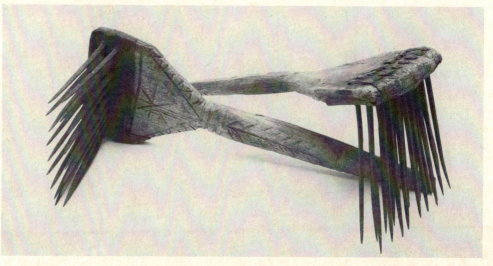

Figure 38: Among the Ukrainians, pairs of wool combs were used to prepare the wool for weaving. They were used in the hand, like wool cards, and were of about the same size but had a double row of quite long, sharp metal spikes for teeth. The wool was laid on the teeth of one and the shorter fibres were combed out using the other. The long fibres that had been straightened out by the combing were then carefully lifted off and spun for weaving yarn. The short fibres were carded with normal commercial cards which were readily available from the mail-order houses and were used for quilts or spun into soft yarns for knitting. The wool combs shown here were used in western Canada during the early twentieth century. They are 35.0 cm long and 13.0 cm wide. The length of the teeth is 12.0 cm. National Museum of Man, Centre for Folk Culture Studies, Ottawa, Ontario (76.605 and 76.606; neg. no. 79-7433).

145 Tablecloth   1915

Twill, 2 x 1.24 m
Woven by Anna Zuzak
Tarnopol, Saskatchewan

Flax and hemp were extensively grown on the prairies for the oil in their seeds. The stems from both plants were also used for textile purposes, but how large the production was is not known. For fibre, the plant had to be pulled before the seeds were ready to be used for oil. A Ukrainian informant told how her mother kept watch on the flax plot and when it was ready she pulled as many of the longest and best stalks as she needed for fibre, leaving the rest to ripen for seed oil. Another informant told how her family never used flax for fibre because, in the area of Manitoba where they lived, there was no water suitable for retting it, not even a ditch, and as cotton yarns were readily available it was no hardship. In the Ukraine a great deal of linen tabby was used for the clothing of both men and women for everyday wear and also for the beautifully embroidered festive costumes. Fine embroidery on linen for special use has been done by Ukrainian women in Canada for a long time, but whether linen was ever produced in sufficient quantity for utilitarian clothing seems to be an unremembered fact. That linen was produced for household purposes at a fairly early period is proven by this tablecloth and several other pieces that are known to have been made in Canada.[87] This handsome piece was woven by the donor and is in a 2/2 twill weave of fairly heavy, almost bleached linen with red cotton borders. The two widths have been faggotted together and the hems have been sewn with handspun linen thread.

Ukrainian Museum of Canada, Saskatoon, Saskatchewan. Gift of Mrs Anna Zuzak (1.979.123.18).

146 Length of bench cover   1900–1910

Twill, 1.37 x 0.59 m
Woven by Mrs Kudyba
Canora, Saskatchewan

Hemp, which grows to a height of six to seven feet, has bast fibre in the stem of the plant that is useful for textile purposes. The fibres can be processed in the same way as flax fibres and when they are spun into a thread they are similar to linen but coarser. During the early period of settlement, hemp was quite extensively grown by the Ukrainians and used for ropes and coarse fabrics, but as hemp is the source of marijuana the growing of the plant has been illegal for a long time in Canada. Hemp can be found in some of the early textiles, such as this length of material that was woven to use as a bench cover. It was spun and woven by the donor and has a semi-bleached 2/2 twill ground, banded in brown and green.

Ukrainian Museum of Canada, Saskatoon, Saskatchewan. Gift of Mrs Kudyka (1.971.01.18).

147 Wall hanging   1911

Weft-faced tabby, 2.02 x 0.86 m
Woven by Domka Panchuk
Arabaka, Manitoba

Traditional furnishings of a Ukrainian house included benches against the wall that had handwoven covers and behind the benches long woollen runners hung horizontally, in order to provide something warm to lean back against. These wall hangings were usually quite colourful and decorative. This is a fairly plain one, woven in weft-faced tabby with natural hemp warp completely covered by wool banding in black and orange with very fine lines of red. It is known that the weaving was done by Domka Panchuk, who came from Bucovina and settled at Arabaka near the American border south of Winnipeg.

Ukrainian Museum of Canada, Saskatoon, Saskatchewan. Gift of Maria Arseney (1.970.01.b.18).

148 Width of bench cover   about 1939

Herringbone twill, 30.0 x 54.0 cm
Woven by Maria Zvarich
Probably Vegreville, Alberta

This is a very attractive sample from a bench cover length. It is all wool, with a natural black warp threaded in a broken herringbone twill and the weft is banded in yellow, orange, purple, green, brown, and white used in a regular sequence and with the additional decoration of pattern rod floats. The piece is fairly late in date and is probably an example of the work of a skilled weaver reproducing the pattern of a length that had been brought by someone from the Ukraine, rather than being basic weaving that was done to cover a bench in a farm house.

A patterning device that is popular in Ukrainian weaving has been used. It is called by the descriptive name "beans" and is made by passing a heavy weft thread in floats over and under the warp. These floats are always of three threads; otherwise it is just the same technique as the Quebec *à la planche* (see Diagrams 52 and 53). Ukrainian weavers today do it by threading the heavier weft through by hand. An old loom at the Ukrainian Museum in Saskatoon has string heddles that have been tied in the clasped way that will allow them to open up, making it possible to use a pattern board behind the shafts in the same way that was done in Quebec and probably in the older tradition this technique was done in that way.

Ukrainian Museum of Canada, Saskatoon, Saskatchewan. Gift of Mrs Kostachuk (1.939.01.18).

149 Wall hanging   about 1930

Tapestry weave, 4.60 x 0.84 m
Woven by Mrs Ktory
Hairy Hill, Alberta

This striking and expertly woven wall hanging is a well-known type of Ukrainian weaving. The weave is tabby, with the multicoloured woollen wefts covering the warp entirely. The pattern has been made by using a tapestry technique with the wefts carried backwards and forwards in the limited areas needed by the design. Where the colours meet, the wefts make a toothed joining, turning alternately around a common warp thread (Diagram 93). Patterns for this type of weaving are traditionally geometric, worked out in steps, and weavers knew them and often repeated the same designs making only minor changes.

Ukrainian Museum of Canada, Saskatoon, Saskatchewan. Gift of Mrs Hanka Romanchych (1.978.57.18).

93 Toothed tapestry

150 Part of a wall hanging
early twentieth century

Tapestry weave, 1.08 x 0.78 m
Probably Manitoba

This incomplete wall hanging is similar to the
previous piece, using the same toothed
linking of the wefts and is most effective in
purples, yellows, and beige handspun wools,
home-dyed with package dyes.

An informant told how as a young girl in
Manitoba, in the early part of this century,
she helped her mother, who was an expert
weaver to weave wall hangings such as this.
Mother and daughter sat side by side at the
loom, keeping pace with each other, and they
sold their weaving to help carry them
through the early, lean years while the family
got established.

Spinning at first was done with hand
spindles that could easily be made by a
handyman and then spinning wheels were
acquired. The most common form of spinning wheel all across the prairies was of
upright form, similar to the Icelandic wheel
(fig. 34), but of heavier build.

Ukrainian Museum of Canada, Saskatoon, Saskatchewan, Gift of Mrs John Chobotar (1.942.01.18).

151 Sofa cover   about 1950

Tapestry weave, 1.72 x 0.86 m
Woven by Anna Hudyma
Rycroft, Peace River area, Alberta

This extraordinary piece was woven by a remarkable Ukrainian woman, Anna Deley Hudyma. Born in Bridok, Romania in 1893 she married, had two children and, at a comparatively young age, was widowed. Her second husband Bill Hudyma, had come to Canada earlier and established himself in the Peace River area. In 1930 he went back to Romania, married Anna, and brought her with her children to Canada. Her first years here were difficult. Her husband was away from home working on the railroad and, with her son, then only fourteen, Anna set about making a small farm in the bush. To her delight she learned that a neighbour had a loom. Anna set it up and wove on it and also taught a number of other women in the area to weave. In 1940 her husband, then a section foreman, was moved and the family went to live in a section house on the railroad away off in the bush, isolated and leaving the loom behind. It was here in this lonely place that Anna's husband made her a loom with saw, chisel, hammer, and her instructions. It had two shafts and it worked! Slowly the dreary section house with its homemade furniture took on a comfortable, cheerful Ukrainian look with her multicoloured rag rugs on the floors and benches, her tablecloths and doilies, and her tapestry-woven covers on the sofa and chairs. At first she wove in the traditional way of her background, with geometric designs similar to cat. nos. 149 and 150 and then the influences of the new country started to reach her in that remote place. Although she did not read English, she saw the farm magazines with their patterns for petit-point and cross-stitch embroideries, and birds and flowers started to appear in her weaving. She never copied a pattern closely or drew a cartoon to work from, but her granddaughter remembers that she would put whatever the inspiration was beside her and then would weave her pattern freely, using it as a guide. Although in the old country she had been accustomed to doing her own spinning, wool in the fleece was not available, so she bought white yarns from the mail-order catalogue and dyed them herself with package dyes. This sofa cover is worked in vivid reds, pinks, blues, and greens on a black ground. The weave is tapestry, with a toothed interlocking of the weft threads where the colours change, as in Diagram 93. At either end she has used a brocading technique for a row of geometric motifs (Diagram 94). Traditional runners would have been made to cover a wooden bench. Adapting to the changing furniture types, this has been woven in the right proportions to cover a sofa back.

As was the case in many a pioneer family, Anna, the homemaker, was the family centre. She managed to create out of nothing an atmosphere of joy and music and laughter with her weaving giving colour and warmth. In the words of her daughter "Anna never did live in a fine house. She worked extremely hard in the field and in the home, with no modern conveniences but always found time for weaving, knitting, crocheting, and embroidering....Her flowers bloomed among the vegetables in the summer and on her floor and furniture in the winter."[88]

Owned by Mrs Tillie Wieczorek, Edmonton, Alberta.

94 Brocading

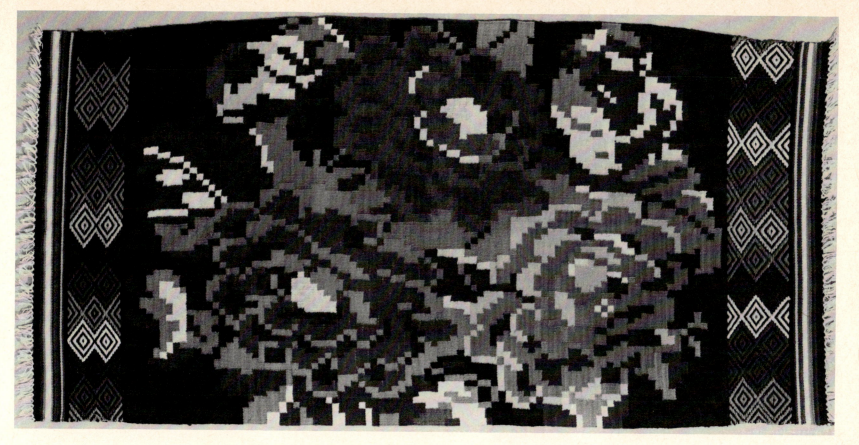

Doukhobor Traditions

The Doukhobors, the name meaning "Spirit-Wrestlers," are a religious group that dissented from the Russian Orthodox Church during the seventeenth century. Their unorthodox beliefs made the establishment view them with considerable intolerance and, as they were also strongly pacifist, refusing military service, they were subjected to periods of extreme persecution during more than two hundred years in Russia. They were moved as a group a number of times, always to less desirable areas of the expanding Russian Empire. Finally, with the support of Tolstoy and his followers in Russia and the Quakers in England and the United States, a mass emigration from the Caucasus, where they were then living, was organized. In 1899 the first group arrived to take up land in Saskatchewan. They were followed shortly by more than seven thousand of their bretheren and still more Doukhobor immigrants came later. Several productive years followed their arrival, while these hard-working people established their communal farms north of Yorkton. In 1902 their charismatic leader, Peter "The Lordly" Verigin, was released from exile in Siberia and allowed to join them. All did not go smoothly. The Doukhobors refused to take an oath of allegiance, which to them seemed like the first step towards military service and once more they ran foul of a government. Many moved on to the interior of British Columbia. The Doukhobors' history in Canada is very interesting but it cannot be gone into here.[89] What is important to this publication is that they were the most superb textile makers and their way of life, which was totally communal and as self-sufficient as they could make it, lead to their supplying all the everyday textile needs and, as time went on, to the making of amazingly elaborate carpets.

(Detail, cat. no. 160)

152 Three lengths of apparel fabric
about 1925

Twill, 2.75, 3.25, and 4.14 x 0.65 m
Woven by Tina Trubitskoff
Brilliant, British Columbia

As with other settlers, at first there were no
textile fibres available to the Doukhobors,
and they simply continued to wear the
clothes they had brought with them to
Canada until flax and hemp were grown and
sheep established. Unlike many other immigrants the Doukhobors had people helping
them to get started. One of the first gifts that
the American Quakers sent to the new
arrivals was three hundred spinning wheels,
and these were followed by another gift of
wheels and looms from the Canadian Coun-
cil of Women.[90] In spite of help from outside,
life was pretty grim. The men had to work
away from the settlements to earn money
and the women were left to keep things
going, even to the extent of harnessing
themselves to the ploughs to break the land,
until the communities managed to acquire
draft animals. Clothing was plain and simple,
but with the use of package dyes colour
could be afforded, undoubtedly giving a lift
to the spirits. These three lengths of fine 2/2
wool twill in bright pink, blue, and green
were woven in the natural white of the wool
and then piece-dyed. In British Columbia, the
land the Doukhobors had was not suitable
for raising sheep but close connections were
kept with the older settlements, and fleeces
were sent from Saskatchewan and all the
processing, spinning and weaving were done
in the communities in the Kootenays.

National Museum of Man, Centre for Folk Culture
Studies, Ottawa, Ontario (71.625, 71.626, 71.627).

Figure 39: The woollen yarns in the lengths of apparel fabric (cat. no. 152) are fine, hard, and smooth and were prepared by combing. Doukhobor men were famous for their wood-carving, and in the early period of settlement textile combs such as these beautifully carved wooden ones were used. They measure 59.0 x 35.0 cm and 23.0 x 19.0 cm, and were made in the early twentieth century. When in use, the large comb was set upright in a slot at the left end of a spinning bench. The spinner sat beside it, laid the fibres on the teeth and then combed them with the smaller hand comb. When the fibres had been untangled and laid parallel, the upright comb was used as a distaff to hold the fibres as the woman spun them with either a dropped spindle or a spinning wheel. Combing and spinning were carried on alternately. Combs such as these were also used in the preparation of flax fibres. Doukhobor Village Museum, Doukhobor Historical Society, Castlegar, British Columbia.

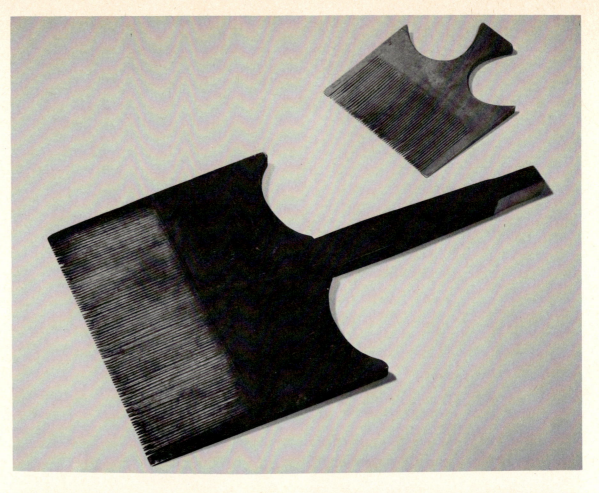

Figure 40: Combs of wood were the early type, but they were superceded by ones like this pair, with paddle-shaped handles and curved metal teeth. The same method of wool combing was used. An upright post was put into the left end of the spinning bench and one comb was held firmly, teeth up, by placing the hole in its handle over a knob on the top of the upright. Wool fibres were put on the teeth of the stationary comb and the other comb was used to work them into shape. When a tidy little beard of fibre, about four inches (10.16 cm) in length, had been formed on the rigid comb it was spun off and the process was repeated. The combs have nicely shaped wooden handles that are faced at the front edge with metal sheeting through which the curved metal teeth project and they measure 33.0 x 21.0 cm. It is the preparation of the wool by combing that gives the rather special quality to the Doukhobor yardage. Glenbow-Alberta Institute, Calgary (C 5265 a & b).

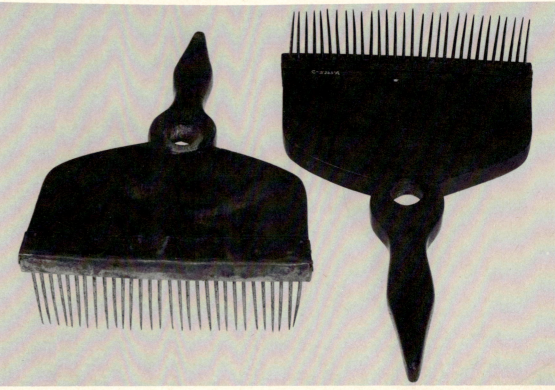

153 Woman's blouse
early twentieth century

Twill with knitted trimming, 0.56 x 0.65 m
Castlegar area, British Columbia

The costume of the Doukhobor women during the early years in Canada consisted of loosely pleated skirts and blouses such as this, of fine wool twill. The blouses were all made in a simple adaptation of the fashion of the period, not as might be expected in the straight-cut peasant style. This blouse is blue and has been very nicely finished with a fine knitted edging in green handspun wool.

Doukhobor Village Museum, Doukhobor Historical Society, Castlegar, British Columbia (977.58).

154 Woman's skirt   about 1910

Twill with cross-stitch embroidery, 0.93 m
Woven by Grace Kooznetsoff
British Columbia

Straight, loosely pleated peasant skirts, usually completely plain and, for reasons of wool conservation, not longer than mid-calf, were made and worn by Doukhobor women during their early years in Canada. This must have been a rather special skirt as it is quite full, made from six widths of dark red twill, is a bit longer than usual and is finished with a row of eight-pointed stars embroidered in wool cross-stitch, just above the hemline. It was spun, woven, and handsewn by Grace Kooznetsoff. The usual costume was completed with a plain blouse like cat. no. 153, a linen underskirt, in winter other layers of petticoats and, over it all, an apron. For everyday, a woollen shawl covered the head and shoulders but for ceremonial occasions, even to the present day, the women make exquisite head-kerchiefs of silk or synthetic, embroidered with floral patterns in a double faced satin stitch.[91]

National Museum of Man, Centre for Folk Culture Studies, Ottawa, Ontario (71.644).

155 Woman's apron   about 1910

Twill with tapestry band and knitted border,
0.86 x 0.92 m
Woven by Grace Kooznetsoff
British Columbia

This decorative apron was also made by
Grace Kooznetsoff. The material is the usual
fine yardage, woven in the natural wool and
then dyed with package dye after weaving.
The lower edge is finished with fine open-
work wool knitting, the Doukhobor's favourite trimming. Probably the apron length with
the knitting attached was dyed scarlet, and
then the black motifs were embroidered on it
and the fine, wool-tapestry band was added.
Similar decorative bands are found on other
items like towels, but it is not certain
whether this type of weaving was done in
Canada. Possibly, bands that had been
brought from the Caucasus were carefully
re-used.

National Museum of Man, Centre for Folk Culture
Studies, Ottawa, Ontario (71.640).

156 Man's shirt   about 1910

Broken herringbone twill, 0.92 x 0.66 m
Probably Saskatchewan

The costume of peasant men in Russia around 1900, when the Doukhobors came to Canada, was linen trousers and a fairly long, loose linen shirt with a sash tied around the waist, and this is the outfit that the Doukhobor men wore. As soon as possible, the women started renewing the clothing that had been brought from Russia. No doubt much of the linen made for work clothes was fairly coarse, but the linen garments that have survived are remarkable fine. The superb quality of this shirt is not surprising because its owner was the leader Peter "The Lordly" Verigin. Most of the Doukhobors lived exceedingly plainly but they did not consider it seemly for their leader to have anything less than the best, and this shirt is obviously the best! The shape of the cut has been influenced by the cut of commercial shirts and the making has been done with the sewing machine, a labour-saving device that the Doukhobors took to shortly after their arrival. The flax preparation and the spinning are superb and the weaving, a broken 2/2 herringbone twill is expert (see Diagram 67). The donor was a granddaughter of Peter "The Lordly."

National Museum of Man, Centre for Folk Culture Studies, Ottawa, Ontario. Gift of Mrs Anna P. Markova (71.660).

157 Man's jacket   about 1920

Broken herringbone twill, 0.80 x 0.69 m
Castlegar area, British Columbia

When the Doukhobor men went out from their communities to do business among their Canadian neighbours they were noticeably different in their linen shirts and trousers. So it became the custom to adopt the camouflage of a suit as close to a Canadian business suit as their wives could make it. A number of coats and full suits survive in museum collections. They are made of the standard Doukhobor handspun, handwoven, combed woollen yardage, dyed black, cut and tailored at home. Usually the sewing is by machine, but all the rest of the work is hand done. The weave of this material is interesting. It is a 2/2 broken herringbone twill with thirty-six warp threads having the twill line running in a Z direction, then the break in the weave followed by six warps, with the twill in the S direction and repeat. It is subtle, and in the black it hardly shows but it does add an interest to the texture of the weave.

National Museum of Man, Centre for Folk Culture Studies, Ottawa, Ontario. Gift of Mrs Nellie Persepelkin (71.745.1).

158 Bed sheet   early twentieth century

Bird's-eye twill with knitted lace.
2.24 x 1.70 m
Castlegar area, British Columbia

This sheet is made from two widths of handspun, handwoven linen of beautiful quality, and it has been trimmed at the side by an insertion and a very wide border of fine knitted lace. Doukhobor living was communal and it was essential for all to work very hard for the good of the community, but a woman's small amount of leisure time was her own, and if she wanted to make something beautiful from the everyday materials that were available to her, she was free to do so. No history is attached to this piece, so we do not know the name of the weaver or what incentive led her to do this work, but we do know that she created a masterpiece.

Doukhobor Village Museum, Doukhobor Historical Society, Castlegar, British Columbia (no. 145).

159 Coverlet 1906

Checked twill with knitted lace, 1.87 x 1.46 m, plus lace
Woven by Irene Rezansoff
Pelly, near Thunder Hills, Saskatchewan

This coverlet, made from two joined widths of wool twill, is one of several similar pieces that were made in Saskatchewan and British Columbia. All are red, checked in black, and are edged at the side with bands of brightly-coloured knitted wool lace. One of these coverlets belonged to Peter "The Lordly" Verigin and is still on the bed in his bedroom, which is now part of the Doukhobor Society Museum at Verigin, north of Yorkton. As might be expected, the knitted lace on it is wider than on any of the other examples. The weaving of all of them was done in natural white and black wool and then the lengths were piece-dyed with commercial dye, which coloured the white parts red and made the black more intense. The knitting was done in narrow lengths in plain white wool and each length, when finished, was dyed a different bright colour, in this case, red, green, and pink and then were joined to make the edging for the coverlet.

Manitoba Museum of Man and Nature, Winnipeg (H9.8.169).

160 Carpet   about 1900

Tapestry weave, 2.06 x 1.22 m
Woven by Grace Kooznetsoff
Saskatchewan

This stunning carpet is a type that was made
by the Doukhobors not long after they came
to Canada. They had lived in the Caucasus
for a long time before the mass emigration
and that area is famous for the carpets, both
flat-woven and with pile. The weave of this
piece, tapestry with slits between the colour
areas (see Diagram 7), is Caucasian, the
pattern is a free adaptation of design from
that area but the colour scheme is pure
Doukhobor. It is woven of very heavy
handspun wool and has a black ground, with
the pattern in vivid pink, blue, green, and
yellow.[92]

National Museum of Man, Centre for Folk Culture
Studies, Ottawa, Ontario (71-614).

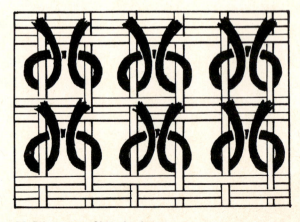

95 Pile weave, Ghiordes *knot*

161 Carpet 1925

Knotted pile weave, 2.16 x 1.17 m
Woven by Helen Hancheroff
Brilliant, British Columbia

Caucasian influences are evident in both the technique and the design of this piece. It is a knotted pile weave, just like an oriental carpet. Rows of multicoloured rug knots have been tied on the warp after every two passages of the ground weft, making a very firm, dense pile. The method of tying the pile knots is the common way used in the Caucasus, the so-called *Ghiordes* knot (Diagram 95). Although the pattern is considerably simpler and sparser than is usual in oriental carpets, they are undoubtedly the source of both motifs and layout. Even the small goat-like figures in the centre probably have Central Asian ancestry. The colours are, as usual, from packaged dyes but the reds, pink, green, yellow, and blue have been very well combined with black and white and the effect is excellent. The piece was woven by Helen Hancheroff in 1925 for her father, Paul, whose initials appear in the outer border. The Doukhobors must have brought their knowledge of rug knotting with them in 1899, but there would not have been a sufficient surplus of wool for the making of such a piece until many years later.

National Museum of Man, Centre for Folk Culture Studies, Ottawa, Ontario (71-623).

162 Carpet   1923

Knotted pile weave, 2.44 x 2.44 m

Woven by Anastasia Lords
Brilliant, British Columbia

With this magnificent pile rug, the textile skills of the Doukhobor weavers of western Canada reached a peak, providing us with a worthy climax for this account of spinning and weaving done during the settlement periods of this country. It was made by Anastasia Lords at Brilliant, British Columbia and was completed in 1923. The technique is the same as in the previous piece, with rows of multicoloured *Ghiordes* knots used after every two passages of the ground weft. It is entirely made of wool, with a bright blue ground in the field, surrounded by two borders in reddish brown and dark red, and motifs in a range of bright, intense colours. The pattern is incredibly rich and imaginative with many types of flowers, assorted birds, from chickens to peacocks, beribboned flower baskets, camels, caribou, centering on a rectangle of grapes and grape leaves enclosing a small teapot. The investment in both time and wool indicates that at last a stage of development had been reached when the struggle for survival was over.

Glenbow-Alberta Institute, Calgary. Gift of Miss Fedosia Verigin, for Miss Anastasia Lords (C.996).

Figure 41: This idyllic scene shows Anastasia Lords, the maker of cat. no. 162, sitting in an apple orchard, spinning in the typical Doukhobor manner. Miss Lords was born 1885, in the village of Slavyanka in the Caucasus, and came to Canada in 1899. The child beside her is wearing the long, loose gown that the children of the community were expected to wear until they were about twelve years old. Glenbow-Alberta Institute, Calgary.

Conclusion

When a collection is brought together by one individual, the selection is inevitably a personal one, and so it has been with the gathering of material for this exhibition. Unlike the choices made when one is part of a committee, there are no arguments. On the other hand, when the decision has once been made, there is no backup either, and doubt may raise its ugly head. Does this very wide range of material of varying levels of skill and quality make sense, now that it has been finally gathered together? Why should a rag rug be combined with an exquisite altar frontal? Why should a garment made yesterday be shown with 200-year-old Indian artifacts? It may seem a curious group, but each piece has been chosen to contribute its bit of the Canadian story. If the selection is wide and somewhat strange, so is Canada. If the material is practical and not very ornamental, so was life in the early days of our country. This unhomogeneous collection has grown from my conviction that it is a miracle that native peoples, who roamed this often inhospitable land, and the wave after wave of newcomers, who became Canadians through difficult days of settlement, not only survived, but survived with a very considerable margin of creative verve. They sought a better way of life and with the sweat of their brows, the skill of their hands, and their desire to create something good, they did make that better life for themselves…and for us, their descendents. This exhibition of textiles, varied as it is, with fabrics simple and complex, early and late, drawn from all parts of the country, does make sense when it is considered as a celebration of the Canadian spirit that would not settle for the dull and dreary. With any new material that came to hand, and with any skill that could be mastered, fabrics were created that reached beyond the simple need for warmth to satisfy the equally human need for something nice to feel and lovely to look at, lifting the practical skills of textile making to a simple but satisfyingly comfortable art.

(Detail, cat. no. 136)

Footnotes

1 For pictures of many beautiful Indian textiles see Brasser; see Coe; see Conn; see also Odle. For basic background information see Jenness; see Rousseau and Brown; see Turner, 1979.

2 See Rogers, 1962, pp.C58 and C62, also Rogers, 1967 pp.40 and 59.

3 See Davidson.

4 See Burnham, D.K., 1980, for further explanation and illustration.

5 In much ethnographic literature, weft twining on split pairs with closely packed weft has been called *twilled twining*. This is a very misleading term, since the weave has no technical connection with twill weave.

6 See Lyford, 1943, p.40.

7 See Bendorf and Speyer, cat. no. 160.

8 For excellent information see Turner, 1955, Chapters 3 and 5.

9 Many of Edmund Morris's drawings are in the Royal Ontario Museum.

10 See Drucker 1963, pp.61-63 and p.83; see Drucker 1965, pp.34-35; see Gunther, p.254; see also Sendey for pictures of people wearing bark garments, including drawings made in 1778 by John Webber, one of which shows a Nootkan Indian woman weaving on a loom frame.

11 Personal communication from Dr George MacDonald, Senior Scientist, National Museum of Man. For weaving techniques used by the Chilkat, see Samuel.

12 See Drucker, 1963, pp.83-89.

13 For an account of Paul Kane's travels, including his diary and a catalogue of Kane's paintings and sketches, see Harper. The painting (fig. 2) is cat. no. IV.556 and the spinning sketch (fig. 3) is cat. no. IV.554 in the catalogue. See also Allodi for listing of Kane sketches in R.O.M. (fig. 3 is her cat. no. 1339).

14 See Wells.

15 See Gustafson, Chapter 3.

16 See Sturtevant.

17 Quill-woven bands are used on the earliest known garment from North America, a skin coat that is in the Ashmolean Museum, Oxford, England. The coat was listed in the 1656 catalogue of the Tradescant Collection, so must have reached England before that time. Its provenance is not known, but it is probable that it has an east coast origin.
For excellent photographs and diagrams of various quilling techniques, see Orchard, 1971; see Odle; and for brief background information see also R.O.M.

18 For excellent information on beadwork of all kinds see Orchard, 1975.

19 See Orchard, 1975, chapter on wampum pp.71-87.

20 For this theory see Burnham, D.K., 1976. For the basic text on Quebec braiding see Barbeau, either 1972 or 1973; see also Massicotte, whose researches on the subject pre-date even those of Barbeau. For instruction for the making of braided sashes see LeBlanc; see also Bourret and Lavigne. The *Association des artisans de ceintures fléchées du Québec inc.* has been formed to promote the study and production of traditional Quebec braiding. Historical research and the recording of existing examples is being carried out by the archivist of the association, Maurice Leduc.

21 See Viola, pp.40, 95, 97-99, for portraits painted by Charles Bird King and dated between 1821 and 1842.

22 See Josephy, p.53.

24 See Ellice for account of their captivity, and opposite p.160 for this sketch, reproduced in colour.

25 See Barbeau, 1972 and 1973, for background and development of the braided sashes of Quebec.

25 See Ellice for account of their captivity, and opposite p.160 for this sketch, reproduced in colour.

26 See Burnham and Burnham, pp.3-10, for brief historical background and also pp.143-169; see Séguin, 1967, pp.386-399 and pp.459-470; see also Séguin, 1959, pp.93-99; for an account of the weaving establishment of Mme de Repentigny see Doyon-Ferland.

27 See Griffiths, 1973 and 1979, for historical background of the Acadians.

28 A wide-ranging and thoroughly researched exhibition of Louisiana Acadian spinning and weaving, called *L'amour de maman*, Louisiana State Museum (December 1980 to July 1981), includes a few parallel pieces from France and from Cape Breton. The similarities are striking. Vaughn Glasgow, the Museum's Chief Curator, has begun work on a publication also to be called *L'amour de maman*.

29 See Chabot for biography of Marie de l'Incarnation.

30 See Marshall, p.73.

31 For further information on this weave, with illustrations, see Burnham and Burnham, pp.144-145 and pp.157-161; see also D.K. Burnham, 1980, pp.71 and 97.

32 The results of the collecting done by Dr Marius Barbeau are now in the National Gallery, the National Museum of Man, and the Royal Ontario Museum, and a number of the pieces are illustrated in Burnham and Burnham pp.157-167.

33 For further information on this weave, with illustrations, see Burnham and Burnham, pp.145-148, and 159-169.

34 See Burnham and Burnham, p.163.

35 For further information on this coverlet and the Bolton ones see Burnham and Burnham, pp.146-148 and 166-167.

36 See Séguin, 1967 Chapter IV, p.459; see also Canadian pictorial records such as Allodi, cat. nos 700, 705, 706, 2090, 2220; and Bell, pp.47, 53, 66.

37 See Burnham and Burnham, pp.78-79 for illustration of these garments.

38 The costume research was done for the *Village acadien* by Jeanne Arsenault. Her findings are published in Arsenault, 1977 and 1979, and also in Doucet.

39 See Burnham and Burnham for illustration of two other examples of Acadian skirt materials, pp.63-64.

40 See Burnham and Burnham, p.76, cat. no. 93.

41 See Warren.

42 See Burnham and Burnham, pp.264-272 for historical background and illustrations of this weave; see also H.B. Burnham, pp.8-9.

43 See Burnham and Burnham, pp.298-316, for historical background and illustrations of this weave.

44 For further information on Fry's history and pictures of his weaving see the many references in Burnham and Burnham.

45 See D.K. Burnham, 1980, p.47, for illustration of pattern draft and threading draft of the Fry doublecloth coverlet, shown as cat. no. 72.

46 For explanation and illustration of pattern blocks see D.K. Burnham, 1980, pp.8-9.

47 For listing of the processes see D.K. Burnham, 1980, p.58; see also Coons and Koob for description of the processes and illustrations, pp.33-49.

48 For threading drafts for a number of the following pieces see Burnham and Burnham, pp.126-139.

49 The account book of William Nelles of Grimsby, Baldwin Rare Books Collection, Metropolitan Toronto Library, Toronto.

50 In Hohenloher Bauernmuseum, Schönenberg, West Germany.

51 For Scottish immigration in eastern Canada see Duncan. For exceedingly useful, brief information on settlements of many different ethnic groups see *The Canadian Family Tree*, Canadian Citizenship Branch.

52 See Langton, p.218. Books such as the journals of Anne Langton and Mary O'Brien, and those written by Mrs Moodie and Mrs Traill, are invaluable to the student of textile and costume history. They provide much specific information concerning textiles used in Canada during the settlement period, and they also place those textiles in their setting of pioneer life.

53 Not long before she died, Miss Ann MacLellan, in whose memory this blanket has been given to the Newfoundland Museum, replied to a fairly extensive list of questions sent to her by the author concerning the making of textiles in the Codroy Valley. She herself was an expert weaver, having been trained as a young girl by the grandmother who wove the blanket, and she well understood the fine points of spinning and weaving. Her answers concerning the equipment and methods that were used provide a very useful document, which has been filed for reference at the Newfoundland Museum, St John's and in the Textile Department of the Royal Ontario Museum, Toronto. See also Pocius for a detailed report of field-work done in the Avalon Peninsula of eastern Newfoundland. No weaving was done in the area of his investigations, but he gives extensive information about sheep, spinning, and so on.

54 See Hoffmann, pp.187-194.

55 For further illustrations of this weave see Burnham and Burnham, pp.172-173.

56 See Teal for information about wool combing.

57 See Buxton Keenlyside for much information on spinning and spinning wheels, and for full description of this spinning wheel, pp.154-155; see Burnham and Burnham, p.33, for pictures and description of spinning wheel signed by F. Young.

58 For further information on this loom see Burnham and Burnham, pp.22-25 and 44-45; for diagrams of the parts of a 4-shaft loom see D.K. Burnham, 1980, pp.118-119.

59 See Traill, 1969, pp.181-184. Mrs Traill, in her admirable volume of good advice for the person contemplating coming as a settler to Canada, gives a full description of carpet weaving in Ontario.

60 For the story of the finding of this carpet see Burnham and Burnham, p.94, cat. no. 114.

61 See Brett for illustration of this dress in colour, p.31, and for description and pattern draft of the cut of the garment in folder, cat. no. 30.

62 See Gehret, pp.50-56, for information and illustration of similar kerchiefs.

63 See Brett, folder no. 86 for the cut of this coat. A black suit of excellent quality broadcloth is in the Jordan Historical Museum of the Twenty, Jordan, Ontario. It is known that the material was woven by Samuel Fry, the professional weaver, and that the suit was worn at his own wedding in 1837. For illustration of Fry's suit see Burnham and Burnham p.77, cat. no. 95, and for further information on fulling see p.62.

64 See Mackley, pp.46-47 and 50-51. The information that materials were sent to Glen Dyer from Newfoundland was contained in personal communication from Miss Ann MacLellan.

65 For cut of garment see Brett, folder no. 84.

66 The cut of this shirt is similar, but with fuller sleeves, to one that belonged to Mr Thomas Coutts, the English banker shown in D.K. Burnham, 1973, p.17.

67 See Pocius for further information on Newfoundland wool and knitting, pp.1-28.

68 For further examples of quilts made from homespun patches see Burnham and Burnham, pp.70-71, 108, and colour plate opposite p.61; see D.K. Burnham 1975, cat. nos 2, 6, and 12.

69 This quilt is from the McKendry Collection, a very large collection of quilts from eastern Ontario that is now in the Centre for Folk Culture Studies, National Museum of Man, Ottawa. For further information on handwoven and other quilts, and as background reading for Canadian textiles of various kinds, see McKendry.

70 For full information on local dye sources in northeast America see Casselman.

71 For historical background, technique, pattern photographs, and threading drafts see Burnham and Burnham chapter on overshot, pp.174-263.

72 For the Cape Breton pattern drafts see Mackley.

73 For further information on Mrs Munro see Mackley, pp.28-31; see also Burnham and Burnham, p.11.

74 Charles Irvin's loom is at Black Creek Pioneer Village.

75 The efficient weaving of "rose fashion" is dependent on a loom with the addition of lams, making it easy to change the treadling order. Since few Canadian looms were equipped with lams, "rose fashion" was quite rare here, compared with the much wider use of the method in the United States. See Burnham and Burnham, pp.180-182.

76 See Reaman.

77 See Burnham and Burnham, pp.275-276 and 283-284, for information on this weave construction and draft of this piece.

78 See Burnham and Burnham for chapter on twill diaper coverlets, pp.285-297.

79 See Burnham and Burnham section on *"Star and Diamond"* weave, pp.273-274 and 277-279.

80 See D.K. Burnham, 1977, for more specific information as to which weavers used which constructions. For the average coverlet viewer, the construction of the weave is only important if it effects the appearance of the piece, but for the student or serious collector it provides a very valuable clue to the identity of the weaver.

81 For information about the operation of Campbell's jacquard loom and jacquard weavers in Ontario, see Burnham and Burnham, chapter on jacquard weaving, pp.317-378; see Heisey; see also Davison and Mayer-Thurman for information on American coverlet weavers and many pictures of their work.

82 See McKendry, fig. 98, p.73, for illustration of a coverlet by this man that is in a private collection. The owners were informed when they bought the coverlet in the Purple Hill area that Moses Cherry was the weaver. It has not, as yet, been possible to discover more about Cherry. For other patterns woven by him see Burnham and Burnham, pp.373-376.

83 In an excellent small paper given at the Royal Ontario Museum in 1976, Anne Lambert gave a summary of field work done in rural Alberta. It is to be hoped that this original research will be carried further.

84 Personal communication from Chuck Sutyla, Multiculturalism, Department of Culture and Youth, Saskatchewan.

85 Personal communication. Magnus Einarsson, of the Centre for Folk Culture Studies, found no memory of handweaving during his research in the Icelandic communities of Manitoba. See *Gimli Saga* for reference to handlooms, pp.225 and 672; for reference to sheep, pp.32 and 592; and for numerous scattered references to spinning and knitting.

86 See Buxton Keenlyside, pp.167-170, for full description of the National Museum's Hutterite wheels and mention of their suitability for the making of knitting yarns.

87 See Catalogue, Canadian Centre for Folk Culture Studies, no. 17.

88 I am indebted to Anna Hudyma's daughter, Mary Kunesky, and her granddaughter, Tillie Wieczorek, for the information given.

89 For full historic background of the Doukhobors, see Woodcock and Avakumovic.

90 See Woodcock and Avakumovic, pp.156 and 164.

91 See Mealing, pp.34-35.

92 See Mealing, pp.38-39.